Leaving New Buffalo Commune

LEAVING

NEW BUFFALO COMMUNE

Arthur Kopecky

Foreword by Timothy Miller

University of New Mexico Press
Albuquerque

10 09 08 07 06   1 2 3 4 5

Library of Congress Cataloging-in-Publication Data

Kopecky, Arthur, 1944–
    Leaving New Buffalo Commune / Arthur Kopecky.
        p. cm. — (CounterCulture series)
    Includes bibliographical references and index.
        ISBN-13: 978-0-8263-4054-2 (pbk. : alk. paper)
        ISBN-10: 0-8263-4054-7 (pbk. : alk. paper)
    1. Kopecky, Arthur, 1944–   —Diaries.
    2. New Buffalo (N.M. : Commune)
    3. Communes—New Mexico.
    4. Counterculture—New Mexico.
    I. Title. II. Series.
        HQ971.5.N7K65 2006
        307.77'409789—dc22
                                    2006014979

Book design: Robyn Mundy
Cover photo: Sandra Kopecky
Jacket design and type composition: Kathleen Sparkes
Body type is Clearface 10.5/14
Display type is Gothic 821 and Gothic 13

Series

A Volume in the CounterCulture Series

Editors: David Farber, History, Temple University

Beth L. Bailey, American Studies, Temple University

Dedication

Somewhere there are people who want a freer,
friendlier world. There must be some in every place
who are not satisfied with things the way they are;
some who believe in change and unity. This book
is dedicated to them, to you, who would propel a
quantum leap into a sustainable future. You have as
great a challenge as any have faced. This is not
a battle of the sword or explosions. This effort to
build on idealism takes a long commitment and a
steady hand. Good luck. If you would be a help,
this would be the time. Brave on.

CONTENTS

LIST OF ILLUSTRATIONS

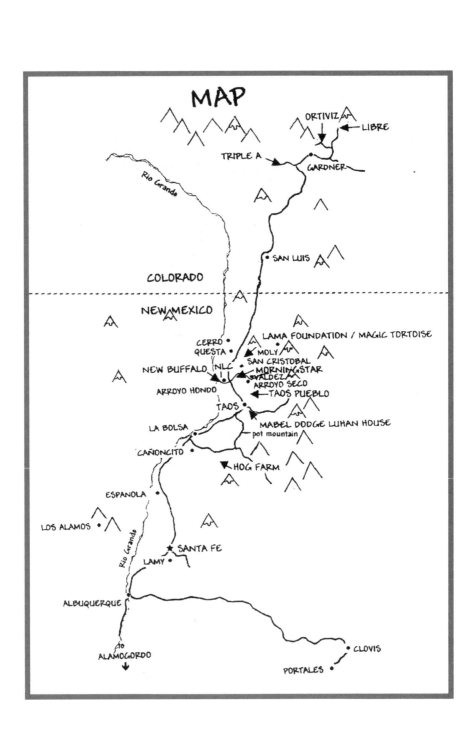

FOREWORD

Timothy Miller

For a decade after about 1965 the United States—and the rest of the Western world—saw a veritable explosion of communal living. Hundreds of thousands of cultural explorers, mostly young and from relatively affluent backgrounds, turned their backs on American consumer culture and moved into thousands upon thousands of communes in cities, college towns, and the expansive countryside.

Communal living is a venerable theme in American culture. Swanendael, or the Valley of the Swans, founded by Dutch Mennonites in Delaware in 1663, is often listed as the first American commune (although of course indigenous peoples had already been living in a manner that could be considered communal for thousands of years). Others soon followed—the Labadist Colony at Bohemia Manor, Maryland; the Woman in the Wilderness near Philadelphia; Ephrata, in Lancaster County, Pennsylvania. In 1774 the first Shakers arrived, and soon they established what has been America's longest-running set of communal enclaves, one of which survives today in Maine. America has not had a moment without communes for some three hundred years.

Communes have always been countercultural, rejecting society's norms in favor of alternative approaches to life and work. Some have taken antimaterialism to extremes, as happened in the occasional commune that deeded its land to God. Nudity was tolerated, or encouraged, at some communes long before hippies arrived on the scene. Anarchist communes in which radicals banded together to escape the confines of the social order were thriving over a century ago. Colonies of artists have long been important centers of creativity. In that sense the communes of the 1960s era were variants on a long-running theme. But they did package the communal experience in a new and flamboyant way.

The communal eruption of the 1960s era dwarfed anything that had gone before. By mid-decade the civil rights movement had exposed grave flaws in the nation's social contract, protests against the war in Vietnam were mushrooming, psychedelic substances were newly available, Asian spiritual teachers were entering the United States as never before, and a new, colorful countercultural lifestyle was suddenly ubiquitous. Communes grew right along with the rest of the cultural revolution: Tolstoy Farm (1963), Drop City (1965), the Hog Farm (1965), and Morning Star Ranch (1966) were among the pioneering ventures that ushered in what by the end of the decade became a vast wave of commune-building.

A stereotype of a "hippie commune" was soon well fixed in the public mind. Communes—and their residents—were filthy. The residents ingested exotic drugs and became hallucinating zombies. Orgies were the sexual order of the day. No one ever really worked, and communards constituted a drain on the welfare system. Everyone lived in squalor. Communes were as disgusting as they were fascinating.

But the actual communal scene was not much like the stereotype. Although a few communes did tend toward the down-and-out, most were energized by a high sense of purpose, a conviction that these new cooperative homes were harbingers of a future society of peace and love and mutual aid. Moreover, the communal scene was quite diverse. There were communes that embodied back-to-the-land romanticism; there were communes of strict religious conviction and discipline; there were communes that operated as social-change centers in cities; there were communes that existed to serve the needy, running soup kitchens and homeless shelters.

No one has any idea how many communes there were altogether in the 1960s era, but estimates that their numbers ranged upwards of ten thousand are plausible. Similarly no one knows how many persons joined communes at one time or another, but their numbers were surely in the hundreds of thousands, if not a million. Some stayed for days or weeks, but some made it a lifetime venture. Hundreds of communes founded in the 1960s era survive today, often with many of their original members still present.

The communal spirit reached every part of the United States. It did, however, seem especially powerful in a few places: New England, northern California,

Virginia, and New Mexico. The latter might have seemed an unlikely communal magnet; it was far from urban centers and economically depressed. New Mexico did, however, have an air of alternative culture to it, especially in the greater Taos area, where Mabel Dodge Luhan had opened her home as a retreat for urban sophisticates and artists and where writers and artists from Georgia O'Keeffe to D. H. Lawrence had found their spiritual homes. New Mexico also had a deeply rooted population of American Indians, objects of great fascination and admiration within the counterculture; communards liked to say that the Taos Pueblo was America's oldest commune. New Mexico also had relatively inexpensive land and, in several cases, alternative-minded prosperous patrons who made land for commune-building freely available.

New Buffalo was among the first of the new-generation Taos communes. In 1967 a group of young Americans, drawn by fascination with the local Indians and by the larger New Mexico mystique, decided to build a commune. It would be called New Buffalo, because it would be all things—all sustenance—to them, just as the buffalo had been for many Indian tribes. They had, fortunately, in their number Rick Klein, who had money from an inheritance and used it to buy the land needed for the project. They soon found a suitable hundred-acre tract at Arroyo Hondo, north of Taos, and immediately set to work building traditional adobe buildings. Although many of the founders soon left, others arrived and New Buffalo remained solidly in operation for several years, as Art Kopecky's memoir recalls so well.

New Buffalo was the pioneer of the Taos-era communes, but it was far from the only one. In 1969 a group of refugees from Morning Star, an openland California commune that had been ordered to disband by local authorities, arrived in the area and started a new Morning Star atop a mesa owned by Michael Duncan. Soon another commune, this one a militant leftist cell called the Reality Construction Company, set up shop next door to Morning Star. A few miles to the north a group of spiritual seekers opened the Lama Foundation, which remains in operation today. Not far away were Lorien and Lila, built on the land of yet another communal benefactor, Charles Lonsdale. And many others dotted the northern New Mexico countryside as well: Five Star, the Furry Freak Brothers, the Kingdom of Heaven, the Family, a New Mexico branch of California's Hog Farm—and who knows how many more.

New Buffalo and its thousands of sister communes embodied the boundless optimism of countercultural youth in the 1960s era. Now, a generation and more later, it is time to preserve the record of that transformative time for posterity. Art Kopecky's first volume about New Buffalo stopped in 1975, just as the commune seemed to be closing in on the self-sufficiency it had sought from the beginning. Now in volume two we see how a clash of visions in the late 1970s era changed the course of New Buffalo and its members over the next two decades. We are fortunate to have Kopecky's journals as primary documents that have committed to history the story of this remarkable commune and its setting.

ACKNOWLEDGMENTS

With the experience of the first volume behind us, my wife Sandra dove into preparing the second manuscript, typing up the remaining hand-written journals and then arranging and weaving the sequence of events of each day if needed. With all the many editing tasks, she always was careful to let me see her suggestions. These books wouldn't exist without her determined efforts. In addition Sandy is one of the main characters. For years she helped keep body and soul together, making New Buffalo a home.

Many people gave life to the New Buffalo community, but I want to acknowledge the contribution especially of Larry McInteer. Quiet, gentle, very intelligent, and spiritual, for many years Larry played an essential role and set a great example.

From day one of my community experience, Carol Egbert was part of my immediate family. She worked hard, enjoyed life, and was such a good mom. Thanks to Carol for helping us live free.

And thanks to several hundred others like Rick and Terry, Kiva and Kemal, Jon and Dee, Pepe, Tom, (alias Ron), Peggi Sue, Kim, and Mike who lived free and gave generously to create this new beginning.

I want also to acknowledge the present generation of community workers. Thank goodness there are thousands who work now for a friendlier sustainable future.

Some of the names in the book have been changed and the viewpoint, of course, is my own.

1. *At the Bolinas commune in California. 1970.*
Photo by Harris Saltzberg

PROLOGUE

"It is the heritage of our age to know that all men are one."

Bolinas, California, August 1970

It is a quiet morning with the fog not yet lifted, this morning that I write. There are four people asleep around me and several downstairs gathered about the wood-burning stove.

Though I would rouse people to change parts of their lives, I would have my writing imbued with this peace that surrounds me. If I would have anyone stirred to some action, it is to achieve this peace in all lives. It is not to add any new destruction or passion to the earth.

I have lived on what many people call a commune for almost a year. I happen to be one of those who have helped put this together, if indeed a person can pretend to take credit for anything so marvelous.

We are living in the future. We are living in a very advanced state of brotherhood. We are living in peace. We have use of all the machines that have been developed as convenience and a bountiful supply of food. We rarely work for a salary; we work for one another. We are black, red, white, and yellow. And we are all having a very fine time. It is all quite natural and is generally what is happening throughout the world. It is only now in our age, really, that run-of-the-mill people like myself can learn so much of history, science, and humanity in so short a time. It is the heritage of our age to know that all men are one.

NEW BUFFALO SITE MAP

SANGRE DE CRISTO
MOUNTAINS

RIO HONDO

ROAD TO HWY. 3

TO RIO GRANDE

LOWER PASTURE

GATE

DRYLAND

DRYLAND

WHEAT / OATS / RYE

COTTONWOOD TREE

TO ALFALFA

LOWER GARDEN

TO PRAIRIE DOG HILL

SEEPAGE PIT

ALFALFA

summer outhouse
site

1st. GREENHOUSE

OUTHOUSE

ORCHARD

TO HOLDING POND

GROW HOLES
kitchen garden site
TOWER

WASHROOM

PARKING

KITCHEN

PANTRIES

CLOTHES LINE

UPPER GARDEN

sunporch site
CIRCLE
CANDLE ROOM

solar site
ALCOVE

PUMP

HOGAN

WOOD PILE

COURTYARD

VOLLEYBALL
COURT

solar site

dairy barn
site

greenhouse site
2nd. GREENHOUSE

TOOL SHED

PROPERTY LINE

IRRIGATION DITCH

POLE BARN

CHICKEN COOP

PIT HOUSE

HAY STACKS

DRYLAND

DITCH DUG BY LARRY AND TAM

ACEQUIA LLANO DELA MADRE

DITCH ROAD

MESA

INTRODUCTION

March 7, 2005

I, Arty AnSwei, a very small fish, do nevertheless presume to have some big ideas. Idealism—visions for the future—is not the monopoly of the high in society.

United States history was started with a considerable measure of idealism. It is my conviction that only a surge of idealism again can reassert our freedom and help us face a long list of problems that are all going critical. We need a new paradigm. I believe in the possibility, even necessity, of a peaceful revolution. Idealism is called upon again—this time to foster greater friendliness, greater generosity.

We have consumed too much. We have borrowed too much. We have elevated greed into a religion. These things will not sustain us. Some humble people will need to lead, not in violence or denunciation but with example. The reward—a romantic life and a role in American history.

I participated in an idealistic burst in the 1960s through the 1970s. My thought is that the Aquarian Age birth, the Woodstock phenomenon, was a precursor of a more dedicated movement, which again is showing signs of life.

Volume 2 completes the story of my eight years immersed in that idealistic endeavor at the New Buffalo "hippie commune." If you want to intervene to change the course of history, you can do it. If you want to promote the humane, the goodwill aspects of human nature, the non-war solutions, you can do it. But it takes more than fine words and heartfelt songs; you need a plan of action. It can't be violent action; there is already too much anger. When young people think, "What shall I do?" we need an additional image there: one of service, freedom, and generosity to a broader family. You can make it happen.

2.
Pepe of the Pride family in the Mind Machine. 1970. Photo by Harris Saltzberg

It is popular to postulate the "end of days," the coming of "the rapture," society becoming so over-burdened that it self-destructs. Counter that. Don't let some ancient fears rule your future. Join with others and imagine a better world. Humanity has made great progress over the centuries; another great step forward is called for. It involves developing a faith in humankind, in human intelligence. You have to prove that greed and selfishness don't need to be the foundation of society. That indeed is a noble task—not easy—not at all a sure thing. This brings us back to idealism. Idealism will be needed. Martin Luther King Jr. is famous for the phrase "I have a dream." Expand on that dream. Create some new dreams. For you may say that we're the dreamers, but we're not the only ones.

Let me, AnSwei Livingproof, present to you an overview to lead into the story. I was a young man from New York City relocated to California. I had dropped out of graduate school at UC Berkeley during the height of the Vietnam War. The concept of the Dawning of the Age of Aquarius and the spontaneous surge of communal living drew me into the new culture. My travels with the Pride family in our Wonderbread truck—the Mind Machine— eventually brought us to the New Buffalo commune in the Fall of '71, where a group of "back to the land" idealists had bought a 140-acre ranch in the mountains of New Mexico. There we settled.

Over the next five years, which are chronicled in volume 1, we grew in knowledge and determination. Planting alfalfa fields (like the local ranchos) was a major breakthrough. As volume 2 opens, we are approaching being fully planted (an arduous task). The group is focusing on dairy as the prime agricultural endeavor. Goat John, who selfishly monopolized the dairy, has left, and a more communal enterprise is in the works.

I often think of the parallel between the early Christian communities and us. These were simply dressed people with big ideas. Much energy had to go into basic survival tasks that were accomplished by a completely voluntary group effort. A spirituality and a closeness with nature pervaded that are as valuable as any fancy possessions.

These journals are in real time—slightly edited—events recorded as they were happening. Now we open the curtains and join this communal family as they continue to go about their daily tasks creating a small piece of history in the making of the counterculture.

JOURNAL 18

The two are very connected in my mind:
communes and world peace.

March 30, 1976: Our saga continues in a mountain arroyo below the peaks of the Sangre de Cristo Mountains in northern New Mexico—a commune being created—a manifestation of many people. Having survived the winter in this high desert valley, our communal family perseveres to become self-sufficient, ever looking for like-minded people to come our way.

We have just enjoyed a genuine storm, moistening the native plants and our planted fields. The little solar greenhouse, butted up against the south-wing adobe wall, gives a new-age look to the hand-mudded buildings. Protected inside their fertile beds are the baby tomatoes, cucumbers, and peppers.

I am slowly recovering. I spoke to Doctor Kaufman, and he agreed I just seriously sprained a back muscle. That is the gamble on wood runs in the wild country; you can hardly do them for years and never get hurt. I can recuperate in comfort with plenty of food and the time it takes to mend. I am anxious to be back building our poor business where we hardly earn a dime. Yet little by little we are putting together a real farm, one run by a commune.

Larry McInteer and Sasha are engaged! Everyone is a bit surprised. This is the stuff of real romance. Sasha arrived one cold winter afternoon. With her shawl, baby Juan was strapped to her back—daughter Olalay clutching at her skirts. Wearing many layers of clothing, she looked like a mountain villager out of an old *National Geographic* magazine.

Wednesday: Our cows stay out at night and get their full diet on the quickly greening pastures. Goats, too, are out a lot—free ranging. With the pastures growing and grain fields in good condition, they behave very well and haven't needed any goat herder. They do have to be chased out of the chicken coop though, but they've learned to walk right by the pueblo without coming in. The animals look so good out there—our two herds.

Sylvie now is milking, being trained as second. She's had experience. Her light brown hair frames her big eyes and round face. The sprinkling of freckles across her nose emphasizes her youthful charm. Her three kids, Jimmy, Monica, and Tony, are very polite, and their presence is a big plus for our communal family.

Mike Pots is working his old route in Taos doing yard work, landscaping, and garden preparation. With his money he buys dairy supplies. Mike is really solid with this new business.

Thursday: Kim Grodberg, along with our newest and tireless partner Jimmy, put some posts in the ground with wire around them for the new trees and bushes. Without this barrier, they would never stand a chance with the marauding goats, which are always ready to discover a tasty snack.

After many discussions, we got a present of an electric fence from Sasha! This is another piece in our dairy concept. Now we'll have a means, we hope, to graze the goats in the lush summer months when they can't be loose.

On the world front, the USSR has attained military parity with the US. The Soviet Union has developed tremendous military capacity to match America in recent years. Big arms race—the world is geared up for battle. I've always cared about this stuff since I was fifteen. The two are very connected in my mind, communes and world peace.

On the home front, Gene McCarthy suggests a solution to unemployment: a redistribution of the available work among more people by adopting shorter workweeks and longer vacations.

I must say I enjoy reading the weekly news magazines, and I think they are of very high quality. They survive because of liquor, auto, and cigarette advertising—three things that wisdom should lead intelligent people to discourage, not to promote. So much for world affairs; back to grass and animals.

Ron sold $20 worth of candles. Sandy made a $20 tax contribution, and from the Sears Catalog Store, she ordered more diapers for our soon-to-be baby.

Friday: Bright warm day. With pack hanging from his shoulder, Ron, walking

3. *Kiva, Kemal, and Jonesy. Photo by Clarice Kopecky*

down the road and never looking back, took off to the Hog Farm. Mike is off to town to grind 150 pounds of wheat. Our own grinder, again, is broken.

Goat John and Carol have hooked up together and are moving to Michael Duncan's land, the abandoned Morningstar commune, to a more private scene! Carol is excited, and John is working as hard as a hardy pioneer for their new home. He gets a lot done at a hell of a pace; there's a real worker.

Larry and Sasha hooked up too, and now they're starry-eyed about the new life they'll start. But Larry seems to want to recede from the commune! Our own president thinking the commune may be a wrong place for him to have "his" personal family. I certainly believe the best future can be with New Buffalo. He is a great asset to us: senior member, very gentle, inventive, and knowledgeable in construction. If we are to raise a barn roof and convert to solar heat, we'll certainly need his kind of help.

Kemal and Kiva? Will they come back with plans to stay? Kemal, of the three—Kemal, Larry, and John—I am closest to. And he, like Kim's recent return, will add a lot of quality and energy to our house. And Kiva, too, can be a very valuable member. Baby Jonesy, of course, is invaluable.

April 4, 1976: I can hardly feel my wound anymore. I went up to Morningstar with John and Rebel and looked around. They have done a lot of work since they moved up there. Corral is up, rooms and grounds are very neat, and there are orderly piles of bricks, vigas, latillas, and dirt. Many fields look well watered. I try running around a little, getting back to my usual self. Away from the buildings, I feel I am deep in the countryside. Only the wind disturbs the stillness among the piñon trees. A quietness pervades that comes down from the beginning of time. No traffic or crowds here as I was used to in the canyons of Manhattan.

I saw some neighbors in upper Arroyo Hondo and talked about the irrigation water. Alfredo Trujillo will not be around to be mayordomo. He is currently working on a solar heat project.

As of today I'm a goat milker. Kim has a fungus infection on one hand, so he's out until cured. Sylvie tried out, but Mike says she's awfully slow. Mike wants a second, so I'm it, which is fine with me. Mike took over as dairy master when Goat John moved out.

Sandy has the little terrace by the outhouse looking very well cared for. There are phlox, irises, and more chives now. The heavily chewed lilacs are still alive.

Tuesday: While in the midst of being broke, Kemal arrived and presented us with a 1969 Dodge pickup with crew cab! When other people are considering leaving, Kemal has brought back something for us—a new family vehicle. This is the first time we've had a respectable town vehicle pledged to New Buffalo. Since I arrived, of course we had the Bird truck (Mind Machine). It was great, but this, I think, is much better and safer.

So here is the man Kemal—no kid anymore. He's a father now, committing himself to the commune. It offers a good future: land, crops, livestock, and good friends to help take care of things. He can dig it. Kemal is quite positive he doesn't want some floating scene here either, this constant change of people. It has got to be productive and offer a home for serious people, rather than a catchall for so many drifters. Still we offer shelter, food, and hospitality to all on the road, and inspiration for any who want this way of life. Inspiration and many practical lessons we can give.

Sandy cooked dinner. Kitchen got very nicely cleaned as it does almost every day.

April 8: Kim has taken on a very professional attitude toward mechanics. He is suspicious of just how communal the new truck will work out. Kemal is very positive about saying it is "ours." Kim certainly has done a real ace job on checking it over.

Sylvie has the new chicken yard enclosed. She doubled the size of their yard, and it also gives them real shade. They're happy chickens now. She stays with Ron sometimes.

Kemal, our master meat preserver, broke out a ham; we're frying it and eating it at our leisure. He contributes to our survival knowledge. Kemal seems very pleased. He was walking around just looking and feeling that we have a really great place here.

Plus there's been a rash of job offers. Saturday, four of us will be working for other ranchers at $16 a day cleaning the main ditch. Kemal and young Jimmy will work for Buffalo. Each ranch supplies workers to clean the acequias once a year in the spring before the water can be allowed down. The full three miles must be inspected and trimmed. Some have nippers or a chain saw, and most have shovels. I know the ditch country well, with its willow thickets and earthen embankments. All the gold in Wall Street can't buy the love of being this close with the earth. We have to line up more shovels.

Saturday: Eight of us worked on the ditch today. Neighbor Leo Vigil, who is about sixty years old, was on the crew. We worked hard, got a lot done, had to put out two fires, and were exhausted by the end of the day. Back at home, friends are playing tunes outside while watching the setting sun.

Sunday: John, Carol, and Reb are packing and moving. And pretty Peggi Sue is here! She's headed for Oregon; a sister is having a baby. Says she was just planning on passing through, but with Jerry and Hap gone she feels she could live here again! She sees it should mellow it even more with John and Carol finding their place in the sun. Sounds like she's seriously considering coming back; we hope she does. Peggi is a very energetic young gal—just what we need.

The Dodge loses and burns oil. Hap came by and put about a pint of Marvel Mystery Oil in. Hap's always good for a few songs. In the kitchen around the table—tapping feet to time—we sang some good ones.

Along with very dark clouds, thunder, lightning, and hail, the irrigation water came on in the ditch. Wow! This is cold snowmelt in abundance; it needs to be a flood to soak the earth of the ditch and move through the sand beds. Mike followed the water for over a mile as it crossed under the highway and headed our way. It reached us just as night was falling. Kemal, Jimmy, and Ron started to run some of the ditches. Sylvie had been cleaning the waterways much of the day. Good timing.

April 13: Event! Today started the New Buffalo dairy rather than John's goat dairy! Boy, oh boy, we all feel good! Mike milks in the morning. Kemal plans to go along, and then I milk in the evening. Mike came along with me tonight. We're going to really enjoy and be proud of this now-communal herd. To back us up, the fields are alive with vibrant green growth from the wet, mellow earth.

New era: We have a real farm, and there's talk around the house to formalize the structure more: institute membership and a procedure for admitting people. This is part of the evolution of the commune—to make a stable household where the residents control the land, livestock, and who lives here—not leaving it so much to the whim of fate.

Kemal says he wasn't for this before but sees it hasn't worked so well the other way. Peggi Sue didn't even think she'd want to live here again, because she couldn't have a voice in who was here. People like Kim and Mike, who are quiet, now would be given a necessary voice, where before, because they're gentle and unobtrusive, simply were not consulted and were ignored by new people coming in. Ladies too, like Sandy, now would have an equal voice and a place to put their opinions.

More than ever we have people who are not drifters; they're not folks who don't know what they want; people who float in because of the free-rent, no-obligations situation.

Feeling good—coming into our most productive year—best year yet in many ways, and we want it to last.

April 15, 1976: It's snowing! This storm is getting to be equivalent to a complete irrigation. Our Mother Earth and Father Sky are combining to be very good to us; help us reap a very bountiful harvest. Our land is set up now to take advantage of this storm. We have only a half acre without a crop on it. All the rest is in alfalfa, brome grass, crested wheat grass, and clover, or winter rye or winter wheat—all hardy plants that enjoy and thrive in this weather.

This afternoon I had to rest. I watched Sandy color the candles many bright colors. A second batch of cheese came off the stove today. Kiva is going to make another batch tomorrow. She's very interested and reading up and asking people with experience.

4. *Arty and Sandy. Photo by Clarice Kopecky*

Sunday: Kim with Jimmy and Peggi Sue covered both the upper and lower gardens with manure. Took a lot of effort all day using wheelbarrows—close to the earth—very careful work. In the lower garden every shovel of earth I examined had earthworms.

Kim then disked the gardens. He finished his plans—took a continuous effort. Sandy made lunch for the hard workers, and at night Sylvie rewarded us with two excellent lemon meringue pies.

April 20: Peg and I doctored Fudge, our calf. Under absolutely clear skies, Kim and I, with the tractor, dragged prairie dog hill. I covered the whole half-acre rather meticulously with seed bought by Sylvie. Kemal, Jimmy, and Kim hopped around, throwing off the rocks. This area was so desolate, it's been like farming on the moon.

In town today, Kemal sold milk and eggs, bought dairy ration, and picked up a copy of milk production regulations. He also made an appointment with an official for 9 a.m. on Friday. Kiva says there is a great demand for cow's milk in town. Her cheese sold right away.

Notes from meeting—proposed: animals, cars, and trucks. Commune has jurisdiction; none leave without approval, and none stay without approval. How to decide: consensus or unanimous vote? We didn't add any rules or written legalities; just met to get consensus—agreement—among us all. If we do have outstanding problems, then we'll meet again.

This meeting represents more of a meeting of minds than we've ever had. We have a more communally oriented group than ever. Mike Pots and Kim both felt good about it. At the same time, our commune consciousness grows, our consciousness of the dairy grows—build a milking house, right to code.

Tax fund is complete.

April 23: A gorgeous day. Surrounded by green pastures and wheat, the family is very busy putting in rows in the lower garden. With flames dancing, dry growth popping and crackling, Kemal burned grass on the one overgrown ditch that brings water toward prairie dog hill. The cows would not go near it.

I went to town for an early morning appointment. Spoke to the health department's chief milk inspector on the phone. He's going to come out to New Buffalo from Clovis! That's three hundred miles away. This is the man whose occupation is to know dairy. Part of his job is to help give advice so that people don't make investments and then find out they've put in the wrong thing. The dairy is a reflection of the whole: seepage tanks, outhouses, water supply, overall cleanliness; all affect the scene.

This is the right thing to do. Grade A raw milk license is the goal. A lot depends on this inspector and what he thinks of our farm. If he thinks we can do it, then we'll do it—whatever it takes.

But Larry, it appears, is out of it lately. One peyote meeting a week takes two days of work out. Then he's spent a lot of time fooling around with his new car and new girlfriend. His mind is on moving, and in this busy season he is not helping. A loss.

Sasha, meantime, has gone to Los Angeles to see her family. Someone died, and she went to see if she could make some money and who knows what. I'm not sure she's crazy about the idea of a formal marriage. Seems it is getting postponed.

Saturday: Teen Jimmy showed he's really with it. Early in the morning he went and got the water and started irrigating the new field. He stuck with it all day until it was finished, not even taking a break for lunch. It's a big job; we don't want washouts.

Kemal and neighbor Carlos Trujillo castrated the horse. Carlos refused payment; a good friend he is. It is terrible that he has some physical problem that the doctors just can't cure. Carlos knows all the moves: lassoing, catching one front leg with a loop, then tightening; the horse has to lower itself. Carlos makes a few more turns, and the horse is immobilized. He is quick with his small knife and knows just where to cut. The blood is very bright. He was fifty-nine today—one of the best-respected ranchers around.

April 28–Wednesday: Kemal and I met Mr. Tom Proctor and Jerry Martino from the Environmental Protection Agency and drove out from Taos with them in their car. Mr. Proctor spent several hours here. These fellows were encouraging. Proctor will send us some suggested plans. He gave us the name of a dairy supply dealer in Albuquerque.

We walked right up to our open-air barn. He stood west of the barn and said, "This is the site." East of the barn is too close to our well and on a main natural drain.

He says three rooms not two; a separate room for milking, one for cleaning, and a third for bottling. Open drainage is fine, and we can use it to irrigate but need to have two catch basins so the water from the milk area doesn't go through our land to the river. We can use the two pits that are out there already. This means we'll have to put in a pipeline to this area. Also we need electricity and a triple sink—for wash, rinse, and a Clorox rinse—Clorox then evaporates. That's it. Outhouses will have to be cleanable and completely screened. A lot of work, but it should be within our ability. The work is no joke, but this is definitely a very good thing to aim for; we could be Grade A— licensed to do what we have been planning to do—sell milk. Kemal's going to make a trip to see the dairy supply in Albuquerque and some other operations.

Visitors: We have some every day. I like meeting the people. Mike asked visitor Griego to leave. Kim, Kemal, and I rather liked the fellow. I felt Mike was too quick with the cutoff. As part of my life here I like working with new people, and we give some a new sort of experience. Anyhow, we invited him to return. No, not to live permanently; we needn't make such decisions after two days.

Thursday: Heavy clouds to the west this morning. I switched the first-gate water to a different field, and then put the fourth-gate water back on the rye.

After that, prepared to seed before the rain. I started out alone, but Mike and Sylvie later joined me in creating the next alfalfa-brome field. We got a very good spread.

April 30, 1976: Big flood in the morning! Later Rebel told us that up on the Seco rim, the Des Montes community cut off the Cochia ditch, and the result was loads more water down here. We haven't ever seen the ditch this full of rushing water. Had to use a digging bar to open the main gates. On our property the flooding didn't do much damage at all; a big prairie dog hole in the second ditch was preventing the flow from washing out the crested wheat fields. Lucky.

We have a scout for a bus called "Project America" camped here, a very nice young man with a backpack. He says we could get thirteen of his friends up here for a few days to participate. They're crossing America.

We like people. We are a good part of the country—a good part of this humanity. We like to make many friends and have them feel this way, enjoying the simple pleasure of the beautiful mountains.

Ron, Sylvie, and gal Clover went with a few friends to get their auras "adjusted" down in Alamogordo, three hundred miles away. It was abortive. They were rejected, and then got into such personal squabbles on the way back that Ron hitched rather than rode.

Sunday: Several of us took the day off. Kim didn't do too much nor I. Ron couldn't even finish his dish assignment. Kiva, Sandy, and Sylvie, though, always make sure we've got plenty to eat.

May 4, 1976: Fairly early I went out in the morning to check the ditch water. It had gone up in the night. The third ditch had overflowed where a bunch of weeds caught. There was some washout in our new field.

Kemal and Mike went to work. Larry and I knocked off one big job that has been lingering. We marked off a new 3.5 percent ditch for Leo's property, where we irrigated for him last year. The locals have traditionally just drawn straight lines for feeder ditches, and they erode massively. They get so bad that people put old cars and trucks in them! Much better to zigzag the water down hill. Next we plow in the lines.

Project America is here. We had dinner together. Bus and many bicycles parked out front. A nice group—showed very futuristic slides and films on the future of Solari in Arizona, space cities, and also alternative energy sources. Perhaps they'll let us put them to work tomorrow.

We received a letter from health inspector Tom Proctor with a suggested plan, some photos, and an invitation to see a small operation in his neighborhood. Excellent.

Wednesday: Project America cross-country bicyclers gave us a hand. Two cut kitchen wood, two cleaned the kid pen, and a team dug out the dirt floor in the room that's to get a new mud floor—a big job done. Griego returned and while giving Sandy tasty tips for red chile gravy, cooked a big Mexican feast for dinner.

Thursday: Very threatening sky in the morning—all clouds and very dark to the west. It rained last night; it's raining tonight. The ditch water is going into our holding pond. The third gate is shut way down, and fourth gate is off. Shovel in hand, with my legs as my horse, I gallop across the gravelly hills above the fields, shuttling water. I was rather tired because I took a hard run in the morning chasing a nervous cow out.

Two French girls and a tall fellow are here. The scout from the bicyclers remains in his tent. He's a very mellow guy—going to bike to Colorado. We're sending him to Ortiviz, our sister commune. I like to see quiet, clean living—no smoke or drink—people that know how to sleep outside. Of course he is welcome to sleep inside in our circle room too. The other thirteen bikers are gone. At my mom's house in Taos they're staying tonight.

May 8: Lama Foundation people came down—excellent company. Healthy, clean, friendly people, they are our closest friends communally. Basically an older group than us, they lost quickly to our team at volleyball. We spent all day looking around, relaxing and playing ball. The kids were hanging out at the holding pond, investigating all the life that water brings.

Sylvie and Kiva made a delicious Mexican dinner. Sylvie once lived in South America. There she learned how to make tamales. Kemal cooked the mutton roasts for an extra feast. They had defrosted; someone unplugged the freezer.

Monday: Sun was out—bright and hot—watching visitors trudging up the drive, each one a potential story. Last night a hitchhiker, Wade, appeared. Three nice-looking young women and one kid—each in a VW bus—arrived, as well as several other people. Sasha has returned from California. How will she relate to our Larry? Carlton is here also—a friend from Bolinas days. Kind of a city boy, he's a very clean, rather slick dressed, tall African from Chicago. He's twenty-six years old and been around.

I worked on the red truck sideboards much of the day. Carlton spent a lot of time splitting wood. Kim and Sylvie put in some extra hard hours making corn and pea rows in the garden. Kim feels quite confident to handle this important aspect of the commune vision—people knowing the earth—knowing how to grow good quality food and plenty of it. Without Kim, this part of our dream would be much harder to put together. With him it is perfectly in control.

We fed seven or eight extras tonight. I'm not anxious to go for any records. It doesn't make it any easier when every scrap at dinner is gone and nothing left for the next day.

May 11, 1976: I'm thirty-two years old today and I feel very good. Reluctantly, I got into the sewer work. Nice black, slurpy sludge; at least a visiting gal, Cornelia, from Germany helped take off the cover and took the edge off the work. Then with some digging, I released the pressure, which let at least a foot of water out. I stepped out of the way just in time. The pit is full of muck right up to the drain from the kitchen. Definitely needs to be cleaned out; it's been two years.

Commune news: Cornelia spent ten days at The Farm in Tennessee. On 1,200 acres they've just admitted their 100th member! These people are the leaders—farming—dedicated to helping people. They have thirteen offshoot communes in the states. Cornelia says they are thinking of buying a boat to ship their surplus goods in. Great! They do not work for money but to help our fellow people and with a definite international view.

Wednesday: Kemal started preparing bee boxes for hives with parts he got in the mail; Mike helped. It's good that he joined in. Really makes the work get done.

Our big wheat field is looking fabulous. The cover crop of oats is greening our new alfalfa fields. The little new alfalfas, which the oats protect, are up too and plenty thick. The land is a visual tonic.

Ron worked all day completing the new summer pasture fence, just in time. It looks very good. He prefers this outdoor work, away from household clatter. Unfortunately, lately when he comes in the house, he just clashes with people.

May 14: Kemal and I went up to Lama Foundation this morning. We're close with this spiritual mountain group and that's very good. We got the $300 loan from them, and if they do come into some money, they're liable to give us some more. It was a good visit—getting us closer—have them feel our strength and idealism. They are a very positive force with a lot of gentle people.

Mike is a bit disappointed we didn't get rich quick. He doesn't quite believe we'll get this big project together. Day to day, anyhow, we know just what to do. The forces will carry us on. We're destined for success; we just put in the work each day, and it will all come.

John, an ex-Questa policeman, ex-narcotics officer, and mechanic, was up. An acquaintance of Kemal's, he's glad to be friends with us. More and more, we have a scene many people can relate to—not just a collection of crazy hippies but responsible people.

With flies buzzing about my head, I continued cleaning out the seepage sewer pit—a bit messy. Sandy is closer to having the baby.

May 15, 1976: Last evening, just as it was getting dark, from our perch we watched a longhaired, bearded fellow walk up the road. Said he's interested in learning about adobe. Pretty quick we learned he's quite an expert on fruit trees! Kim and I took a turn around with him to see our orchard. He showed us how to prune a little tree. Sounds like he knows his stuff. Jim is his name. He said he would help re-mud the floor in John and Carol's old room, which Sandy will be moving into.

In the dazzling afternoon, we took our all-star volleyball team to Lama Mountain to visit the Tortoise-Techs, some of our closest commune friends: Bill and Annie, Rollo and Beverly, Justin and Joanne, Tucker and Nellie. We trounced their team, even loaning them our guest ringer, tall Dick McKracken. He and Kathy, our friends from downtown Hondo, came with us.

So, our solidarity is greater than ever. We've played host to Lama, and now we are warmly received on the mountain. We're all into some group endeavors; it's sort of tricky, but we're doing well. Our cause is getting a lot of good, mature, skillful people.

Also we hear from Rebel that Michael Duncan, owner of the Morningstar mesa, is back. Reb is impressed that Michael is very mellow and interested in advancements for the farm and is thinking of forming a corporation! This would be the way to liberate the land and create another commune.

In the dimming glow of the evening light, two Arroyo Hondo Commissioners came over and offered me the job of mayordomo for the Acequia Madre del Llano. I took it. We shook hands outside. This puts me in charge of collecting the fees and distributing water for one thousand acres of irrigation owned by eighty families. This is quite an honor actually for a subway-riding boy from New York.

Sunday: I recruited Jim, and we finished cleaning out the seepage tank. Took about two hours to get the rest of the sludge out. Mike and Kemal, meanwhile, put up the electric fence, got it working, and put the goats in it. It will take two of us to herd them in. Wires have to be marked with ribbons so the entrance can be seen.

Lotsi the goat has a problem. Her teat holes seem to be getting smaller, making it very difficult to milk her. It's not healthy for the goat, because we've got to squeeze so hard. Plus it takes so long.

In the afternoon, I got sworn in as mayordomo at Manuel Ortiz's house in Upper Hondo. He said I don't have to run the ditch every day.

Monday: Sweet corn was planted—three types—our major planting. I went and kept a food-stamp appointment as "head of household" of unrelated people. The cows are in the summer pasture. Nelly spent the day at the barn with her new bull calf; I saw him sucking. Very good. He gets three days on the mother.

Visiting Jim had his lesson in adobe. He and I mixed two boats of mud and started laying the new floor. It's not easy—pushing and pulling the hoe in the thick mud—to mix in the straw. No cheating; not too wet or the mud will crack! The mud gets hauled in with buckets and then smoothed with a trowel. This fellow Jim is a very fine person. Like many of us he has quite a big head of hair. The result, no doubt, from not cutting it. He's a country-raised boy who knows a lot about rural living. He sleeps on the circle floor.

Ron went to town and sold candles. The volleyball net went back up, and one backpacking young fellow, to whom we gave a bit of the bum's rush this morning, has returned.

May 19, 1976–Wednesday: At dawn I brought Kaplan's share of water to us. Onions, potatoes, corn, peas, and lettuce got watered. Our short growing season has commenced.

On Monday Jim and I started mudding the floor. Tuesday we did five more mud boats. A mud floor, coated with linseed oil and waxed, makes for a hard, cleanable floor—better for the baby. A visiting photographer, Bill Owens, asked if he could take some pictures for a book he is making called

Working. Sweating in the still air, mixing mud, we posed with the mountains as a backdrop.

Eee yikes! Last night, a little after 10 o'clock, Sandy went into labor. I drove out and picked up friend and midwife Tish and then got dressed in clean clothes. By 12:30 a.m. he was born, a five-pound, eight-ounce baby boy. Tish and Kiva were very busy, and Sasha served coffee, tea, and some good corn bread. Little fellow's temperature was a few degrees off though, and he had to be warmed. Exhausted, we put him down in the little homemade cradle and all fell asleep. My arm around Sandy focused me—I felt a little dazed.

By about 7:00 a.m. the baby seemed too sleepy and was getting blue. When we made him cry his color would return. We went to the hospital, stopping quickly to show my Mom and our longtime friend Shirley Roman. Clarice was truly startled to see us walk in with a newborn baby! No time for "oohs" and "ahhs." At Holy Cross Hospital we found a friend, nurse Sharon, and she called the doctor who had examined Sandy and had approved of the home delivery.

The doctor came right in and told us just what we felt—that it was possibly very serious. They started right away to admit him and examine him. The little fellow took a bit of a beating. They were having trouble with some needles. When I left, mother and child were both resting—a bit haggard but with very good prospects of doing well.

Back at Buffalo, I quickly got back into the swing of things. Spoke with Jim, Kim, Alfred, and a fellow from *Newsweek* whom Alfred brought out. Alfred Hobbs, patriarch of the hippies, is definitely a good man. He knows how to loosen a tongue a bit.

So, good luck baby and good night.

Thursday: I called the hospital this morning. Sandy sounded pleased; baby looks and acts well. Sounds good.

While I was out—no phone at Buffalo—I went as mayordomo, all the way up to the church and back. I ran mostly and felt great. Got some lunch at Melacio's and advice from commissioner Manuel that I need not be so thorough every day looking at everything.

Cooperation: Ron, finally in a good mood, cleaned up all the sludge that we got out of the seepage pit. It will be a fertilizer stash for the big wheat field. He put in a new viga and new metal cover and put dirt on its roof. The pit is covered up for a few more years. Great. I started the job—he finished—it's done.

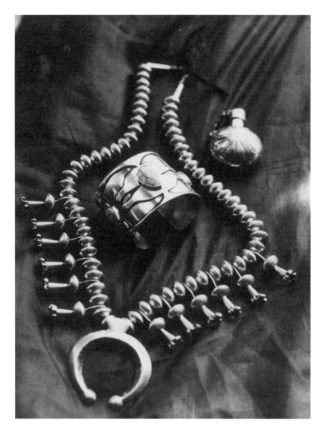

5.
Dodge House creations: squash blossom necklace, medicine bottle, bracelet. Courtesy of Dan Cohn

Pepe the revolutionary drove up to see us. He is always so excited, involved in at least seven collaborative projects with people at the jewelry commune. Jennifer is his current squeeze.

Friday: Made a June 14th appointment at 1 p.m. with Mr. Tom Proctor. Found out some rules for seepage tanks and outhouses.

Next at the hospital—complications! Sandy and baby were taken late in the night to Los Alamos Hospital Baby Clinic! She's a bit out on the street—no friends—no money. An ordeal for Sandy, who should be resting.

Back in Hondo, I saw several people on the ditch: Joe Cordova, Eliu Vigil, Orlando, and Manuel Martinez. They congratulated me on being a father. Somehow I feel very proud to be among these suntanned men with their cowboy hats and weathered hands.

Home at Buffalo, I saw Tomas Vigil, who came out to put in the new ditch we laid out at his dad's. I changed clothes, ran over, and we put in the ditch with the plow in forty-five minutes. We're trading for some sheep.

Today was the first day we saw a little bloat in the goats; Greta was throwing up and had a big belly. Chandra wouldn't eat nor would Lotsi. Reason? We just watered their pasture, I think. Book says to watch out on lush, newly wet fields. But two hours later, Greta was eating hay. Tomorrow we'll restrict them to less time out.

Sunday: The baby's "doing fine" is the report. Good, good. Next week, then they'll be back.

We are giving Lotsi's milk only to the baby goats. She shows some mastitis reaction in the teat we've been treating. She is on special care, and we'll have to think of some good things to give her, like garlic and comfrey. The mistake was that as soon as we saw a bruise to bag or teat, we should have separated the milk and tested for mastitis. We were too slow to take precautions. Now Pepe's mad, (from blood in a bottle of goat's milk), and we could lose our number-one customer, which would be a big setback for us.

May 24, 1976: I treat Lotsi with Kim. Kim is showing an excellent hand with the animals now that he's given the chance. We now have a sheet in the milk room for milk records. This is a big step forward to develop our treatment for mastitis.

Jim, our newfound brother, is sick of working for money, but he's a real "farm funky" as he says. He spends long hours quietly in the garden—very persistent worker and quite meticulous too. Sunday he went fishing with Mike. Great if they make friends. This fellow has been a big help and is the best newcomer we've met in a long time.

Action: I took Larry's Ford sedan with V-8 engine and went through incredible mountains to Los Alamos. Saw the hospital—the whole setup. Very excellent. Sandy met me at the door and—zoom, zoom—we took little Emil home to New Buffalo. Both mother and child look good. The baby was very popular—"little doll baby"—very patient and quiet. He was sick (spinal fluid infection), and the doctors and medicine probably for sure saved his little life. Lots of people helped us out with very expensive methods and machines. Doctor's secretary put Sandy up as a houseguest after the doctor was called in and reprimanded by his higher authority for scolding the nurses and putting the exhausted mother in a hospital bed. Thank you.

Earlier, before my arrival at the hospital, I went up to Polito's to see his "out of business" dairy. He's got a cooler and a storage tank both for $100! Very exciting. I'm feeling good. Things are moving.

Kemal and Kiva saw Pepe and friends. They're happy to see cow's milk and accepted one extra gallon free. Kiva and Kemal—not quite sure on how they would be received—got a very good welcome.

Larry: I spoke to him, saying he should really get with us—feel that energy. He wants to be more productive—doing his best—this a great place to do it.

Got an offer to trade Pamela, our beef cow, for a Guernsey milk cow. Things are going to happen for us.

May 28: Progress: Sandy's floor was finished being mudded today. Gardens are getting all the water they need with Kim very much on top of it. Sandy is finally getting to rest.

June 1, 1976: Yesterday I was on the community ditch, making a careful survey all the way, looking at the weak spots. I brought the commissioner to one place, and we did a repair that might have been a terrible break. I could see several improvements: cutting out the horseshoe with a culvert, where the water crosses the highway, is the first priority for more efficient water transport. We're speeding right into the short and crucial planting and growing period.

Washout! What a fool. I advised Kim to leave water on the rye to get it done. Bad spot, because the water gathered and washed out a foot-deep arroyo in half of one unplanted bean section; a ton of dirt, at least, got moved. Sorry, sorry. Tomorrow I turn down the water in the main ditch.

Strep throat! Monica got it; Jimmy should have moved out right away. But then he got it. Sylvie took them in for tests and cure. Now Jason seems to have it. He's quarantined, especially from Sandy. I took both Jason and Tony in for tests but couldn't get them done. Kemal is sick too but not bad enough to keep him home. Plus baby Timor is sick. They should be separated too. Hope it doesn't spread and have another Buffalo epidemic . . . duh.

Friday: Mike Pots is making a greenhouse attached to the south facing end of his room. He dug a hole yesterday and poured concrete today. Our hardiest man is going solar.

Sasha is gone, a sigh of relief from many of us. We took her in, in cold winter, a homeless gal—destitute—looking for a funky place to get on welfare.

Consensus rules from now on! We don't want the commune to be a catchall for misfits. She did provide Larry with a love affair, which he certainly needed. And it appears, just in the nick of time, she took care of her ill son. We do appreciate that she got it together with the purchase of the electric fence. She's another person we've met and lived with.

June 7: The cow is going up in production. Lotsi is still not declared well. It's hard managing the goats. Here, only three weeks after we put it up, we're taking down the electric fence.

Wednesday: Under blue skies, Ron and I got some of the electric fence back up; we've got a beautiful field surrounded. In the afternoon I took Mike to the clinic for strep test—extra care for our milker, and we don't want to have any epidemics. Hopefully it's only a cold. He got a little overtired—run down. Mike works very hard, here and in town three days a week.

Happy commotion outside! Tall Neil Svenningson and Holly just drove up in their new flashy '59 Chevrolet panel truck! These are our good family. We just happen to have a room they can use. With them is their new baby, Max, named after our grandpa Max Finstein.

My mayordomo ditch duties are taking a lot of time. Manuel Ortiz is a good man to work with. He's president of the commission for which I work. I stepped up the water and had it dammed at Tieder's head gate, so it wouldn't reach the washout at Leo's. The water had created a giant chasm, and the entire flow eroded into it. I'd been watching that place. The moment I saw the ditch entirely dry, I knew just what had happened. Nobody knows the ditches like I do. Spoke with Leo in the evening. Tomorrow we fix it with a bulldozer.

Each night I stay with Sandy and the new baby Emil. Big trip coming up to Clovis—see a bit of the state.

A new day: We looked at "our" Guernsey. She won't be ready until after we come back. No rush. Felipe will milk her until we make the exchange.

Neil and Holly set up house in the abandoned room, the one that Sasha left. Holly is one of the all-time heavies in the homemaking department. They had both gotten burned out on the commune, but I hope they can now see it more as a stable, normal, and very good life.

The big circle room is clean. Sylvie doesn't forget to make it look pleasant in here. Open space—no furniture except for the big cedar table and benches— nothing to gather dust or collect left articles. Its clarity reflects a clarity of ours.

6. *Outside the candle room. Photo by Clarice Kopecky*

Down from Morningstar came John and Rebel to borrow our mower, a very essential piece of equipment for us; yet we let it go. The Pitman arm and a blade, they broke right away. If worse comes to worse, we'll get Al Kaplan to mow for us.

Sandy painted tierra blanca on the new room walls. It goes on dark and dries a brilliant white. The floor is dry enough now for filling the cracks. My ax needs sharpening.

Sunday: Before going on our long-planned journey, I checked the ditch; it was way down; I found a new and major break. I fetched Celestino Vigil and a power saw. Neil and visitor Jeremy went and retrieved O. G. Martinez, and in two hours we repaired the hole with trees and sandbags. Then I took off with Bob Dowling, from the Ortiviz farm in Colorado. We're invited to learn to be real dairymen by the chief state milk inspector himself. We're a little ragged, Bob with his kooky hat and me with worn clothes, but people want to help us.

We looked at two dairies on the way down. Stopped to see friends Paul and Millie in Albuquerque and made it to within fifty miles of Clovis by midnight. Slept on the grass.

Early, before 9 a.m., we met Mr. Proctor at his office. He had errands to do. We went to a park for some morning exercise, then off to Portales and to Ed Burnett's dairy. In her country kitchen, Mrs. Burnett served us lunch. The whole operation is for sale for $52,000. No individual cows for sale. They milk just four cows at a time. But here is the basic setup. Back to Albuquerque in the afternoon. At Paul and Millie's we had a light dinner and went to bed.

Next morning, we were given an extensive tour at Price's Albuquerque dairy with nine hundred cows milking. We talked with the manager, Homer Morris—famous for dairy cow judging—and the young foreman Butch, who took us around and showed us the operation.

Next to Macalhaney Dairy, our Crystal's birthplace. We walked around in the several hundred head of beautiful Jerseys. Saw the cooling, homogenizing, pasteurizing, and bottling all in a pretty small room.

We then saw Mr. Thatcher—seventy-five years old—running his whole operation himself, even throwing the bales! He has twenty milking and fifteen heifers ready to calve. $17,500 for the thirty-five head—priced to sell—probably has them sold. Mr. Thatcher, as all others, was very pleased to talk with us and show us around. He is the state advisor for pasture. With a lot of fencing he rotates fifteen individual areas, leaving the cows on each only two days a month. He still refers to his wife as "my bride."

Then on to Billy Jones Dairy Supply. We bought bottles, ninety cents apiece, one hundred throwaway tops, two stainless steel five-gallon cans to milk into, bottlebrushes, and soap. A cooling tank of 200-gallon capacity is the smallest Bill Jones knows of.

Proctor, who is the law in these things, for now wants to encourage us. He seems to accept hand bottling.

We want business—no more food stamps or welfare or being so broke. We've got a lot of people, so we'll have to think bigger.

Thursday: Peggi Sue is back! Sunny and vivacious, she wants to settle in and stay. Tonight she cooked an incredible meal with two of our own chickens and made a super cake. She wants to get in on the milking too. Great!

Kemal butchered a sheep we bought. Mike, Jim, and I slaughtered the biggest cabrito: skinned, gutted, and hung it in the cool night breeze. After fantastic dinner Peggi Sue joins me singing Bob Dylan songs. We got that "Subterranean Homesick Blues" just right. This little celebration was also a fond farewell to Jim, who has been so helpful.

7. *Carol and Zindor. Bolinas, California. 1970.*
Photo by Harris Saltzberg

June 23, 1976: Storm last night. We had a fair amount of rain. I set out to complete all necessary mayordomo tasks. It took all day.

Dan Cohn and Jessy, along with two friends, came to visit. Also three good-looking gals from the Mabel Dodge House jewelry community and Sarah Baker, ex–lead singer of Oriental Blue Streak band fame, add to our very lively home.

Dan Cohn is a blast from the past. He's a handsome man with short, wavy blond hair. We were acquaintances at City College of NY. He moved to Berkeley, and a year later I entered a Masters program in international relations at UC. Far from home, acquaintances become close friends.

In the excitement of the psychedelic revolution, a group of Wisconsin boys moved to Berkeley. There was tall Kirk Imse Sleazy, short muscular Zindor with a long beard, and a half dozen others. Dick Shu—fastidiously clean—rented the apartment above Dan Cohn. In this crowd was a very eager Indian, Pepe Rochon. One day Dan introduced us, and that started a partnership, which carries us both on this wondrous path that neither could travel alone. Later Dan moved to Bolinas, and our forming tribe gathered at his house on stilts before starting our first commune on Laurel Street back in '69.

Just about overnight our farm has changed. On Friday morning a bunch of us herded Pamela the cow and the two Herefords up to the barn. As soon as we put them in, Felipe drove up. He backed right up to the ramp, and Pamela and one Hereford went very easily into the truck. Now we get Jenny the Guernsey.

We asked Felipe if he wanted a horse. Kemal made a deal, trading the remaining Hereford, horse, and $25 for a beautiful Holstein that should drop a calf in July. Saturday she was delivered.

Next we went out and bought Polito's cooler for $60. Larry is starting on the repairs; some bearings need replacing, but the refrigeration works. Basically it's a metal box, five foot by two foot on a metal stand. It's open at the top, and filled with water, which is cooled all the way down to 34 degrees. Right after milking, you filter the milk into bottles and place them in the cold water. Proctor says you have about an hour to cool milk; we will now be able to do it much more rapidly.

July 9, 1976: At 6 a.m. Kemal woke me up. Dead cow! Must belong to one of our neighbors. We constantly live with this phantom of bloat. Kemal went and asked around while I got the tractor and rope.

The two cows that constantly break through our fences belong to Steve Vigil's brother. We dragged it out. Then Steve and I looked around Buffalo as we chased the other cow out. We saw how they ate a lot of developing oats, which we'll get to cut after the alfalfas are all up.

Wet, succulent, leguminous plants in pasture, being grazed for first time, are particularly capable of producing bloat. We always feed dry hay before grazing and make sure the pasture is not wet. To get nourishment out of graze, cattle have huge digestive systems, and when too much gas is produced, it can kill them quickly. Below and forward of the hipbone is a place you can puncture to give relief if one gets there in time.

Emil, our little son, is doing quite well. He certainly keeps his mom occupied. A luxury, really, for the women to be able to spend so much time on the little children. Very nice for the kids. I like the world we live in despite certain problems we face.

July 18, 1976: After several days of not doing too much, I'm feeling good and rested. I've been on the ditch fairly often. I hear the pounding of hammer to nail as it is carried off the mesa wall; Larry's building the new outhouse. Sasha left, and he is back to being stuck with us. Well, we love him. A shame that gal didn't want to stay and support him right here. Her loss.

The cows are in a fuss at the barn. The vet was here testing for TB and brucellosis; results will be available Monday. We're going to start selling milk at the co-op as "pet food."

What! A bit of a shock—Kemal and Kiva say they're moving out! Kemal suggested they'd like to take a few animals: pigs and Crystal. The cow gets a resounding "NO!" and maybe it'll be the same for pigs.

Mike is pissed. He's tired of people copping out and then wanting to take a piece of the farm with them. Well, no way we'll willingly let go of a cow! And then there's the truck. Though they've got near a dozen vehicles where they're going, they want the Dodge truck that Kemal was so insistent was "ours." Kim was very skeptical; now we see. For me, I didn't expect it. Kim says he's seen it coming from the start. Kemal has been a major partner of mine, and all of a sudden he's out!

This will be a very major difference for this winter though. No move could help us out, wood wise, more. Kiva lacked conservation consciousness, and Kemal, outdoorsman that he is, couldn't do anything. Though I felt a bit stunned in the morning, I had a great day. Once again, we're looking for a vehicle.

Tuesday night: Full flow in the ditch all night, and we're ready: Kim, Peggi Sue, and I started out, and Larry took my place at 2 a.m. Like beacons in the night, one can see three storm lanterns and one handy little flashlight bobbing around the landscape. You can't buy a pill to feel this good. The sky is full of stars; the night animals move around and talk; the water gurgles bringing life to the fields. Someplace people in the city are sleeping so they can arise, put on a suit, and go get stuck in traffic. I'm in a different galaxy far, far away from that. This watering is right on the money.

Kim did the town trip; six gallons of cow's milk sold and $15 collected for lettuce from Joe's Restaurant, a great market for us. We have a lot of produce coming up. Kim has seen it a long way off; his vision has been good. Sylvie and Peggi milk the goats in the evening.

July 22: I delivered milk this morning; Holly came along. Also went and talked with the vet about vaccinations.

Event: Now I've started a real ledger. Kemal and Kiva gave me the binder they established for the milk. Now I'll take it over and put a section for all

8. *Herding Fudge, our steer. Photo by Clarice Kopecky*

expenses too. This is something I believe is essential to a real commune: a central treasury and central account. It is necessary so we can see what is actually happening—help other people understand what it takes to run the place. We are finally making some real money.

Kemal will take some bees, the bee equipment, and two pigs. He'd like the cow Crystal, but we won't let her go. Also cheese pots, thermometer, cheese books, and "our" truck will go. But this is clearing the situation. This will be "the last time," we hope, that pieces of our scene are taken that we don't really want to see go. We had a meeting where we said as much, but this will make it more definite.

Second cut of alfalfa looks incredibly good—thicker and lusher than last cut. This is when our alfalfa fields are really getting prime. It's taken several years for them to look this good.

Sunday: We gave shots; I did the shooting: Crystal, Fudge, new Carnegie, and Nelly each under the skin. Felipe had vaccinated Jenny and Julie. Six head of cattle—four dairy and two steers—just a beginning. From across the valley, New Buffalo looks alive, vibrantly green.

Commitment—that's it; we want very great, sincere commitment to communal living. If you loose faith—decide to leave the fold—no reward. Stay in, and it's all yours. The whole belongs to the New Buffalo Corporation. We can't have a strong ongoing scene and have everyone who's built it have claims on pieces.

July 28, 1976: Sylvie made a mozzarella cheese today; it's in the press. We're eating a Muenster cheese that Peggi Sue made; I like it very much. There's a ricotta cheese in the making and a Parmesan cheese hung up drying. It's good and hard.

Friday: I've been thinking I'd like to put a solar collector on the south wall of the wing, where Sandy has her room. The doors of the three rooms will lead into the collector, which can second as a greenhouse. Mike's solar collector is coming along very nicely, being very carefully done.

We have a tall and quiet fellow, Michael, from South Carolina, who says he traveled out here to specifically visit New Buffalo and see if he could maybe join. He's been very helpful and has set up a little camp in the circle. Ron and Kim said, "We're open for new energy." And we are. We lose a strong man, and we'd like to get another—someone more committed. Kiva and Kemal are set to leave tomorrow.

Tuesday: Very dramatic, this weather; there must be a hundred completely different skies. All day they swirled around. Across the river Leo and son windrowing and baling their bottom field.

August 6, 1976: Heavy frost. I see it in the early morning when I get the cows before sunrise; I hear the vegetation crunching beneath my boots.

Mike Pots: He puts his money toward the animals: goat feeders, buck purchase, milking equipment. He financed his passive solar collector, and now he's invested in the Buffalo apiary. He swears his desire is to buy the stuff for New Buffalo. Now we've got a mask, gloves, and smoker.

He inspected the hives. One is making queen cells. He extracted ten frames of honey—sixty pounds—and got ten very nice frames with foundation and cells; so now they can use the same frames to make more honey. Great that Mike got right in there when we needed someone in charge. Got a few stings in return.

But Mike's single life is fraying him on the edges; he has episodes of spouting out abrupt loudness for no apparent reason. Maybe it's for attention, I don't know. A woman in his life would be just right.

Saturday: Before dawn had begun to lighten the sky, Kim and Peg, equipped with flashlight and lantern, continued the harvest of peas, carrots, turnips, radishes, and lettuce to sell at this morning's farmers market. Lettuce was poor because of frost last night.

A big cloud threatened us as we picked up the second truckload of hay off the two and a half acres we cut yesterday. Plus we picked up forty-six bales at Leo's. Some of the bales we didn't like much—too dry and stemmy—others are wet but whole. We'll let them air out.

Lama picked up a gallon of cottage cheese that Sandy made, plus seven gallons of their own milk from their cow that is temporarily here.

Best week so far—made $78.50!

August 9, 1976: Into Dick McKracken's truck we loaded our big 500-pound sow. Worked out a good method using truck sideboards to corner her in. Ornery and excited, she just about climbed onto Dick as we drove to the Mariposa ranch to get her bred. Good thing she's halfway tame!

Developed a good method with Julie the cow too; she's got a rope hanging from her halter; grab it and then hook her to the long rope, then into headstall.

In late afternoon, armed with shovels and strong backs, Al, Larry, Jimmy, and I worked on the leak from the Acequia Madre—the air intoxicating from the surrounding piñon and juniper trees. We made some overdue repairs. Jimmy, with his joking, youthful exuberance, helped to make us feel good.

JOURNAL 19

So dreams do come true.
Struggles are rewarded.

August 10, 1976: The evening has settled in, the mountains purple in the colorful sunset. Our days are full with daily chores, milk runs, and early morning irrigations—Peggi Sue handling the runoff. Sylvie and helpers preparing peas for a late night freezing. A real treat—handled like precious gold, and precious they are.

August 11: Two men from the Soil Conservation office were over. Very good. Wayne Fesita thinks we can drain and improve our swampy pasture and also says the border areas can be improved—plant better grass. An agriculture expert, he's a very good man to get advice from. We have a date to get him out here again—knows people and knows the state. Fellow Wayne will be able to help us with many aspects of setting up the dairy barn. I really gravitate toward meeting these professional people.

Later, out on the ditch I spoke with Malacio. He has a thirsty farm. Saw Tieder and his sprinkler system. It's really great. Soil fellows were right out there—measuring—needs three more hours on that spot. Tieder is to pass on the water at night, so one other person can be irrigating at the same time. Cooperation.

Julie cow is coming into the headstall on her own! She'll drop her calf real soon. We seem to be doing quite well, taming the wild beast. She is a beautiful animal.

Looks like we'll buy Dennis Long's Dodge pickup. We'll have to do clutch and engine repair and add new shocks, but we ought to get a good truck.

Kim is a bit injured—his back. It's been building up constantly for weeks, but he hasn't been able to stop; just like me, drive yourself until the body forces a rest. My milking has improved, and I don't mind milking three cows. Sylvie is trying to break into the cow scene in the mornings. Peggi Sue is doing the goats at night, alone, and she prefers it that way.

August 14, 1976: Julie dropped her bull calf. I left her in the pasture in the morning because she looked like she was going to have it. Then Babe came into heat. Very good. Jimmy and I cut another acre of alfalfa.

August 16, 1976: We now have three truckloads in. But we are perpetually feeling short of hay. We're cutting down; cows' milk production is going down too. I'll give them a few good meals of hay and see if that helps. Brown Swiss are supposed to be good converters of graze to milk.

Talking with Mike and Kim: "What happens if our hay does run out?" I say we can always let them out to live off the graze, as we have done with Nelly and all the beef cattle. Then we decide what to do.

Holly is moved into her new room, but Neil is gone, looking for work. He's experienced in working the oil fields. Maybe he's over looking around Farmington. He left her a car but said not to let it get used. Monica moved into the room she left vacated.

Young Jon, who was here in April, returned after living and working in Oregon and Colorado. Jon had once been "vibed" out by Ron for no obvious reason. This young man is big and strong. Only about twenty years old, he has a very deep voice. He helped pick up hay and cut pigweed, and he did some major landscaping work. Ron is accepting now; we have no future without people joining us.

A new day: New expanded milk run today. We have some very nice new customers, I hear. The Mabel Dodge House wants another four gallons. More and more people are asking us for cow's milk.

After milking, I went over to Leo's. I have almost all the new ditches completed now—a very thorough job being done, if I do say so myself. I look out with satisfaction; I also shudder at seeing a little dirt road leading up there. When I first started this project I took that road, not seeing the correct one. Half way up it gets terribly steep. The tractor actually started to go over backwards—not a good thing. My reflexes gunned the accelerator; it threw the tractor forward enough to get the wheels back on the ground—better for steering—and I made it to the top cross-country. My heart was pounding—my body shaking. Once in a while you need your luck.

Visitor Anhighon from Germany is here. Young Jon very anxious to help and work into the group.

August 18, 1976: Harvest time. The golden wheat is fat and ripe and standing tall; it's ready. With Manuel Martinez's 36-year-old combine we are thoroughly modern—no more cutting by hand. Larry has done an excellent job greasing and repairing the rickety old monster.

Letter from a friend in Vancouver, British Columbia: "Another set of busy months coming up. Well, I've been loving it so far and as long as that keeps up, so will I. . . . Life is good and I feel very grateful for the gift of a lifetime in these most strange and wonderful times." Precisely my sentiments—the way to feel—that's our spirit.

Wayne Fesita from Soil Conservation was here, giving out a lot of ideas.

Saturday: Larry and I finished combining the big wheat field—several thousand pounds. Spinning and rattling, the combine broke down. We made a wooden bearing using our new lathe to replace a brass one that came apart. Good work.

Young Jon left. I'm not sure why. Anhighon from German commune still here. He and Sylvie pulled all the sunflowers out of the wheat field. They are so beautiful with yellow faces all turned east, but they can't be in the wheat. Must be careful not to trample the grain.

Mike Pots made a gate for the new pig corral. Now they stay in. Mike has added a car hood for a pig shelter and has made a pig feeder from a sink. He wishes someone else would take more responsibility with the pigs.

August 25, 1976: Michael Pair—good brother from the Huerfano Valley—and I raked the cut hay, and then we went out on the ditch. Hay has to be turned several times to get it pretty dry, and it has to be in rows to be picked up. That afternoon big storm clouds came up and brought rain.

Larry and Kim are taking the truck engine apart. Mike has started yet another big project putting a cement retainer wall on the one wing. First the

9. *Carnegie, Kim, and Mike*

top of the wall has to be remudded, then covered with chicken wire, then concreted to keep the mud from deteriorating in the rain. He also put in four canales to drain the roof. Good work.

Everything is not always so smooth. Larry had to repair the motor for the wheat-aerating device. Peggi Sue got a car stuck in the garden while getting lettuce for sale to Joe's Restaurant. Tractor ran out of gas while combining. Red truck ran out of gas—had to siphon from the car. Tractor wouldn't start when out in the field—had to take the truck out to jump start it. The other day I had to take the carburetor apart to get a piece of rust out. Our biggest field got rained on twice after being cut. Worse yet, the bales we got from Leo are terrible, terrible. We took the greener ones, but we should have opened them up to sun dry. Just leaving unstacked was not good enough. The big pain-in-the-ass is having to stake out our steer, Carnegie, because he sucks our milk cow Nelly—one more extra chore.

Emil has a low blood count. Maxy, Holly and Neil's boy, is teething and cries a lot some days. Tony, Sylvie's youngest, had asthma for a day. And our man Kim, his back is hurt, but he's getting professional help from the hospital.

Our wheat is in and the dryer seems to work now; it saves a lot of effort. In our milk room the cooler from Polito is working well; that is essential to us. The milk is so fresh. And now there is plenty of cream for butter to go on the bread we make every day. No complaints on the milk run. The baby chicks are doing well. All in all, we're staying right in there, working hard. Difficulties, yes, but we've got a lot of good things to keep us going.

The contradictory of a welcome probability will assert itself, whenever such an eventuality is likely to be most frustrating, or the outcome of a given desired probability will be inverse to the degree of desirability. There is no such thing as a free lunch. Whenever things appear to be going better, you have overlooked something!

In a crisis or emergency situation, which forces an immediate decision between alternative courses of action, inevitably most people choose the worst one possible. Nothing is as easy as it looks. It will take longer and be harder than you think. If anything can go wrong, it will. Mike Pots, the optimist.

This fellow is not discouraged though. He works hard every day. And actually, though we do have problems and setbacks, we are still here. Neither the bugs nor germs have killed us, nor war or the vigilantes.

Thursday: We almost got the hay in but rain hit briefly at 3 p.m., so we'll let it dry a bit tomorrow morning.

Larry, our scientist, is going to start an experiment creating and capturing methane gas. He made that water heater and has made dozens of innovative improvements: wooden bearing for Manuel's combine, dryer for the wheat, and fancy cabinets for the kitchen. And he removed the noise from the cooler. This will be the greatest challenge yet. It's a bit tricky, since that methane can EXPLODE! Great hope for the future.

August 27, 1976: It took three trips to bring in that hay. We're making better and better stacks. In the old-fashioned method we stack the hay on the flatbed truck. Three or four people with pitchforks pass the pungent greenery to the person on the truck. That one gently places hay on top of hay until the stack is too tall to reach. The kids love to ride on top of the stack, bouncing along. Heck, I love to ride the stack myself! Back at the barn we create a giant bread-loaf-shaped stack about twelve feet tall. This later can be sliced with our great hay knife so the hay is not disturbed as it's fed out.

And from Lama Foundation came David to help with chores. With us he helped to remove the sand and sawdust out of the root cellar; we want the sand drier and the floor too. He and I mowed our last and second cutting of alfalfa. We'll continue cutting hay tomorrow if the sky looks clear.

Joe Gomez, food stamp worker who was out today, said he heard the weather's due to clear now.

Monday evening: I'm feeling very good. We had a meeting and pep talk and out-front discussion of dairy: where we're going, milking machines, and how many cows. I spoke enthusiastically about my drive to see the commune establish high-quality and good-quantity production—business.

Sylvie, Holly, and Peggi Sue went in to get food stamps, and they got them, but not easily. Each had to speak individually to the worker—a real grilling.

We're just too successful. Food stamps aren't meant for us, they're trying to tell us. So, we're not going to apply any longer. We have three steers, two pigs coming up and one 500-pound sow. Our bin is full of wheat (2,000 pounds), and there's a big flock of 130 chickens, though egg production has badly dropped. We have carrots, beets, a good root cellar, and plans for, hopefully, a ton of apples and about 600 pounds of potatoes. We have three cows producing milk and six goats—eleven gallons a day. We've got about 100 pounds of onions, frozen peas, canned apricots, sauerkraut, dried zucchinis. Still, we feed a lot of people, including anyone who comes up the road.

I checked out the chickens because Holly was in town. I killed and butchered one that had a very broken leg; we ate it right away. Since I've been at Buffalo, I learned how to do that simple chore: head off, feathers off with boiling water dip, clean guts out, spleen removed from liver—carefully— gizzard out, and gland on tail cut off.

Under threatening skies, Larry, Sandy, and I brought in the alfalfa hay, and it looks pretty good.

Tonight, as I was milking Julie, I jumped up to cover some hay as a rain started. Nelly cow came in while Julie was in the stall and BAM! Julie got nervous. When I continued, she wouldn't drop her milk, upset by my allowing Nelly to enter while she was stuck in the headstall. I returned later and milked her with no problem. She comes right in the stall by herself. I have to turn my head so she can keep her dignity for she is bowing to my will to satisfy her greed. Courtesy demands I turn my head. She even expects to be hobbled a certain way. Handled right, she's a good cow.

David returned to Lama. He is a fine man. I've been wondering where more of my compatriots are. Well, here is one not quite available to live here, but a close neighbor from our closest commune. Really great to have him here and talk with him—talk about what we're working for: brotherhood, clearness, mellowness, closer to God, to earth, to each other. Unlike John, who hated to have anyone near him, we have our friends see us milk, throw hay to the animals, be there with us, and see how we do our most productive thing— milking time.

A new day: I talk about business—success—making money. Will success spoil us? No! What do I want? I'd like to see us lower our prices if we found we had our essentials covered. I'd like to make gifts of our fine product to some people. Gaskins's Farm is a model for me; they're buying a boat so they can ship their surplus anywhere in the world they want to. There is no end to how much we can help, no end to how much we can contribute to helping communes grow. I'd like to get to the point where we have so much abundance. *Arty deserves the BEST!*—Writer unknown.

Terrific Sunday: Hot and clear—the rain has stopped. Lots of visiting friends for a Buffalo afternoon of volleyball, good eats, and homegrown country music. Saturday night Sylvie, Holly, and Peggi Sue put up a peyote meeting for Larry. Three venerable elders from the Pueblo were here: Teles Good Morning, Frank Samora, and Joe Sandoval. These fine men step right out of the pages of history: homespun blankets over the shoulders, finely beaded moccasins, long braids, and a lilting accent speaking short sentences. Also Bobby Pedro and wife Laura are staying with us for a while.

With lots of other friends, we had over fifty people for the feast. They were pleased that the people living with Larry feel so much for him that they'd put up a meeting for him, quite a distinctive way to honor our good friend and helper. Coincidently, Daddy Dave and Rick Klein were here. My mom came too, enjoying the company at the party. I think New Buffalo felt very good to these people.

New fellow arrived tonight from France. Anhighon, from Germany, is back. He's very helpful around the kitchen.

Tuesday: Yesterday, as clouds appeared in a tumbling fury, we planted the two fields with winter wheat—continue the cycle.

The kitchen stove was smoking terribly. Who comes along to take the stove apart and give it an elaborate cleaning? Mr. Pots. He also gave the milk room a once-over and got the calf out in the morning.

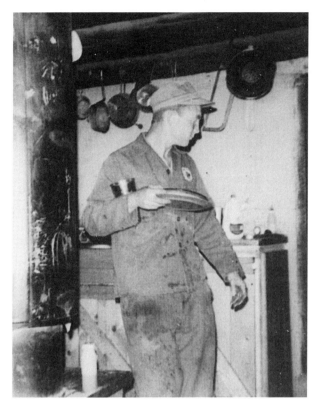

10. *Mike Pots*

I finished making the outhouse seat and began to assemble it to the platform. The new outhouse is further from the house and well screened. In this bathroom there is no mirror. Instead we look out to the hills of native trees, green-gray sage, and chamisa bushes, a reflection of our effect on the earth—minimal—not destructive. Why are so many content to see concrete and buildings?

Wednesday: After morning milking, Mike, Larry, and I put a pole and firewood run together. We took off a flat, got the tools, fixed the hydraulic jack, bought a bow saw blade and dropped off the tire. Also before we left, Holly got very upset over something to do with precious eggs and quit her job as chicken master.

The transfer from Sylvie to Holly was one of the worst demonstrations of communal competence. The egg production went all the way down to zero before a review was made of the feeding schedule. Holly, it turned out, had no idea the chickens were to get ten pounds a day of mixed grains and laying mash. But all the chickens, except three, are still alive, and we're trying to rescue the trip. We've got a good house and yard, good chickens, and a 500-pound stash of food for them.

Tieder said he'd sell his grain for $6 a hundred pounds. He also said Lupe Young in Cerro de Questa has wheat for sale. Food, it's very important. In this willy-nilly world, the scales can change very rapidly.

Sharing instead of greed, this is the crucial point. Abundance and scarcity are always there. The thing is to share whatever it is we have. We show that by sharing responsibilities, etc., we hope to create a good life. Big article in *Time* about the profit motive. This need not be the central theme of America.

In proving herself "queen of homemakers," Holly—in a canning rampage—put up beets, turnips, tomatoes, and pears. Steer clear of the kitchen; you may get run over!

After his "need to leave," Ron has returned. He sees we need the help, and this is his scene. He wants to contribute. Good. He hopes to be mellower and says the time away was devoted to dedicating himself to change. Ron now is herding the cows in and out, cutting all our kitchen wood again, harvesting the smoke. He's willing and conscious to water the winter wheat. We're really plugging away.

And there is a rumor Sylvie will quit—leave! We drive her too hard with so many things to do. We're not good company enough. She's got welfare. Boy, she's a great woman though: pitches hay, great cook, she's neat, lives very frugally and simply, good with the chickens, getting good at cheese making. Real country.

In the news: Mao Tse Dong died; one of the great leaders of the Chinese— "Serve the people." In *Newsweek* on the consciousness movement, it "reinforces social traditional American beliefs; the innate goodness of man, the inevitability of human progress." Now these are beliefs I have, not the capitalist vision but an American belief nonetheless.

Wood run didn't get back until after 9:00 in the evening. Rescue mission was about to set out. Perfect timing, we arrived home as they were about to leave to find us. We got a big load of wood, but it certainly wasn't easy.

September 13, 1976: Quiet day. I milked all three cows this morning, and I guess I'll continue that for a while so Sylvie can be with her kids in the morning and help them off to school with a good breakfast. But she's not leaving; not now and that's very good. She just had to generate a little excitement—some emotion.

I helped Holly move canned goods down to the root cellar: apricots, tomatoes, sauerkraut, turnips, radishes, a few beets, and pears, all in quart jars. She already put beets away in sand in the root cellar. Holly's a bit moody; she misses Neil.

In the pantry are six cheeses now—beautiful round loaves getting a yellow rind. In the wheat bin still the blower is on; the wheat is gradually drying and getting hard.

Tomatoes are coming in. Sandy preserved nine more jars of them. With more greenhouses yet, we'll start to get enough tomatoes to really supply our demand. Larry and I put the irrigation lines in the new wheat fields. Larry laid out proper three-percent sloping ditches for the first time in those fields.

We're feeding 140 chickens, four pigs, four milk cows, three steers, eleven goats, and one sheep.

A new day: Peg, Larry, Ron, Sylvie, and Mike went down to the orchard at La Bolsa. We picked seventeen good-sized boxes of apples—plenty to eat now and plenty to preserve. We've got more prospects.

Kim bought four bushels of green chiles today for storing and 100 pounds of pinto beans for $22. He and Peg picked a bushel or more of little but tasty wild plums. Kim and Peggi Sue seem always to be side by side.

Weather—what a tease—very threatening all day but not a drop of rain. Wheat is coming up fast. Irrigation water is nowhere near.

September 19: Mike proposed a wood run; I said okay. Peggi Sue and Ron came too. I led us to a dusty road in San Cristobal, the very closest place to get wood. We got a load quickly, and it was easy. Had a nice lunch of our own bread, cheese, tomatoes and were back home before 4 p.m., even with a late start. At home Sandy canned more tomatoes from the greenhouse with more harvests to come.

I went out for a short run when we got home. But because I strained a muscle while working on the outhouse, I have had to slow down some and rest. Then I went dancing with Pepe and Peggi anyhow. Heard Joe Cota and Rick Klein's band, both very good. Pepe just returned from Wisconsin with a very unusual report. "Cro Farm is sold!" he says, and "Curly Jim and Mike Torgeson relocated to Wisconsin" very near the Grotto farm where we were five years ago. A 500-acre farm they bought this time with dairy facilities, just no cows. I hate to hear Cro Farm is sold. That's a great piece of land.

Sylvie spaced out the cow trip for two days; her own mental confusion she felt was more important than her role in the dairy, so she quit showing up. Result: Nelly gives three quarts less every day.

Just as people say, put those cows through changes in the routine and down goes production. Cannot recapture it until next season. Goat John says you can't have more than one person run the scene—see what happens. Other people, too, point to our example and say you try but you fail. Me? I say we're still in an infant stage—lots to learn and a lot more commitment to be given.

September 21: Sylvie is back with it. Great! And Nelly is up. Hard task we have before us. Can't achieve something great though if we don't have a real challenge.

Friends of Sylvie are staying with us: three boys, a girl, and the husband and wife Claude and Sue—good people. Claude is a farm worker, a milker, but he's had enough of it after ten years milking 120 to 140 Guernsey cows twice a day.

Many voices mingle in our busy kitchen. The smell of roasting chiles on the iron stove top permeates the air. It wafts down the few stairs into the great kiva room, our circle. From there it drifts through the open doors to the courtyard where the air is taking on the autumn chill.

September 23: Pretty heavy frost now—time to finish cutting. Kim went to town; he's feeling better. Still he has to stay away from heavy work. But he's been cooking, canning pepper relish, and taking the milk runs. Other day he went to Santa Fe with Hap and put a deposit down on an engine for our truck—a good move.

September 24, 1976: Event: Mike Pots finished concrete-capping the three rooms of the west wing. Looks great—excellent workmanship. He used many long nails woven into the chicken wire with a technique Larry taught us. Four canales got set in too.

Today pears got canned. This is much more like the farm life than a few years ago. Stocking up for winter—potatoes and carrots coming in—freezer filling up and over 100 quarts of canned goods in the root cellar. Wheat is in the bin and about 1,000 pounds of grain put away for the animals. Some cheese and butter being put away too. We still need more milk just to maintain our sales and supply us for the year.

11. *Lumber roads with aspens. Photo by Clarice Kopecky*

Monday: Ba-zoom! We go from a real dry period to a long storm. All the land is thriving with rain. Enjoyed the mountain landscape on a wood run to help Dick and Al, our good neighbors, to bring vigas down from the high mountains. We got snowed on at the end, but the weather held off until we were finished. There are no windows in our truck, and there's a problem with the brake's air assist and a problem with electric fuel pump. Fuel pump corrected itself, thank goodness, and problem with the brakes never appeared. Aspen trees are very yellow in the beautiful and cloud-shrouded mountains with us rumbling along some lumbering roads.

Our house is cool; two windows are completely missing—one kitchen and one circle. One circle door doesn't really work, and only the screen door is on the kitchen. Soon time to winterize. Our kiva is adorned with braids of onions and ristras of chiles.

Tuesday: I saw Kemal. He said he heard of a Holstein six-year-old for sale—seven gallons supposedly for $300. I'll check it out. We could perhaps get $300 for Julie, who is disappointing, and be milking a better cow. Sounds like possibly a good deal.

On the world scene: Secretary of State Kissinger says that in his talks with Mao the Chairman said that nuclear war is very likely. This I became very aware of when sixteen years old and that has shaped my life. I believe it is not inevitable. One way or the other, greater sharing, understanding, generosity, and agricultural skills can help. It was my consciousness of wanting to work for world peace, I feel, that really got me into this communal business. Defeat greed—promote sharing. Here is the source of the problem and the solution.

Mike set up an apple run for tomorrow. Efficient man he is—tonight he is preparing the lunch.

September 29: A perfect day—Exhilarating! Snow on the mountains contrasting with the yellow aspens and green woods in a perfectly blue sky. Kim, Peggi, Dope John, Michael, and Ron picked apples, and what apples! We get the best half and return the rest in the form of cider. The circle again is lined with boxes of apples—the sweet aroma hanging heavily in the circle.

Back here Larry and I cut one field of alfalfa and raked what had been cut and rained on. Sandy canned up twenty more quarts of our tomatoes. It was my dish day. I even helped to make dinner.

In the world—munitions—lots of vested interests in war machines: big ships, planes, rockets, etc. Are the people in these industries more interested in world peace or a high standard of living? Plush suburbs and mansions—plenty of money in the pocket. The military-industrial complex is a part of American prosperity. What a delicate game we play; the future in the balance.

The world changes very fast. I'm reading about the 1830s in the West. There was hardly anyone in Texas or California. How quickly we covered the landscape with cities and suburbs. When's enough?

September 30, 1976: The nights are cold and the frost is like snow in the mornings. Then very quickly we warm up and thaw out. Alfalfa and lettuce both recover. We helped Tomas Vigil out with a little cutting today to speed his work along—show our appreciation.

New fellow here, John, helped sort a few apples and picked up some hay with us. He wants to fix the pit house to live in. And Sylvie has really quit this time! She just isn't cut out for the scene as it is, I guess. Son Jimmy was very mature and helpful. Jason will surely miss Monica and Tony. I'll miss them all.

Kim has stepped back into milking Nelly. Nelly doesn't like these switches. Now she's down—holding her milk. We had a good regular thing going, just what we want in the dairy, and boom! One committed member splits. By the time we have a real dairy, we'll need more commitment.

October 3, 1976: Buster, the nasty buck goat, is here. Easy to tell who's in heat with him around! Some does are getting bred. But boy, does he smell! He got out yesterday and Larry roped him and got him back. He is just like a human-sized devil. Unfortunately I had to hold him in while Mike brought in a doe to be bred. He is sticky with his smelly ejaculations.

Running late, I then went to town to get my glasses fixed—poor people—while I was in the office the secretary came out with a bottle of air spray, and then she turned on a blower and walked over and opened the door. I got my glasses fixed. Good move.

Back at the house Holly is not happy. Refusing to let her car be used for a town trip this morning, she got hysterical, calling us all a bunch of heathens. She retreated and is now holed up in her room.

October 7: Rich, rich society we have and very free. Sylvie and Holly both have welfare and can afford to live separately—keep their own hours—have a more comfortable, quieter private scene. And they have chosen it. Just why it didn't work out well with Sylvie, I don't know. Dedication was lacking.

Holly, too, lacks the dedication. She does have a good understanding, but her personal trip with Neil dominates her. She possibly can get back with him. He won't live here; so if she separates from us, there's a good chance she'll be able to reunite with him.

Peggi Sue and Kim sat down to the apples and did the entire job; all that are for us are individually wrapped. Now we have to press Steve's share. That was a big job that can hang over us for a long while, but it's done.

Kim did a very good piece of carpentry today repairing one of the circle doors. Now it is like a real door and portal. Terrific. Mike put on the kitchen door today, and it was a cold day. I had very carefully preserved the Dutch doors and the screws and bolts. There is so much traffic at our home that it is traditional to take the door off in the summer.

Saving the parts was the opposite of what Sylvie did in the chicken house. She lost the mechanism that turns on the early morning light. Kim says it is necessary that they be woken up early to lay eggs; fourteen hours a day they need. Food isn't enough. So we need the mechanism. Have to buy it.

At Buffalo we've got some flu. Jason has a 104°F temperature on and off. He's in bed with a fire. Sandy's cold was bad two days ago, but she's feeling much better, thank goodness. Sandy tends to get annoyed and overwrought about our constant everyday problems. She is not the constant source of cheer and competence, though she is a very good homemaker. She's sticking with us though, and that's good. Most other women have deserted the ship.

Now, world peace needn't be your motivation or dedication. Take Mike— it's survival. We're doing it, and it takes a big group effort. But that's much surer survival if you have the knowledge and means to produce food in quantity and maintain home and machines. Just like in a tribe in the forest: in the modern jungle of machines and humanity, as a member of a strong resourceful tribe, you have a good chance to survive.

October 10, 1976: Yesterday the apples for Steve were pressed and ten gallons of delicious juice delivered. Today the last of our hay got picked up. Now this is it. No more free hay until next June. Cows will go out to our lush upper pastures after we harvest the carrots.

I ran a few miles in the moonlight. I hear coyotes off by the Rio Grande but never see them. I always carry a shovel as I glide through the surreal landscape. In the mountains the sky is impossibly full of stars, and the moonlight creates a gray, ghost world. I drink in the silence and the tiny sounds.

October 11: I organized a wood run since the weather is so clear. We went to San Cristobal—me, Peggi, Kim, new John, who seems a good compatriot, and visitor Neal, who's been here over a week now. A pleasure to find wood so close to home—pine and some really big oaks that had to be cut to get them out. We're getting a respectable stash.

Friday: On the wild side: Dope John is our new man, a fairly clever, mellow tall fellow. He is handsome with dark hair—Peggi's new lover. No skills, no money, no job—that's what we get. I hear rumors he has a big debt to pay off. Not your ideal situation. Oh well . . .

Also Sequoia—a friend who used to live here—abandoned a car near us because of a flat, no gas, and maybe other problems. He said we could have it. So Kim, Neal, and new visitor Lee Richmond towed it up with the tractor. It's got to be worth something, and we sure need the bucks.

In a two-day effort, most carrots are in, packed in the root cellar. We wet the sawdust and sand to keep them moist. Ron had organized a wood run for today but it didn't get off. Another batch of candles got made and Sandy colored them. New cow feeder is delivered to the cows. It looks good: just poles, a dollar's worth of nails, baling wire, and some scrap lumber—simple and inexpensive—handsome actually with the skinned pine poles.

Tuned into the land, I am. I love to run around our fields, see the alfalfa and abundant brome grass. I've got water on here, there, and other places too. A real little paradise where a few years ago there was a barren waste heavily populated by prairie dogs.

October 16, 1976: Clear blue skies. There's more water than we care to run, the excess cascading down to the Rio Hondo and on to the Rio Grande a mile away.

Very good wood-running days, and now we have a job offer to earn $300 cutting teepee poles, and I have a $68 permit all set to go! But I offered an Indian acquaintance the use of Larry, the truck, and me for Monday. Then Tuesday we can start.

The barn is sounding more real. We know enough now to draw our own plans. This is my little immediate dream: a milking barn, corrals and then a winter barn. The bigger dream: more land being communalized and those communes being models of good farming and consistent production. Bigger dream yet—more sharing.

In the news, Ford workers are striking to create more jobs—share the jobs—sharing right on to reach world peace. Share the jobs—share the land.

Dreams do come true. For many years the liberation forces in Vietnam struggled against incredible odds and with incredible sacrifices. But they won. What a dream come true for them. And the war did not escalate but was stopped by the triumph of all the growing forces of democracy in the US. Another great event. I think of these dreams, then my own are hardly so spectacular. So why shouldn't they be fulfilled? They too are on the road to world peace.

In *Newsweek*, it was reported that Mao could not understand how the US could have been defeated. He couldn't understand the extent of democracy in the armed forces and at home; a few or even many warmongers could not drive the nation and the army to fight for capitalist ideals forever. President Kennedy saw the error and foresaw exactly this outcome. Then he was mysteriously killed, and the war went forward.

To me this end is a victory for America too. The pulse of our democratic nation shows up more clearly than the propaganda of the "leaders of society." We changed; did not escalate forever.

So dreams do come true. Struggles are rewarded. Mankind makes great strides toward democracy, peace, and freedom. And peace would help dissolve boundaries that keep people apart—that hold in check the freedom to travel and enjoy the world's cultures. Peace would let us use all resources for human culture. So much is used for war machines.

On the immediate level of our struggle, some new heifers, I think, are our most pressing need. Probably it will be slow. The people here are very cautious, very conservative in a way—don't change too fast. Don't want to lose the magic—the essence. My faith is great; I won't lose it. I see the important immediate task: establish a legal dairy, real production of high quality. I'm excited and thank God I feel very good.

Monday: Despite this pressure to get the teepee pole run finished, yesterday Larry and I went on a regular wood run. We looked for Tommy Gomez but he wasn't home so we went alone. We got a load of wood high in the Taos Canyon. Then we drove into the magical Taos Pueblo, cruised around some dusty lanes, to give half the wood to the Gomez's for free. We do get a lot for ourselves, and we should remember our neighbors.

New people: Larry's sister was here for about a week, a very good-looking young woman. She stayed in my room and helped out with kitchen chores. Tall friend of Dope John's, named Bob, has been around sometimes—prosperous looking—well-kept long blond hair. Neal, who has been here several weeks, is a friend of John's too, and John's got one more friend staying here since yesterday.

John reportedly is on the verge of another move to go earn money to repair his damaged dealings. He says he'll remember us when he gets a job and not quit just when he's broke, to return empty-handed to his family. He is a friend and is very close with Ron and Peggi, and I rather like him myself. On the physical plane he hasn't much together—no money, no tools—but he has a good mind and body. He's very likely ready to change away from his present business—not really—he's not for us.

A bus arrived two days ago with a young family. The man with the pale red hair said they're interested in living here and heard we are interested in new members. It is a bit awkward, but they say they'd like to move in—get out of their bus. This gives us a chance to go through our new procedures that we discussed—trial period—consensus of the people already here. I tried to explain about possessions, as we would have them.

These people seem much more likely than, say, John. This family has two kids and a woman, young and attractive too! With only Peggi Sue and Sandy here, we don't necessarily improve the situation with more single guys. Mary cooked up soybeans for us—soybeans à la Tennessee—a vital and important food, and one we haven't used much. Jim and Mary used to live at the Farm in Tennessee where they grow lots of soybeans.

The man of the family, (Red) Jim Kehoe, has carpentry and mechanic skills and has a few essential tools. We had one fool here before who had a broken hammer and said he was a great carpenter. Jim though, is for real, and it is reflected in his tools.

Jim has the time to swing full-time into our tasks. One needn't be a dairy expert to live here. He has milked cows and goats on a homestead in British Columbia though. One needn't be committed to cows. Most welcome if he's good and productive at something.

I talked to Mike as I helped him clean up a big lumber-and-fencing mess in the pasture where a few years ago Catalina and Paul built a goat shelter and where John kept the first goats of the new herd before we used the present barn. I said very cautiously that these new folks were interested in living here. He caught the tone and said, "Art, understand that I'm not against new people joining us."

I'm glad he pointed that out. He wants us to be fussy and he wants to be asked. He shouldn't have to butt in; he is a veteran here and just because he minds his own business is no reason he shouldn't be consulted. And with the case of John and John's friend Neal, he feels he's been left out completely.

Out front he doesn't want any dealers; he's seen it at Morningstar. John is heavily into dealing. He even borrowed our commune car to run his errands. "The last time" for that, I say. In fact it was Larry's car. I still tell Larry whenever I want to use it. In this case though, Larry was not consulted. We helped Tommy Gomez with wood and John with food, shelter, car, friendship. Enough!

So will our new people work out? I hope so. Peggi is feeling great—a real tremendous person. She and Sandy, who is feeling pretty well herself, made more candles.

Kim, on my suggestion, arranged to bring Julie over to Eliu's Hereford bull. It was done in time, I believe, for free, and we solved the problem of how to get her pregnant when the A.I. (artificial insemination) man says she's too difficult for him to do. He tried and failed.

Tuesday: Yesterday, Larry, our new guest Jim, and I went to the ranger station in Questa. Along with their truck, we caravanned up to near 11,000 feet, and the two forest service men marked 126 trees for us, including a special-ordered flagpole. Beautiful country. We set to work. Got nineteen poles on the truck. Thirty-foot poles are heavy; carrying them out was tough, and me with a little back strain again for last two days. Not much, but I don't quite feel like superman.

We push ourselves. There's nothing like such desperate endeavors to get some money to convince me we have to establish our own business at home. Last year I worked for Armando—bummer—and for Wendy in some cold weather. What I want is New Buffalo to have something permanent, reliable, which we can do right here.

We didn't get back from the forest until dark. Great beans and rice dinner and then utter exhaustion sent me to bed.

Wednesday: Off to the woods again. Peggi was up real early and milked the goats so Mike could take a break; he has a bad cold. Larry, Kim, and Red Jim unloaded the truck, and we got going at 9:45 a.m. We were at the site before noon and working in the enchanted woods. I was moving a little slow and hurt a little; then in the silent forest, God touched me and I found all my pain was gone—euphoric—lucky and just right. By the end of the run I felt so tip-top that I ran part of the way out instead of riding. Rest of the way down, Peg and I rode in the back in the open. We got forty more poles, working very hard. Larry is feeling very well also. Great.

October 21, 1976: Plenty happening—an exciting life—new people. A hitchhiking visitor from New Zealand is with us, and our new and very attractive, latest lady, Lena. She's a neighbor from across the river who is building a house. The house isn't done, so she's going to stay with us for the winter if all works well. She has a son, about six years old. She knows a craft—silver work—has good tools. We're lucky. Of course we've been working for a fine home, and you'd think it would attract more than your hardcore, unattached males.

Each night goes below 20°F now. We had a fire in the circle. Still very few fires in the rooms. Rooms with babies sometimes get an hour's fire in the evening.

Sunday: Ta-dah! Snow in the mountains above us—a good rain and hail fell here. That was a long dry spell, and we gathered a lot of wood in the interval, and with two consecutive days of pole cutting, we finished that job. Our new-found friend Lena was on both of them; she brought her panel truck along the second day. Quite a gal! Peggi Sue came too. They're both as much help as any of the guys.

New people: There is Jim, Mary, and now our neighbor Lena. Another woman with two kids has appeared and asked for shelter and, separately, a dude—long hair, no bedding, poor shoes, no shirt—a very unlikely guy. So we've got to figure how to receive the new gal.

At dinner Peg is telling the dude our policy—rules—way of handling— we decide. But Ron interrupts and says that's all "past bullshit!" Terrible to interrupt our fine young lady as she is trying to develop her verbal ability to deal with this frequently asked question: "Can I live here?" The answer is not automatically "yes." I wish he wouldn't be so belligerent.

Monday: Then Ron was in a great mood today, as he often is—soft spoken and all smiles. He is an open guy and wants us to give this new gal Anna a chance—she's French—been in Canada. This fellow David is a friend of hers. She could go with him back to Canada or to Toronto to a sister, but she'd rather try something with some people here in the USA.

Well, we are "some" people, and she's in for the moment and very likely for some months. Her friend David says he'll help put a floor in, make a bed, and bring a bit of firewood. Good.

Ron went to town and easily sold $30 worth of candles. Mike and Sandy skinned teepee poles. Larry and Kim took the engine out of the Dodge, and Larry put it back together, so the engine is in one piece.

October 26, 1976: Life certainly isn't dull for us. Good man Mike has recovered; he skinned two poles Sunday, six poles next day, and twelve today! He is look- ing good too, getting strong. What we need to survive—vigorous health. He can really do physical work. Peggi Sue, too, recovered very quickly from her in-bed condition yesterday. She does exercises at night. Mike had been knocked out of it for several days. These country kids are tough. They bounce right back.

We got paid $250 for the skinned poles, a terrific hit for us. I buy grain tomorrow. Larry spent $40 on parts for our new pickup.

A heat lamp is installed over the baby chicks. The hens laid fifteen eggs two days ago; then twelve, and now nine today. We picked up a new timer light, specifically designed to use with chickens. Kim put in that heat lamp. He's upbeat too these days.

We are only at the beginning. In the Amish country of Pennsylvania are hundreds of the most prosperous well-kept farms; they are my distant ideal.

Years ago I visited their country fair and saw what must have been one thousand different breeds of chickens. Each was odder or more colorful than the next. The deep meadow greens, the horse-pulling contests, and especially the kaleidoscope of chickens create my most-memorable recurring dream.

This new girl Anna has been taken in. So all of a sudden, we have three babies under five months old. Anna has a new baby and a little fellow who can hardly talk yet. Mary has two sons: the baby Silver, and Solomon, who is five years old. Lena has a son, a little younger than Jason, our veteran kid. This is a big responsibility. I hope they get enough attention, lots of care, so we have a mellow home. We certainly are open; two weeks ago we had two children; now there are seven young ones.

Sol is sick with a bad cough. All three babies have had illness but are doing well now. I hope we have no more epidemics. We'll have to keep kids warm and be sure they are eating. And I think we'll have to be stricter about isolating the ones that are particularly contagious. Maybe we can't help but be exposed anyhow. Weather turned really cold; we had a fire all day in the circle stove.

Over at Nick and Adriana's (Taos Learning Center) a new group is living. They always manage to get a group of far-out people to share their place. Ron said we'd help them thresh their grain. I drove over, loaded up with grain on the stalk, and brought it to Michael Duncan's. The job got done just before an inch of snow fell. Good timing. It wasn't much grain for all the fuss, but we helped out. It's a long learning process for the 95 percent nonfarmers in the population to relearn about grain, meat, and all types of food.

Kim and Peggi retrieved the engine for the Dodge. They had a lot of fun talking on Hap's CB radio in his truck. They picked up some lumber for Mike and boots for Peg.

Emil: Little son is a real doll; he looks good and is quiet for hours on end. He smiles a lot and often wakes in the morning and doesn't cry. He just lies there and looks around and talks.

Pollen: Anna's two-year-old is quite a doll too—quiet and very bright—no whining and he's good at entertaining himself. I haven't heard him cry much at all.

People: We meet quite a few. Involved with people—I certainly am—the commune definitely is.

Jeff from Ortiviz came by. With thick blond hair and beard, he looks the part of the pioneer. Ortiviz, our Colorado sister commune, is very much like ours. Jeff is like myself in many ways—my counterpart at the ranch. He believes in planning. He's in the forefront of getting people to respect communal property; getting it understood what "is" the commune's. The livestock has been the main thing to be resolved in the last few years. Both our places have made great progress in this area. Razberry, our very close sister from Bolinas days, is living up there now too.

More and more we're solidifying the idea that there are definite members—control the commune—make policy on livestock, building, vehicles, and crops. We both now have, I'd say, a more congenial group, with much more acceptance of the commune as the actual home. At New Buffalo with Goat John gone and other changes, there is much more unity—more a sense of a common struggle and a group effort.

This is the energy that will make productive communes; we can take a piece of land and have very high-quality and high-producing trips. Rather than being on the bottom of the scale in use of the land, we move on up.

Halloween: I finally got my wizard's cape back that has the lightning bolts and moons sewed on it! I undid my braid, and Sandy tangled and meshed twigs in my hair for a wild look. She made a faerie costume for herself. People came over from the Mabel Dodge House and the Seco Brown House. You can always find a good party at New Buffalo!

We had a terrific party: two bands—300 people—lots of colorful costumes and smoke in the air. Even a giant dragon came. It had a great orange head with green designs and a tremendous yellow smile with foot-long white teeth! It had at least four people in it, and just fit through the circle door. It mixed well with the several Count Draculas, the wizards, clowns, generals, witches, and the Statue of Liberty, which was totally fantastic. Some very good-looking people—strong men and beautiful women—who know how to party hard. Lovely Lenore Vigil came as a dirty old man in a trench coat, complete with a concealed three-foot penis, which she used very deftly.

Next day: The old Mind Machine is back with a new owner, Joseph, who came as Carbon Man, a tall, very resourceful fellow. He works in town as a machinist and is looking for a place to park the van.

Three all right fellows are here from California. They left on the spur of the moment. One has a big Harley with a considerably extended front wheel. They don't even have any bedrolls or much money. They might switch their orange pickup for Jim's bus. That would be terrific. That bus has got to go. A pickup is useful and very easily sold.

November 4, 1976—Thursday: We retrieved the marked forty-foot flagpole—a special order—a full load of firewood and a load on Jim's new pickup too. It has a very bright paint job and runs well. The bus is gone and the trade made.

I got $30 from Armando for some past construction work, but it took five hours. I did a few exercises while I waited. At home I put in the last circle skylight with Lascolite. It took many years to get decent windows on the circle roof.

Mike took a few supers[1] away from the bees and collected a few more stings and some more honey, about thirty-five pounds.

Everyone ended up with some sticky honey on their fingers. Every once in a while you'd see someone take off running; a bunch of angry bees came down to the pueblo looking for their honey. A few of us got a sting or two.

Mike also slaughtered a pig, one of the smaller ones. They eat a lot. Our 1,200 pounds of rye has got to last a long time. Better to feed just one. Still we'll keep the pig scene going. We learn about this part of agriculture; we get money from selling baby piglets. We get experience butchering, and we get the meat.

Larry put his new solar-collector extension on, more than doubling the collecting surface. He concreted the retainer wall above the greenhouse collector too. Made fast work of that.

Mike's face—eyes just slits in a puffy face.

Saturday: Timing: A good day for timing. Brother Mick came up and walked into a feast. Our neighbors at the New Light Center (new name for the scene at Nick and Adrienne's) had arranged to bring food over and we'd share dinner. An army of people came up the road; unbeknownst to us, the Center also invited twenty or thirty more, all of whom arrived first. Terrific and delicious feast—plenty for all—a very nice group. Myself, as long as there are no drunks, I love these happenings. It was indeed a "human be-in" happening at Kennedy airport in NY (where I met the Mad Hatter in '67) that started me on this path.

Even better at timing was our Red Jim. We discovered three days after the big wood run that the two-man saw was missing! High up into Taos Canyon, Jim went after it—got it out of someone's pickup! A few hours later and we would have lost our most important saw.

Mike and I branded the two new steers plus Crystal. Gave Christopher a seven-way shot. Then we skinned the flagpole. We're just vibing the people in

---

1. Frames of beeswax in which honey is stored.

12. *Flagpole and teepee poles: Larry on top; Art, Kim,
and Mike sitting*

these days. The evening's party mellowed into a drum session in the circle. Singing and chanting around the fire, the dancers cast mystical shadows on the white clay walls. I went to bed late as the last of the evening guests said their goodnights.

November 12, 1976: People: We're not cut off. Two fellows up here asking about communal living. A pretty, young woman here from South Dakota wanted to see a "real" commune. Don't see many attractive gals hitching around these days. She keeps herself clean, has a good sleeping bag, and is very modest. Real country-western looking. Kathleen is the name. Also a straight-looking fellow Mel up here with a VW bus. He took Peggi Sue to Vail, Colorado, just for the hell of it—a few hundred miles of drive. She wanted to go visiting.

Lots of home improvements in the making. Larry doubled a few kitchen windows with clear plastic. Jim started making a foundation for a greenhouse collector. I got some pieces of wood in place for the solar collector in front of Sandy and Jason's room. Ron is making a window for Anna's very dark room, a window that eventually will connect to a greenhouse. It's coming along fast. A good move.

Kim, Larry, and Jim today put the new engine in—great work—but one exhaust manifold is wrong so we need to get the right one.

We're broke—just about! The one girl who is staying disparages money; says she got rid of a bunch just to be free of it; a bit of a wild story. Of course, she's all out now that she's here. Mel says he might like to find a place here for the winter. He's got some kind of money.

The famous Bi-Centennial belt is on display at the Chase Manhattan Bank in New York City! Big time: Pepe's making gold conchos now. He turned me on to a taste of cocaine, which we snorted with a $100 bill the other day. But money for the commune? No. And we're waiting on Nelson Big Bow in Oklahoma to pay for his load of teepee poles we've still got. He owes us $1,140! And Armando doesn't come across with my pay from thirteen months ago though he says he will. So, something will break. We just made another batch of candles. I just sent off a letter to try and get two heifers.

If we don't establish a business that can take care of us, it'll be poverty forever. Buffalo would fold. Just the wood collecting alone is too much. When I first got here, they had quit, and then it took two years before we got the steam to build up a good pile. How long can the few heavy wood gatherers keep it up? We'll need to purchase alternative systems in the future to make an acceptable life here. And just living in continuous poverty is a bad way to feel. We can hardly show the commune as an alternative if it means waiting on handouts and welfare. That's no alternative.

Mike fixed a big feast dinner with pork and many other dishes for us. Sometimes we have our prayer "Circle" before dinner in the kitchen around the stove where it's warm; tonight we said grace with fifteen around the center fire in the kiva.

November 15, 1976: Cold wind this morning. I say I like my faith renewed. If all this heavy peace, love, and sharing vibration is getting stronger, some of the ripples should be bouncing back to us; bouncing around, they should touch us now and again. Peggi went out and fished in some good ones.

Mel's a straight-looking fellow in a VW bus. Independent and successful, he feels the need to give—to share. He's not a bad fellow at all. He can really dig where we're at. "Say, this is great!" he said. I tend to agree. He has some skill too. Right away, he saw me putting up this solar collector and lent a hand. He helped me stick to the work and speeded up the process considerably. Then today I accompanied him to town, and rather quickly we spent about $100 of his on materials.

I need some of that old magic. A similar act of generosity sealed our fate back in Bolinas in '69. Back then we were true gypsies staying with friends and living out of our bread truck and teepee. On the coastal mesa a sturdy fellow, Bill Beckman, was building a dome home. Pepe, a skilled worker, jumped right in helping him for the fun of it. Of course he's rapping a mile a minute when a neighbor, Woody Ransom, comes by. He asks Pepe to take him up to this marvelous Cro Farm "commune" in Oregon. They go, and Woody decides to restart a commune in Vermont called Rock Bottom on a maple sugar farm he owns. That left his house in Bolinas vacant that we rented for $50 a month, and we had our first commune. How the magic worked in those days!

Gray skies above—the light has a yellow cast, creating a glow and intensifying the green of the juniper and piñon trees. Mike cut the sheep's tail off, which was necessary to get it bred. He sees it's got to be done and he does it. He washes the milk-room towels every week too. Coming along is the solar crop dryer he's making. With many big racks, it is very impressive looking. It can be used for jerky, but it's mainly useful for drying quantities of fruit.

I was saying that Peggi Sue met Mel and brought him over, and he took her to Vail, a 400-mile lift door to door. Couldn't phone for better service. Then she returns and brings in a couple with a little girl. We feed them some of our excellent dinner and then the guy picks up the guitar, and they sing some songs—just about the best bunch of songs I've ever heard! They really transport me!

This now is the genuine article. I've seen the East Bay Sharks near San Francisco and heard Santana live in the park. These humble folk are not the usual. I live to hear such things. It's not the singing so much though but the songs. I always want to hear songs that say something I believe—to know that it's really happening, that it's not just in my head. I'm hearing it from other people. Cosmic Comfort is the name of the group, and Simeon writes songs, some of which have got to become famous.

These people are a clear source of consciousness that is trying to break free—become more our daily consciousness. God, did they sing a funny song about LSD. And my innermost thoughts Simeon enunciates clearly: missiles exploding, people starving, and yet the vision of peace in our lifetime—real peace felt by people all over the world—making it real. I'm so pleased to meet these folks, just out of nowhere, who are putting into good songs so many ideas that are part of our new consciousness.

Next day: Larry is proving himself continuously a tremendous help. He installed the timer light; the chickens jumped to 23 eggs that very day! The pickup would not start—duh—our new engine! So Larry takes the starter apart, fixes a connection, and we have a running pickup truck that truly belongs to the commune.

A word about brother Ron: Anna has just moved in recently, a lone woman with two very young children. Evidently she's seen some rough scenes in the northwest of Canada. Ron is the very chivalrous gentleman and revolutionary brother. He helps her cut wood and has made now a vast improvement for the dark cavelike room that Anna moved into. He also comforts her baby at many times.

Carter won the presidency. Those responsible people had better keep this boy alive. It's hard to say how much progress he can make toward world peace—a good life—freedom and prosperity for all. But I certainly get the message that a lot of good changes and higher, more concerned consciousness, are on the move.

Wednesday: Mike set today as the day to slaughter our biggest steer, 800 or 900 pounds. I like working with people, and Mike and I work well together. He has a very sincere drive to do properly; he sees it is what makes survival smooth. He got the knives sharp, the bone saw out, and the wheelbarrow, ropes, come-along hoist, .22 rifle, and tarp. The steer was corralled at night and easily roped in the morning, tied to the truck and led to the tree. We said a quick prayer to Mother Earth, Father Sky then I shot him; he went right down without a sound. Mike cut his throat. Larry helped us hoist. I slit the underside. Loads of fat we collected. We're rendering it. We skinned the carcass and then cut it up. That was all well done, quickly. I'm glad I've had enough experience to be able to do a righteous job.

But all is not completely well. Our new truck already is seriously broken. Larry quickly traced the problem to the distributor shaft. It is broken—a major repair—a piece of bad luck.

What spoils the day a bit for me, however, is Ron: Mr. Pleasant. I can find a lot of good to say about Ron, but he does have one major drawback with his on-again, off-again anger. With me, he has picked a few ludicrously insignificant incidents. Yesterday, in front of Mel, he got angry over an incident a year old, when I wouldn't buy brown paint because we had beige paint that had been given to us by Hap. Then he became himself, sold candles, and gave me the cash right down to the last quarter. Now for our man Ron to go and sell candles on the street is just terrific; street peddling is very honorable. It is also a way to meet and stay in touch with many friends. It also shows how we value this little but very important income from our own endeavor—a very communal endeavor. Ron is anchorman; he sells 'em.

Then today Ron got upset because I let the steer Carnegie "witness" the slaughter at about twenty yards, not that the calf was looking. Of course, he spent his usual time grazing. Well, Ron was angry because I hadn't brought the calf up to the barn so he wouldn't be near the killing. I think Ron was just upset that we killed our longtime friend. I loved him too. We did it very well though: silent—with a prayer—quick and clean. Instead of helping or appreciating the effort we make to provide hundreds of pounds of highest-quality meat, he snaps at me.

I see Ron coming; usually it's a hug and smile, but I cannot be sure. I have to be on the lookout for that anger. He may be approaching me seething mad. He said he's not going to carry water for Carnegie steer anymore as reciprocation for our slaughtering at the only tall tree, which happens to be near the steer's pasture. I won't mention it, but it does demonstrate some of the pressure we live under.

Ah, life though is good—outrageously so. I heard Mel giving this rap to someone who was saying how something was kind of bad, and he had to point out how good so many things are. He sees us as an example of some terrific trends.

Two girls from a Santa Fe hostel here—big group-action project. They heard about the place and came up to establish contact. Rifka from across the valley came over several times. Tonight Leslie, who is somehow related to our quiet Anna, was here, again, with her six kids. A bit of a riot when her six joined our seven. We do listen to a good deal of babies' crying.

To all these people we've been able to serve up good country meals.

Fortunately, we have a few good cooks and a lot of food. We had vegetables from our summer garden and good French bread from our wheat. Mike cooked liver from the steer. We serve milk from cows and goats and fresh cheese that Kim made. We've got a lot of people to feed.

Monday: At about 15°F, these days start off quite cold. I took the baby for a walk early after milking where the irrigation water is solid ice; the ditches are hard on top and hollow underneath when you step through. The cold wind makes our checks ruddy. Emil takes well to the cold. They say that in the old days, in the far north, Indians would put the babies in the cold ocean momentarily; if they couldn't take it they would never make it in the freezing climate.

Pretty quick Larry and I got the red truck running by pulling it with the tractor. Then Mel helped us put the eighty-five poles on. Mel is being a big help. Thirty-three years old, he now has one of the rooms. It's a bit bare, but he cleaned it up nicely. In the morning in the kitchen he picks up one of the babies and holds it if it's crying. This is really important because it is not so mellow to hear those crying kids. They like to just be carried around.

We delivered the poles, ordered a distributor, got some roofing nails, and returned home in time to milk. A quiet, sort of spacey gal, Jessy, has been here frequently. She finished my dishes and made the evening circle fire. I appreciate that. Anna milks at night and often does the cow buckets and strainer cleaning. I rather like that too. With her long hair in braids and her French accent, Anna makes a storybook milkmaid.

Mike finished the butchering. The freezer is full. Peggi Sue busy with plans for Thanksgiving; we're having company. The girls are in the kitchen, chattering away, figuring who's going to fix what.

November 24: Yesterday the roofing paper was put on Sandy's greenhouse sun porch. Today, Kim and I made more progress. Canadian David cut a bunch of logs with his chainsaw. Are all those kids of Leslie's his?

Since the slaughter, Ron has been a recluse—very silent—thinking things over.

November 27: A foot of snow—the land transformed. It's very bright out, with the world almost entirely covered in white. This is one of the biggest storms I've seen here. All our efforts are sort of geared to preparation for this: all the wood, hay, and food we have gathered. Now we're stuck here with it—rather than being stuck here with nothing!

There is a cheese making on the stove, some meat out of the freezer, plenty of milk and cream. I sure feel good about this. I remember hitchhiking back here with a little package of beef from the supermarket a few winters back, to feed to the weakest people. Now we've got eggs, milk, meat, and vegetables like never before. Last year was good too. This year even better.

Sunday: Days are short—15° below zero last night. I sure hope the animals do well this winter. This is just the start.

And I hope the kids do better. Pollen is now on penicillin for an ear infection. Emil's latest infection, in the ear, has not cleared up. This is very bad that we have such a bed of child sickness. It certainly does add a problem for mothers and fathers not knowing what or how many kids are living here. The kid population went up, and we have more sickness. Sad but true.

I just love the deep breaths working outside. As I worked I could watch the frosty mist on the mountain dissipating until the snow-covered mountains were left shimmering in their crystalline coldness.

Lena got her truck started with Jim's help and took me on the milk run. Without this earning, we'd never have any hope of saving some money. Now with candle sales for Christmas, we should be able to put a little away toward more stock. No chance without some kind of break that we can save enough to build the dairy though. Either someone has got to give us some money, or we've got to go out and earn it someway.

The conventional way is to borrow. According to our hippie code, this is out. Who would lend us money anyhow? We do not want to put up the farm as collateral; if we fail, then it's the end for New Buffalo. We will not mortgage the place. No way! The early Christians were against lending too. I really go for that: generosity, charity, and hard work is what it should be.

The US government owes 400 billion dollars or so. Now why can't those super patriots who are collecting the interest on the money (ten billion each year or so) just say, "Uncle, forget it. You have other important things to worry about besides what you owe us." The government and these big, wealthy businesspeople are willing to see young men give up their lives and health for the country, so what's so big about asking the wealthy to sacrifice money? Those patriots who die on the battlefield have cheap lives, that's what. The government more easily gets them to lose two legs than to have Mr. Banker lose a night on the town. At any rate, borrowing seems not to be a choice for us.

From *TIME* magazine about the election: Ford was not in the tradition of change that is at the center of American life. This is a very good characteristic and bodes well for the future. As I see it, the country will have to change a great deal—a revolution of consciousness.

November 30: Only –8°F this morning. Mike dug up the barn faucet from the frozen ground, and Larry helped him fix it. Some mechanical fault made it freeze. Mike jumped right on the case.

Kim and Larry put up the outside layer of plastic on the greenhouse sun porch. Kim finished the door. Then those two put the new distributor in the Dodge pickup—a lot of progress. Mary and Sandy colored more candles.

The cows were out foraging in the snow. I notice that when cattle graze they do not mow. They leave bunches of grass tall. In the winter then it is possible to find graze.

December 2, 1976: We got a letter from the agriculture engineer Charles Hahn in Las Cruces answering a few questions about our barn plans. I'm sending off a letter to Tom Proctor to get some more questions settled.

Our solar rooms are not using wood. Today Larry, tempted to make his first fire, started to mud up the one end of the new solar heater. It is going to be a great addition.

December 4: Petunia gave birth to ten piglets, just the right number since she's got ten good teats! Their first night was a cloudy one and therefore warm, about 20°. They survived quite well. When she lies down, the piglets are absolutely frantic to suck.

I spoke with Bob Apodaca at the agricultural exchange office about pastures. He's perfectly familiar with that sedge grass. "They'll eat it," he says, "but they don't like it best." Since about the first of December, we've been cutting into the second cut of alfalfa.

December 9: We've come a long way from John's goats to Buffalo's dairy. This year Mike, Peggi Sue, Kim, and I had each a major role, and also had Sylvie and Anna participate. We've had good luck pretty much and a new and very improved milk room to work in. Now to make some more big steps forward. We're going to have to raise some money. A fund-raising tour to some campus might be a very good idea—get to meet some of the college people—see if our ideas can catch on a bit. The experience for me would be good. There must be some people interested in social change—world peace—organizing some meetings. It takes a lot of energy to get out there, break through the screen of not knowing anyone.

Part of our karma, New Buffalo's and mine, is communication. We've been in several books, mentioned in *Penthouse*, been on television, and we've explained ourselves to hundreds of people who come here. Find a new way, yes, but not in isolation. Commune living—contribution to world peace.

And we certainly haven't been isolated. Fellow Bill here for several days now with a van from NY state. He made tasty pizzas for dinner last night. Fellow Drew was here for two days. He was well equipped for the cold. A bit of a funny guy, looking for natural cures for his gallstones. Seems to me he probably came up with the symptoms to give himself something to do. Somehow when he left, he'd computed the food he'd eaten at $1.20 so he gave me a dollar.

Larry made some plans for a solar heater. I took $35 out of my stash, and he bought some materials. Then he started right in on construction. This one is for the circle and goes up on the roof. It will be the first roof collector. This will be our first demonstration trial model. With only two more rooms with south exposure for the greenhouse type, we'll have to move to the roofs for more collecting.

Also significant, I got an answer from Mr. Proctor, the milk inspector. As I thought, he said build whatever type of barn you want—two coats of concrete inside—last one has to be smooth and then painted. Four-inch slab for floor—foundation that goes to frost line (three feet for us that would be). No cattle doors on north side, he suggests, "too slippery."

Kim and Peggi are having an exquisite time together nowadays. Kim is very muscular, but shy. Peggi finally noticed. Terrific. It shows on Kim; he even prayed at Circle, and he's got a lot of smiles. Kim's one of my best partners ever. They should be enjoying their life here. Today they sold candles on the street and sold eight gallons of cow's milk. This is the first time I've been able to save money out of actual commune earnings.

Note: We sold $1200 worth of milk and consumed $3600 worth; two-thirds of our production went for the home. Still the one-third sold paid for all dairy expenses and then some.

December 17: A big break I've been looking for, I hope! I ran into three very good friends, Peter from Ortiviz and Tomas and Pablo (Paul Mushen), all from the Huerfano Valley. Tomas gave me an ad from a Colorado Livestock paper for a farm selling Brown Swiss cows!

Jim, Mary, and two kids left for a pilgrimage to relatives in California. Should be a good trip for them. Okay for us too; a little wood saving and fewer kids for a little while. Sandy sad to see Mary go. Those sizzling soy sausages

13. *Kim and Peggi Sue*

sure tricked us good! But Jim never quite finished the greenhouse collector foundation. Larry and I tried to get him to change his plans, but he didn't. Next year for that, I guess.

Those two left and young fellow Neal from Brooklyn just arrived. He seems to be of some means: clean clothes, flew out, and he talks about making movies. Peggi and Kim feel close with him. He stayed here for a few weeks in the fall, and therefore he might be staying here now. Also fellow Griego here for a flash. He was visiting last spring. Road bum—mellow rap but a nervous laugh. Says he was in a California penitentiary for seventeen years? Not too clear.

Lena left. She was a neighbor we did a favor for. I'm glad she has other things to do than burn wood here all winter. We helped her, and now we get to save some wood too.

Winter Solstice, 1976: Finally, now for real winter. Food supply looks good: wheat, apples, carrots, potatoes, beef, pork, rice, beans, peanut butter, honey, eggs, and milk. We've never eaten like this before. Mel off to skiing—visiting New Yorker Neal is off too. No circle wood cut—hardly any kitchen wood.

Anna cleaned the kitchen. Sandy cleaned the washroom and recently the pantries—this is the way to live—neat, clean, and orderly. It's chaos enough. Our old motto "funky enough!"

With the help of Jason, Larry cut a Christmas tree. As though it was so important, they trudged about in the snow all over, looking for just the perfect one. They just cut a top, not killing a precious tree. It now has lights and is beginning to get ornaments. The kids certainly like it. Peggi's making fine gingerbread ornaments for the tree—kids helping out—little squeaks and chuckles as they naughtily nibble at arms and legs. David and Leslie's kids are here while Anna and baby Jangle are taken to the doctor for checkup.

Here's a real bad one: From *Western Dairy Journal* 12/76, milk in Massachusetts and Connecticut: higher than usual radiation levels from a Chinese September nuclear test. All health departments order, "No outdoor grazing!" Uh, oh! This could put us in a very bad situation. What about the little people who are dependent on graze? We need peace—no arms race.

Kim, Mike, and I were talking about our very vital assets, mainly hay. How can we support a dairy? It's a tough situation. We can see the moves necessary but not much funds. Still the test is to do best with what we've got. Kim gave me a big hug. I like that.

I feel just a bit tough out running through the snow—no complaints from my body. After traveling across the frozen landscape for hours, I sit and eat dry biscuits and mutton on the bone. I perch right on the edge of the gorge; far below me the Rio Grande continues to cut into the earth. It must be over 100 million years ago that it first started to carve this path.

December 23: Getting close to Christmas—cinnamon and cedar drifting in the air. Larry and Peggi Sue singing duet Christmas carols—true Christmas spirit.

I get up when it's still a cold blue-gray color outside and rather dark inside. Clean the wax vat and put it on the fire. Go milk and feed a little to Crystal and the two milk cows. After milking I go open up the chickens and feed them. Every day I wait anxiously to go check—very few eggs. I'm still quite certain one day soon they'll go back to laying.

We slaughtered and butchered five chickens this morning. I sharpened my knife and helped. Went fast with five people. A little wax in the boiling pot makes feather removal much easier.

While Kim and Peggi were selling candles in town, Sandy was on the case, coloring the next batch right after we stopped dipping.

I put a kerosene lamp in the root cellar. It's getting too cold. Good news! Carl Hagan may come and stay with us for a while. If we could only win him back. Carl the pioneer, he lived here for several years, started the bee trip and was my good partner.

We're doing something big. We should be able to attract some high people who can see what a quality thing we could make. Come on! Where are some good craftsmen with a bunch of idealism? So to town tomorrow for me to sell on last day before Christmas.

A new day: Didn't have to go to town—sold the candles right at the house to a pretty Japanese girl and a young man. Spent a fairly relaxed day therefore— cut a little wood—smoked a good reefer with Canadian David. Chickens started to produce again—fourteen and going up.

Finally we fixed the front kitchen door. It was full of cracks and leaks and very drafty—a great Christmas present for us. Living and sharing together—the whole world could do it. So many individual situations—so much property.

I've been thinking about fallout. It's no science fiction invention; it exists and can hurt. Take cold showers frequently if exposed to radioactive fallout and don't drink milk! Cows gather an awful lot of vegetation to turn into milk, and they filter it. Filter it right from the environment into the milk.

We are hoping for peace—working for it. Fate though is capricious; we can't say what will happen. Reading science fiction can make a person think of the very real possibilities. Anyhow, the door got fixed and the chickens started laying.

I've started to really like the barn scene: feeding cows and bringing in hay, watching the animals grow and being able to see their health. Walking among such tremendous producers of food is exhilarating. I'd sure hate to have to cut out this way, but if fallout radiation becomes a problem, both milk and then meat would be bad choices. I don't want to give it up, but we must adapt to the changing circumstances if it comes to that.

We need peace, as do all the people.

December 26: Continuing clear skies—hot days in the solar collector. We had a very nice quiet Christmas—pine boughs hanging from the ceiling, big paper cutouts of angels, birds, and snowflakes. The tree looks great. Outlining our road, Larry put out about twenty candle-and-paper-bag lanterns that are a New Mexico tradition. Fellow Dan, who played the guitar well, spent two days. We had a half-frozen, strong-looking but very odd fellow for a night. Our new-found brother Mel has gone back to his job in Fort Worth, Texas. He says he'll be back after saving some money. Terrific.

Anna Blueblood's boyfriend David—Leslie's old man—says he doesn't see how we can do it—put so much food on the table. It is an effort. I'm glad he notices. That's the country life: at the source of the food there should be plenty of it.

And we do a lot of entertaining. We had guests last night and tonight too—two couples—our friend Jimmy brought them up just before dark to our warm fire. Listening to Leon Russell in our modern cave, we dance and stomp around as people have since the dawn of humankind. Except now, for the first time, we are freed of ten thousand superstitions and know humans are basically one tribe, not divided as they have been.

January 2, 1977: Dramatics: Leslie and her old man David had a domestic quarrel; they have nasty sessions. Chivalrous Larry got involved, and Dave lost his reason. He then accused Ron of doing several hundred dollars damage to his truck—sugar in the tank—a paranoid ridiculous notion! The screaming and threatening are very unpleasant. We ordered him to leave, and finally he did. Leslie is gone too, and they're back together—craziness we don't need.

We now have with us a very nice couple—big fellow with a beard and pretty wife, daughter, dog, and a pickup showed up, looking for a place and something to get involved with. Kim spoke to them first, and I've rapped some. This fellow knows about building and might have a job in town working for an architect.

Larry called a meeting about us being together—focus especially on Ron's relation with Sandy and me and about belligerence. Ron thinks Sandy should participate in the peyote church more. Hey! We have room for all spiritual ways; need not be only one of the thousands that exist. Sandy as a vulnerable girl has had some people lay trips on her, and she has done well to maintain her independence. Then someone said that Ron and Sandy should sleep together; then they would like each other! No way! Nothing forced here! People were satisfied it was a good meeting. We want to be a together group—good feelings, respect, even love.

January 3: Had several talks with fellow Gary, who returned with wife and daughter to spend the day. He's a pretty strong guy and articulate. We went out for a moonlight run. Says he could once do a four-minute mile. Good time to talk under the vast universe of stars. Trouble is, it's so easy for people to sound so idealistic, but then what they do is something else again.

Taking a couple in, in the wintertime, makes it harder on us. It means we use up more wood, more of our food. But still, we come on strong as wanting more people involved—strong resourceful people.

The "we": Kim definitely, because he invited them up, Peggi, and me for sure. If this commune business is going to be big, it's going to involve more and more people. Ron, too, is very aware of this. We are stagnant if good people aren't attracted to our scene. And we're a small group: Art, Larry, Mike, Kim, Ron, Peggi Sue, Sandy, likely Mel, and maybe Jim, Mary, and perhaps Anna.

And the bad: War hanging over us, uptight world, always increasing super-production, our wild and green world shrinking and being eaten by the culture of ever-vaster growth. And still so many people not benefiting from the world's new prosperity.

January 6: Soft snow—ethereal lighting—white world aglow with a slightly blue light.

In town I saw Pepe. He's all excited and fast-talking. They're going to form a corporation at the Mabel Dodge House and buy the house! He's got a lot of energy. I discussed an order for $240 worth of candles. Sold four gallons of milk and $20 worth of candles.

Poverty—blah! I had to put on chains because the Ford car has such lousy tires. With the chains, the car served very well. I desperately want chains for the Dodge. We can't use our own truck.

American history: April 1846—war between U. S. and Mexico. First detachments went swinging out of Fort Leavenworth on their way west accompanied by miles of supply trains, long files of cavalry, and canvas-covered wagons glistening like banks of snow in the distance—reacting to population pressure. So many men wanting to escape from their poor lives, combined with lots of money for war; America expanding its real estate.

This army, headed by frontier Gen. Stephen W. Kearny, headed for Santa Fe, New Mexico, with that year's Santa Fe caravan. Took it without a shot.

Then January 19, 1847, rebellion by the people because of the conduct of the occupation army—revolt at Taos—Governor Bent killed on visit. Battle at the Taos Pueblo, but unlike most, these American Indians managed to hold onto their ancestral home.

Completely clear at sundown. Pink and purple reflect off the frosted mountains, newly revealed in their frigid splendor.

January 9: Back at Buffalo—modern history—another storm blew in. Fellow Bob visiting for two days. And two guys stopped by here in the blizzard at night and climbed into the covers of my empty bed. I'm usually with Sandy. Then they were off in the morning pretty quick; we had to shovel and push their car out of the snow.

On marriage: "I'd rather marry the cause," says Peggi Sue, "rather than marry one person." That's my idea too. In an age when you are really caring about all your brothers and sisters, marriage to one is very narrow. Devotion, especially just to blood relations—I want a broader experience. That's freedom. We provide the security aspects of marriage as a group: wood, food, and shelter. And new people can come in.

Pepe says the esthetic state—the things in the house—the quality, the cleanliness, and ease of cleaning matches the level of consciousness. You can't have a neat shop and not have it reflected in your personal surroundings.

Peggi and Kim working in the glare of a bare bulb, turning out earrings fashioned from silver dimes. Every night up pretty late, listening to good sounds on the radio. First they'll go to San Francisco. Neither Peg nor Kim has been in California. It's a real treat coming up for them.

Now, why don't they think of enjoying a visit to raise some money for "our" commune dreams? I see it as a rush: the whole world madly spinning, and we playing our little role in the fine balance. I'm "crisis conscious," says Kemal. I see we have to get things done.

Ron, a while back, asked, "What is Sandy doing here?" If she wasn't here, we'd know; we'd miss her terribly. It would be very hard to make up her energy in food preservation, cooking, and keeping our central house nice and clean and organized. The same with Kim and Peggi; how could we make up the loss if they weren't to return?

Mike is working hard getting beehives together. I hope this year will be good for him. Often when jobs need to be done, he's the first to take care of them. No sugar, tobacco, coffee, or pot for him—only a concentrated effort to see how to do the job right. He gets off on the cleanliness of effort and the result. Here's a hundred-per-cent involved man who can make things happen. A fine woman has got to fall in love with this clean-cut guy. As is, there's a deep-seated frustration that comes out in his abrupt, LOUD, ungentle manner and yelling at no one. Look at my poor dad. He had to wait until he was fifty years old! Mike won't have to wait so long.

This is it! Like a navigator in a storm or a pilot streaking through space, we are in cold winter; and after a while, we'll sail out all together if we know the right moves now. At 15° below zero, our Mother is not fooling around. Still our farm is producing food.

January 16, 1977: Sunday Mike and I said a prayer and slaughtered our big sow. I shot her—Mike cut. Then we brought her down near the pueblo and hoisted her up: gutted, dehaired, and cut into six pieces. Mike is right on the ball. He had wood and water ready and hoist up and knives sharpened. We worked very well together, doing a clean, quick job.

We took in for a few days a real hardship case: crutches, overweight, terrible tobacco habit, no money, no home, not much of a plan. Taos Social Services sent her out. Also took in Carol Egbert, our family member from the start of the Pride family, because on the Morningstar mesa her and John's truck is broken and water is frozen. Little Kachina comes too—a bonus. She gets right with her old buddy, mischievous Jason; they lived together for years here—best friends.

From our northern sister community came Angela and Jimmy and two other friends. We played music in the evening—Jimmy throwing longing glances towards Angela. Angela, so perfect a woman, once liked me a lot. Louisa diverted my attention with a flighty but passionate romance, and I always felt a little guilty for not returning Angela's more sincere affection. So I am deeply pleased she has found a true love with Jimmy from the Colorado family.

Some mornings are 10° below zero. Reportedly there is not a lot of snow in the mountains. Ron has been swimming regularly in town; he's found something he likes and enjoys.

January 18: Larry will have the circle heater with the latest design operating tomorrow probably. He got a lot done today—our first roof collector.

Sandy took Emil in to see grandma, who so adores her little grandson. It really has added a thrill to her life; she just loves him. My mom, at age sixty-five, adapted so easily, moving from New York City to the wilds of Taos, New Mexico.

January 19: Deep winter. I went out to run, crashing through the snowdrifts.

Consciousness: Just as Kim is aware of the chicken coop, I was conscious of the meat hanging in the cellar. I read up on pork, and the book recommends freezing it right away. So I got ready to butcher: clean pants and clean shirt. Mike switched over to butchering too and got the table all clean. Then Kim and I started cutting—Mike and Sandy wrapping. To top it off, Ron played a role by being in town and overhearing someone enquiring about pigs. The fellow came right out and bought three!

I was talking with Kim, "Why do people keep buying those items that depend so heavily on advertising"—cigarettes, liquor, soda, and new cars—millions of dollars spent each day? If people were to be more brotherly, really considerate of what is happening to their fellow humans, they could use this conspicuous consumption money to help out their many friends. Why don't they? "People are not happy enough to give up these things," says Kim. So are we happier? Maybe. I feel secure. It is part of our daily consciousness to be thankful.

Some words of wisdom from Henry Kissinger, colorful Secretary of State: "We saw our successes as the product not of fortunate circumstances and considerable effort but of virtue and purity of motive."

Kim and I had a meeting about the walkway for the greenhouse sunporch interior. I've been asking around for advice. For setting stone outdoors: set in sand or gravel or grader fines and concrete between stones or just leave. Indoor: Ed Morgan suggests setting stones in concrete; then finish by filling between the stones with a fine concrete: one cement, two fine plasterer's sand, and one-quarter lime.

People: Mr. Lee is over, a big friendly guy from Sacramento, California. We like him. Also fellow Steve was over yesterday—new chiropractor healer around—short hair and strong looking from Los Angeles. He seems a very decent person. He experimented with my new sledgehammer cutting some wood and broke the handle. That piece of repair work I did lasted about eight days. I got on his case about it—so hard to keep a decent bunch of woodcutting tools together. But I made him understand that I like him; I just didn't appreciate having that broken by a novice who didn't ask if he could use the tools.

Bob, a long-hair quiet brother, comes over quite often and also the very cute girl he lives with, Ellen. She's here even more often than Bob. Good.

Hay: Our second cut is going very fast. We're going to have to do something. It's a heavy pressure on our hay to feed four goats that we do not want. If we could sell them, it would be different. There's three notices up now in town. And we're looking for a better cow that will freshen soon. Got a lead out that Sandy is following with my Mom's phone.

January 25: *This is Mike Pots. I'm 24 years old and I've been unemployed for two and a half years. But I didn't get my usual leaf-raking job as I found out someone in town had gotten it. I asked someone on the street, who told me sometimes Jack Denver's Motel will hire someone so I went there. Not once, but twice I hitched down as he was not there the first time.*

I went back the next morning and as Mr. Jack Denver was not there, I saw three longhaired young Taos Indians raking leaves next to the apartment. A thought entered my mind, and I strolled over and asked if I could get a job from Jack Denver raking leaves like they do. They seemed friendly, seemed to think that I could probably work with them, but they were not sure as "Mr. Big" was not there at the time. The Indian fellows asked me for a joint, and I said I don't have it, but if I did I would give it. I talked to them and we came to the subject of wages. They said he pays $1.50 an hour, and they brought an extra fellow from the pueblo to work. And like I know this is below minimum wage and here he works them like slaves. The new fellow was not even told what he would be paid before starting work. And as we were talking a white pickup truck pulls into the parking lot, a man with short black hair and black pants and vest and hat leans out the window, points to two Indians, and says, "You and you come with me." One of the Indians nods his head and says, "That's him" and I walked over and started to ask for a job and before I'd even finished listing my qualifications, he cut me off short and said, "Nope, I'm getting ready to lay them all off," and at my look of surprise, he told me to get on my way. And so I say and not just because of what he did to me, but also because of how he treated those Indians, —— to you, Mr. Jack Denver!

It has been said that our own worst criticism is how we criticize other people's faults. Although as I am sure you all know, No Human Being Is Perfect. My own feelings are that one can be dead or alive in this respect. I have seen and realized that all people revolve or tend to work together to keep this place functional as a farm and commune. This is very much like a chain in that the strongest of chains is only as strong as its weakest link. Also I am writing all of this, I don't CARE who reads this. If it seems sloppy, it is coming straight off the top of my head and heart into the pen. The Moving Fingers Write and maybe someone will be interested to read. Yet someone may righteously ask, Why do I write about how you feel about other people's good qualities and your own feelings? Is this putting your nose in other people's business or is it an EGO TRIP or WHAT? To ask a question or remark directed to me, Mike Pots, 24 years old, I can only answer that sometimes if you live on close terms with people observing and working with them on a day-to-day, year-in, year-out basis, one can almost say he knows them better than he knows himself. So this is just what it means. How could I help but notice the more desirable noble human qualities present in each and every one?

First fallout in Massachusetts and Connecticut. Now more news about PBBs (polybrominated biphenyls) in Michigan! Oh terrible. "Eight point nine million people poisoned," says *Newsweek*. The stuff was distributed in animal feeds. Must have gone on for years.

In the news also, some seven giant tankers in the past few months have spilled millions of gallons of oil. Still the practice of flushing oil hulls with seawater and dumping it goes on. Dangers of the modern world: chemical pollution, fallout, and covering our whole ocean with a slick of oil. Jacques Cousteau worries that it will kill off the algae, plankton, and other greens that are the basis of all ocean life.

Ron must be feeling well. He did what is right on; on his dish day he cleaned the circle and the kitchen and cooked dinner. Sirloin steaks are what he fixed, and were they good! No trip to the store—just to our freezer.

As a guest, we had a raw-milk yogurt maker; Arthur is his name. Very nice to meet a fellow like us who is into dairy. He has a regular business in Albuquerque. With a gallon of milk, he made us some very good yogurt in four and a half hours!

Also here for dinner was a pretty, young girl and three guys: Day—an acrobat, Richard—a strong, tall, clean Texan, and a longhaired fellow. We served us all a terrific meal. Feels so good to have the prosperity to treat a little crowd every night. We're way advanced of where we've been in the past. Ron is very impressed at how far the one steer has gone. Me too. This is a very important advantage of our cow dairy. We get good steers.

I am working on the walkway—coming out better than I imagined—going to be a first-class job. Peggi Sue is sick and Anna is off somewhere.

No more food stamps; we're eating better than ever. A great achievement and it feels good.

February 2, 1977: The time proceeds. The cows and goats get closer to freshening. The hay season gets closer.

Good brother Mel sent a letter and $150. On the spiritual level he is very conscious, and he manifests his belief on the material plane. He's thinking of us and understands our need. This is what is supposed to happen. There are several levels; we've seen hundreds of people come and go. Most sort of forget our cause or they never knew it. But Mel is doing what many could—love our scene and stay with it—be tight with us and help the community to grow.

JOURNAL 20

His mind is tripping out,
thinking about communal ways.

February 7, 1977: In our rough world we try to forge a mellow, productive, peaceful, and loving scene. Trials come our way. One is hepatitis, a dangerous disease that several people in the neighborhood have gotten. The New Light Center had three or four cases. Then pretty Ellen at Duncan's house got it. She was over here, and Peggi and Kim were over at the Center.

All would be fine for us, except Peggi Sue came down with very mild symptoms, from which she has just about totally recovered. By an odd coincidence, she was at the clinic with Ellen—bad timing—and we suspect she was transferred the flu with hep by the intern in a sloppy procedure. Peggi got the flu sixty minutes after leaving the clinic and was near delirious eight hours later. Anyhow, that brings the disease very close to home, and Kim is so close with Peg. Both are neither cooking or washing commune dishes nor milk dishes. We're going to stop selling milk for a while. We've all gotten gamma globulin shots.

Larry left for Kentucky. So he can apply himself, Ron went for a long journey in search of greater peace, which somehow he is not finding here. He is conscious of it; that he lacks incentive and peace of mind. It's Mike and me as the healthy farm boys doing farm chores. Mike's milking Lotsi, the goat that aborted a very deformed fetus. All other goats seem fine. Mike discovered one hive of bees was dead from starvation, and he got stung six or more times feeding the others with saved honey and sugar water put in empty combs.

Worried about hepatitis. Usually we're confident we'll stop it where it is. Once in a while, we get a flash of paranoia. Hep is especially insidious because the most contagious time is before the symptoms show. Best precaution is if you come in contact with people who have it, or may have it, then limit contact with people who need not be involved.

We, of course, want to sell milk, especially because we need to buy hay. Then again, we should never feel bound economically. There are alternatives. Dry up the cows, sell a cow, or fall back on our savings. I was thinking of alternatives to dairy; a furniture workshop would be one of my choices. Dairy or no, I'd like to see a good shop.

Another incident that was a bit unnerving: Pepe came up here after a fight with some folks in his commune. He tried to rush me into moving him in, but we got into a confrontation right away and said, "No!" Sandy couldn't stand it; Pepe's too self-righteous, and she's seen him in three or four fights here. Kim feels Pepe would kill him if he lost his temper and will not live with him. I don't blame them a bit. I hate to live under that tension. Pepe does get too self-righteous and very angry. I know he lacks respect for Kim and Larry. Yet Pepe is my closest brother, whom I lived with for many years. He's got a great thing going in town, but he has to stick with it or it's meaningless. He should make amends with his family there and continue the idea of buying the house and forming a corporation.

Pepe talks about self-discipline, but he hasn't developed it himself. Every so often he flares up and bloodies some people. We don't want to live waiting for the next incident. People can't trust him, even me in a few instances. We've got to have a controlled mellow scene where people say, "We want to live this way."

Also to do with discipline, Pepe goes through thousands of dollars in fun, booze, and drugs. He has contributed though and a great deal, really. I sure wish him peace of mind. So many restless, angry people—drunkenness and ego.

It is very important that we use ideas of consensus; of group control of who lives here. More and more it is shown how it must be ingrained, that we decide as a group, with relaxed time, who is to live here and what we do.

A small bind at the moment, we decided to stop selling milk so we have no income until I sell candles. We will sell some pigs this weekend.

February 10, 1977: Larry gone, Ron gone, Canadian Blueblood Anna gone, Jim and Mary—soybean queen—stranded 1,500 miles away. Of these, Larry is sure to return. The others were somewhat peripheral to the functioning scene although they help. Kim and Peggi Sue getting ready for takeoff. They are central figures and ones we'll miss every day until they return.

Sandy is making plans to start tomatoes, cucumbers, cabbage, and broccoli. These are chores Kim is the leader of, but he is dropping out. Sandy is fixing up the plant beds now that most of the walkway is finished in the new collector. She's pleased to work with the soil. She could replace Kim's energy in starting vegetables. March is the planting month, and wintertime is good for getting the ten-ounce cups ready.

We had fellow Tom just out of the Coast Guard for an overnight guest, a courteous guy from an Idaho farm. He liked our barn. When he saw the ungraveled portion of the road to here, he thought no one could be living up this way! But he kept on because those were the directions, and he found us. Another guest was a real sorry case, drunken Don. He was all cut up and could hardly walk, but he had a sleeping bag and left nice and early.

In our local news, Pepe is right back at Mabel Dodge Luhan House where he belongs. Kim asked him when he came up here, "What about your big plans to form a corporation and buy that house?" He's there, and everything is back to normal now. Except I've never before had a confrontation with Pepe like that. Always where either of us lived was home for the other. This has the feeling of a bad omen. . . .

At the Healing Center, Jane, Rifka, Jennifer, Tim, Doug, Valerie, and others I don't know set up houses. Into the mystique of herbal and exotic cures and massage, they attracted Steve the chiropractor. But these people helped spread a hepatitis epidemic. Evidently they had Tim as a case for a long while. Then others got it, and Ellen, one of their frequent guests, got very sick. Kim and Peggi Sue were going there for treatment and so was Ron. Thank God we're probably in the clear. We've had little traffic lately, and we told New Zealand Chris to quit eating and sleeping here since he's been over at the Center.

It is hard to deal with this epidemic problem. We need to be cleaner, have better communal cooking and washing areas, better habits, and be very alert. I hope Ron is well. He does not often get sick. As a health precaution only Mike and I are handling dairy cleanup. Kim and Peggi are being kept a little distant.

February 13: We kept all the milk just for three days, and quickly we've got homemade butter—Mike learning the technique from Sandy. He also made about eight pounds of good cottage cheese. Sandy made three quarts of yogurt.

Kim and I went and looked at that cow for sale. She looks good and very soon to drop in about seven days.

I made another 108 pairs of candles with Peggi's help. Then I put in more concrete and the last walkway stones. Mel expected shortly. His mind is tripping out, thinking about communal ways.

February 14, 1977: Mel left today after a short but very good visit. His friend Steve is a fine man—does his yoga—says he doesn't live in quite a commune but is part of a "New Age" family with ten people on one acre. He has a job with an energy systems company. We served up some of our country food, and even pork fried rice made by me!

Mel said he's going to continue working in Fort Worth while he has the connection. He sees that if he moves here, he'd like to have some real money to help make things happen, like a ceramic tile floor or a new kitchen stove. He gave the treasury $90.

I heard that Felipe has his big Brown Swiss for sale. We looked at her today. She is a giant cow and looking in fine shape, very soon to freshen. I just about have the $600 to buy her. With her head in a stall I tried out those huge teats. She did not like that, and gave a lightning kick. I rocked backed on my heels just in time. I think I almost got killed. I can still see that hoof, seared in my memory, about one inch from my forehead. Will have to be more careful.

We sold two pigs to Kemal, one pig to Felipe, one goat to John, eggs, and a few candles, so we are very close to making a deal.

February 19: Clear day—bright hot sun—no good storms since November. Around the barn it is really muddy from thawing out. Graze is just appearing out from under the snow. If we ever had to go without hay, our animals could survive here for years on yellow graze.

I've been reading about the Napoleonic Wars. When Napoleon entered Moscow, all the very beautiful farms for many miles around the capital burned their hay—scorched the earth. They destroyed their farms but forced the famous retreat of Napoleon. At the close of that decade of war, so many horses had been killed that no more replacements could be found in all Europe. In our own era, clever US generals try to defoliate thousands of acres of Vietnam. As a result many thousands of people live tragic lives. Oh shame. Wars are such a huge waste. I hope we are writing a new chapter.

Lena is back and in the groove. She made excellent fry bread with beans and salad. And Sandy topped it off with homemade vanilla pudding and whipped cream from the dairy.

News: Exceptionally cold in the East—lots of snow—industries closed and people cold and out of work. In the West, California is in a very severe drought. In Minnesota no snow cover, and north of us in Colorado, no snow.

In our own sphere of water controversy and cooperation, I say go for the principal of equal distribution of water according to acreage. Drop the inter-community fight over priority and concentrate on us all surviving. Be aware of conservation and ditch improvement and help each other irrigate to get the job done quickly.

February 22: We got a little storm—lots of wind in a partly darkened sky. We received a letter from Ron. In Florida he stayed with past comrade Michael Glassman and is now heading north to Virginia and is enjoying his travel.

I've discovered a terrific book by Tony Herbert on Vietnam. It was very, very bad how people treated each other over there. The Vietnamese are asking for repayment for all the damage. Carter did pardon all the draft dodgers—good—but he couldn't go so far as to say honestly we made a very bad mistake, and we'll own up to it by making a contribution to the reconstruction.

All those generals, colonels, majors, and captains and lieutenants living in relative luxury. To say nothing of the helicopter manufacturers and muni-tions makers, shipping and construction magnates, etc., who made out so well on the war. Do they think to make a contribution to the country they helped maim? At least we got out. America is democratic enough where these people will lose a lot of influence, I hope.

I'm making preparations to move the candle factory over to where the jewelry shop is set up—plenty of room for both. Then I can work on this funky room I've been living in—put in a decent floor.

February 24, 1977: *Hey you guys—SMACK! (kiss) I love you all. See you, who else? Peggi Sue*

February 26: For days a storm built up and yesterday it snowed about two inches down here—the real thing. I went out running in the winter landscape after the milk run. Felt good. Temperature went down to 0°F.

People are very happy with our produce. They make sure to tell us how much they like it. We've got plenty of business waiting. Maybe soon we'll have more milk.

Kind of nice here with just us four adults. Now if we can only add some special people who can dig the opportunity here.

February 27: Almost into March and we finally have a good storm. Today the mountains have that incredible look—few clouds above them and crystal white—so clear. It's cold here—below 0° at night. After morning chores sometimes I take off my boots and put my feet in a pan of warm water to get them back to normal. Ah, that is so nice.

Four goats have freshened now. We've lost three kids because we didn't get to them soon enough. It's been cold, and they couldn't take it. The goats are very poor mothers. We keep two healthy kids at the barn and three more in the kitchen that aren't walking yet. They are cute with big floppy ears and huge eyes.

March 1, 1977–Tuesday: A fine day for me. I've been feeling very good. Mike and I loaded the pig and I took her to the boar. Mike had to do some fancy rope work, tying her around the neck and behind the front legs. It's a little like tying up a bowling ball that fights back. The two of us were just able to haul her into the pickup. I brought the four remaining goat kids along and traded them for nine heavy bales of good hay. So glad we can now make these decisions. John now has his own scene and can immerse himself in goats; he's expecting eighteen to drop!

Speaking of dropping, the bottom is out of the goat market around here. It's hard to sell goat's milk.

March 2: After she left here with Kemal, Kiva smashed up their truck; they got it fixed now. Carol, after she left here, smashed up John's truck; it works but is still smashed. Now Lena goes for an evening out with Ron and gets hit on her driver's side with the car she wants to sell. When we're really together, we'll have insurance on our delivery pickup truck.

March 3: The day did not dawn clear. Clouds and fog hung in the mountains, and now at night the mountains are shrouded and the sky is white from the moon behind a cloud ceiling.

Larry is back! He had a pleasant trip. Spent two days at the Gaskin Farm in Tennessee—a thousand-person commune on about 1,000 acres—average forty visitors a day. I feel our commune is more complete with Larry here.

Sandy finished digging out the adobe from the plant beds. I brought the very best dark crumbly soil up to the new greenhouse with the truck, and she unloaded it.

Ron came and went. Both Sandy and Mike were very unenthusiastic about his staying. What happened to him? I guess it's the contrast. Mike and I, on the one hand, and Sandy too, work constantly. He couldn't get behind a craft or a project. Well, good luck, Ron. He likes to talk—be propagandist. "We," we don't like to hear it. Place to talk is to the outside people who don't hear all that radical stuff.

March 4: Storm continues but little snow. Parts of New Mexico declared "emergency drought"—government pays for one-half feed price. Not here though. We're getting the weather. Winter wheat looks great. Alfalfa fields are soaked and frozen.

Having received our first seed order, Sandy, with some help from Mike, made up six wooden starting flats for March planting. Mike filled the red truck all by himself from our barn and dumped the load of manure on the field we're now preparing.

March 8: Mike is moving our adobe dirt stash away from where it is eroding the west wall by holding in moisture. We move tons of dirt, rock, and manure using our shovels. We both see it as a perfectly good means. It does mean, at times, we do some hard work. Mike can really do it. He thrives behind it.

Through a slight bit of cleverness, Larry and I fixed our water-bath cooler to hold the maximum amount of bottles. Very handy—we had two refrigerator racks that did just the trick. As we add bottles of milk, we remove water so all but the tops are submerged.

For forty dollars we're going to graze Leo's cows here for two weeks.

March 10: Mike cleaned up and moved bricks and lumber from the south wing. Some of the guys were sloppy workmen—didn't clean up when done. Mike has established a new site and all three adobe brick stashes are now away from the house at their own area, and they're covered.

Red Jim's job was a real example of bad work—absolutely wrong design—then a lousy cement job. I pulled his foundation apart with one hand. Hard to believe we were such nice guys and let him do such a stupid job.

Felipe says okay for Sunday delivery of the cow.

Friday: On a very wintry morning—snowdrifts, cold wind, and heavy clouds—I did the milk run. Looking out for new customers, I picked up three. We now have customers for about thirty-five gallons of milk a week.

Jason is home from school sick but getting better, and his baby brother is doing very well. That Jason is a tough little kid. Mom sends him off to school all bundled up, and he trudges down the road gaily in the below-zero air.

Saturday: Today was warm and inviting. Ron is back from camping out at the Grand Canyon. He's thinking of a teepee and maybe helping Lena build her new house.

Felipe delivered the cow to us in his very nice stock trailer. He brought his curious wife and two cautious granddaughters to see our place. Proudly, we always show off the solar attachments.

Back up at the corral, the huge brown beast—eyes intense—charged down the ramp—full udder swaying. Felipe quickly tossed me the rope: "Here, she's yours!" I held on for dear life; the cow did all the leading. This, now, is a real milk cow. Felipe gets the calf when born, which will be very soon. Best to freshen here.

March 16, 1977: Ron is making the effort to get in the swing. He cooked dinner the first two nights he was back and did the dishes and kitchen cleanup. Went out and sold candles and then made another set of candles last evening! Also he is staying with Lena. Will he go with her or continue to make a good impression at the commune? He's kind of changeable—say one thing and then do another. Time will tell.

Tuesday milk run went very well. Larry has made a new delivery cooler out of a refrigerator. He took out the motor, laid it on its back in the pickup. Then we put in the bottles of milk and pour in ice cubes that we make and store in our large freezer. Milk covered with ice—nice. Reclaim the unmelted cubes when the run returns and store them in grain sacks in the big chest freezer.

Wednesday: A very pleasant day. Carl and Janet here with three kids—our old friends who moved away. Carl was such a good partner, but he left for a private scene down in Cañoncito.

I sorted apples. We have good ones, but they don't get eaten if not unwrapped and put out. Friend big Adrienne helped. She is interested in living here; sounds like a possibility. She approached us in the proper manner.

Mike said no. For now, anyhow, she's off to see her mother. Then we'll have to decide in about a month.

I'm feeling good tonight—energy coming up. I did a few good runs today and a little jumping exercise. I've been milking the new cow. We're getting along quite well. Doesn't take long to get her into the stall and hind legs tied. She doesn't jump when I release her and stands completely still for milking—a good girl.

Sandy refinished her new mud floor—more wax—a thorough washing first. The floor is being improved; a nice cleanable surface is very desirable. This one has lots of texture—golden straw. Periodically she has added linseed oil, cut with kerosene, to the weak spots and cracks. Our happy baby has a perfect, simple room to be raised in. It is kept very neat with fresh hanging plants, cheery curtains, and clean, shining varnished furniture.

Our guess that there is a demand for fresh cow's milk is quite correct. I got orders for seven more gallons on the milk run. We're going to have to do some figuring on how to get all the milk in the cooler.

March 18, 1977: Saw Daddy Dave, one of our revered founders. Sitting on tall bar stools in town, he and Pepe and I had a short discussion about that incident where Pepe was rejected at Buffalo. I tried to be persuasive. There was a tremor in my voice, for I sense that this is an essential element for our survival, yet I go against the grain of the hippie idea of being very open. Not practical; we must learn and adapt, I said. But I felt I was not convincing; Pepe's resentment overshadowed any words. I've never been separated from him like this.

The other day I started working on the new greenhouse site in back of the south wing, and today Ron picked it up and did a bunch more. I joined him for a while and loaded more adobe.

Mike is working on the old self-standing greenhouse. The western wall fell off, and he's repairing it—needs a lot of work. In there is where Mike raises his red wiggler worms for fishing. They eat coffee grounds. Spinach is coming up in there now.

The cheese Sandy made is all eaten. She made butter, and a cottage cheese is on the stove.

March 21, 1977: A very pleasant spring day today. Brome grass is really starting to show. I fixed fence this morning so we can contain Leo's cows better. We've been getting some areas grazed that really need the trim. Good to see. Tonight Larry and I marked all the young generation of chickens with red bands and

14.
*Daddy Dave
Gordon. From
the personal
collection of
Chamisa
WeinMeister*

collected five roosters to be killed. We've got 108 hens. The youngest twenty-nine are just starting to lay. Forty-four eggs a day on average last week. They're coming up. Larry has been increasing the feed. He worked down at the chicken house today, cleaning and fixing up some more laying nests.

I stayed up with Daddy Dave until midnight last night talking. I was looking at the buffalo skull on the wall; the light from two kerosene lanterns cast a yellow glow on the whitewashed circle walls. We got very mellow, smoking local homegrown, talking about old times and all the parties we'd been at in this room.

March 26, 1977: Two weeks are up. Leo's cows are gone. Our sedge grass is well mowed. Looks very good. They're sure not crazy about that swampy sedge broad grass.

Leo wants to keep his cows here. We said no. Wayne Fesita of SCS mentioned that grazing alfalfa fields heavily cuts production. We can believe it.

Another milk run successful. We paid for our plowshares, have money for seed and tax funds, and bought feed. Some candle money in there helping out. We are operating from our income. That is what I'm looking for.

Great problem in modern society is unemployment. We've all been signed up for five, six, or even seven years at the unemployment office. No one has ever gotten one offer. And the pressure to keep what little work there is going adds tremendous pressure to destructive tendencies in our society: the tendency toward war; toward cluttering our earth with the ever-expanding construction of cities, and toward waste of natural resources. Many industries need the continued extreme consumption without conservation to maintain their level of production. People on the land; that's a dream of mine.

Sandra found the time to transplant tomatoes from the flats to cups. She mixed up more soil mixture—a loving job she does. The plants go in and out of the rooms each morning and evening. The tomatoes are each individually placed in their cup, marked as to what they are, and watered. They seem to be doing very well.

Ron cooked ham for dinner—a real feast.

Sunday: We got a letter the other day from Peg and Kim. They're thinking of us—buying a three-burner stove for the candle room! They're earning $15 a day where they are. Also got a letter from Mel and an order for candles. He could be a good outlet if we can safely send them.

Goat John was over making goat's butter—needs the separator for that—gets $2.50 a pound. While he was here, a couple drove up to order cow's milk. John just can't help himself; had to snicker disapproval about their choice of milk. The fellow, Steve, is a builder. Works with a local solar heating expert.

Larry is suspicious that the plowshares weren't fixed correctly; they don't have quite the right bend in the point. We'll see.

March 30, 1977: A sunny spring day—ice thick on the water troughs. We came home with six gallons of milk; first time we didn't sell out. Sandy steps in though and uses the milk to make a four-gallon mozzarella cheese, and four gallons for cottage cheese and three quarts of yogurt and two pounds of butter. Sandy hasn't been sleeping well lately. I'm glad she feels good enough to go ahead with using the milk.

Question arises about our tenth birthday celebration. Ron would like to see a bash—a big party with rock 'n' roll band. But the consensus is not for it—turned off by the idea. We're apprehensive—not really our idea of a good time. We were discussing it. What do we want to promote? What do I want to promote? Not another party to have a chance to get "high" and spend too much money on booze.

I see drinking; I don't like it. Neither does Larry or Mike. People want to get loose; well, I'd rather see them get straight—get together. If they need escape from their hard life—not very hard really—well, we have an alternative: the commune's day-to-day work for the community.

Our friends who want the party, they say, "Let us have Buffalo for a day!" Well, I want greater friendship where they commit themselves to New Buffalo for a longer period of time than one party. Out front, I'm scared of a bash of large size in my own home where I either ignore drunks or have to try and tell them what to do.

Our situation, I feel, is very tenuous. We're taking a gamble doing a dairy. We have little else for income. We haven't lifted ourselves out of our poverty yet. We're committed to trying to do something in agriculture. We could have a nonagriculture industry like woodworking: door and cabinet and bed construction for more income.

April 3, 1977: And now the Heavenly Father is taking care of us with the storm we've been wanting. There is nothing we can do to compare with this gift. We can rest a bit, for our earth is being watered.

Sandy and I cut a little wood in the snow—pleasant to be out in the elements.

April 4: Storm is over—very foggy this morning. Puff! It cleared, and we have spring snow panorama. And into this pastoral wonderland chug some Ortiviz hardcores: Susie Creamcheese, Jeff, Razberry, and kids. Both Susie and Raz were with us in the bread truck when we set out from Bolinas in '71. Lots of hugs and kisses all around. So high to hear Susie's laughter—always excited. We have empty rooms for them to stay in—pretty neat and clean if crude. Not much need of a fire these nights—only 20° outside.

While I am repairing the candle room floor, I am staying in Peggi's pad. Here, too, stay the baby tomatoes, broccoli, cucumber, and cabbage plants looking very good. These are our little friends. If this is together then we have homegrown vegetables of top quality. Then if this is not together, we are a great deal poorer. Sandy made it happen.

April 5: Larry took the milk run in alone. He got back about 2:30 p.m. Not bad. He unpacked all the bottles and ice and gave Sandy four gallons for cheese from the milk he didn't sell.

I went with Mike, and we sold a load of manure and hauled a load of organic trash for $75. It was pretty warm and smelled very good. We did, however, get stuck in the barnyard, which did not smell so good, and had to put on chains to get out. Pretty messy—there's just no good way to put on chains in the middle of wet manure.

Larry got an order for our extra teepee poles. We'll make $150, and it will be the start of a building fund! Now if we could sell three goats.

April 6: Larry loaded the teepee poles alone! Quite a job. Then he tied them down and we delivered them. In town traded a rooster for a refrigerator and bought fifteen bales and more seed oats and paid the taxes. Very nice.

Larry's been right on the case these days. In the afternoon he greased the plow and tuned the tractor and plowed. Plowed fields look very neat. The soil is just right.

But, we lost one plowshare; so we are crippled. One John Deere dealer told me he couldn't get those #215 shares anymore.

April 10: Milk run yesterday went great—sold out—got a few more orders. We saw a whole new plow for $100. We've been thinking of getting away from our two-man plowing setup where the tractor pulls the old horse-drawn plow with a seat for the operator to raise and lower the plows. Now here is a plow one man can operate! For Buffalo we bought a new plow.

Larry finished plowing the area below the orchard. Mike, with a little help from me, spread out manure on the garden—took about only an hour, and then Mike plowed with my help and instruction. He is new at the plowing. He kept at the controls and is getting the idea. That tractor is a lot of horsepower, and the new plow is a heavy piece of steel. It takes a little practice to coordinate the gas with a smooth clutch release and steer at the same time. Then one has to get used to the turning ability of the equipment and understand the different patterns that can be used. After plowing part of the garden, Mike dragged the soil to smooth the surface.

April 13: Nelly dropped another big bull calf. Mike fetched them in and milked the cow.

Larry has made a new field drag. He used one half of the metal engine-pulling stand, the school-bus bumper, and a bunch of long metal rods with threads and bolts on the ends. Very clever. It seems to work well. Goats we've been keeping in because our neighbor Kaplan complained about his trees getting attacked. Larry caught them in our little grove—trees just starting to fill out their buds. They are a pain in the butt.

April 15, 1977: Stormy weather—beautiful smell in the air of fragrant spring. Larry put in another terrific day. In the morning he worked on the community ditch. In the afternoon he put oats in the half-acre field already plowed and disked them in. He laid out lines for proper irrigation. Then he worked on the new shower stall using our pop-rivet gun and fiberglass that Sandy bought.

When the old wooden shower stall comes out, it will be made into bee-hives. It was very large and noncleanable. In this room north of the kitchen are also a long sink and long mirror above it, and our venerable washing machine and a table. There's quite a collection of toothbrushes on the shelf. This is the washroom for everybody.

With considerable effort we got the Friday milk run off with thirty-two gallons of milk. We make such an elaborate business out of seventy gallons of milk a week—a humble beginning.

Saturday: I went up the mountain to Lama Foundation, taking Jason with me. Quite a fine place; they're down to about a dozen people. Very beautiful up there. The view to the west is the quintessential panorama of the "Land of Enchantment."

I saw their big cow, the chickens, and the greenhouse with lettuce, cauliflower, and broccoli starts. They have a special place for their seed stash in there too. The big garden has a picket fence all around it. They just finished a garage project; it took one season. That's about the same effort as building a barn: a floor, walls, leak-proof roof, electricity, and inside water.

David, Jason, and I took a walk in the woods. Snow was falling, dry crystalline flakes creating a wonderland. It felt thrillingly fresh out. The soil is so black; the top forest layer is so light and rich with organic matter. We dug up some little pine trees to bring home.

April 19: And here's a new man, Jim Preston, recently out of high school from Buffalo, New York. Tall and slender with brown wavy hair, plastic-framed glasses, he seems gentle and eager. He had read about New Buffalo and was curious to see it. He's very willing to help out and was impressed that he could stay. One day he worked with me: dumped barn manure, gathered rocks off a field, and picked up a load of old grass that had been raked up; we'll use it for bedding.

Lena cooked a very good cheese, egg, and chard dish with baked rolls. That's cheese, wheat, greens, and eggs from our farm. It's not quite good enough to have these things; they still have to be put together so we can eat them.

April 23: Larry went off to the auction after I returned from delivering Lama's milk. He spent $2.50 and got three bargains: a double kitchen sink, an ice chest for milk delivery, and an electric three-plate stove! This may be a basic item for an improved cheese-making setup.

New man Jim rushed out to the garden to make more rows after we returned from la Lama. Lena went out to make rows, and then visiting Virginia, here with three kids, went out and helped make rows too. What a big job, and we've only got one third of the garden plowed. Day after day of work—still it's getting done.

Sunday: This gal, quite attractive, named Virginia, asked if she could move in. We told her okay! She's got three kids: a baby—Rom, a boy—Spirit, and Heaven, a girl about Jason's age. Very energetic, says she'll "work hard in kitchen, field, whatever needs doing!" She reminds me of that ball of energy, White Light. At the same time we asked College Jim what he's into. He said he really likes it here and would really like to stay for spring and summer. He's got college to start in September. We told him, "Great!" Love to have him.

Jim's helping out at the dairy. Always with a smile, he's looking for more to do. He does the cleaning, fetches the cows, takes the milk down, filters and bottles it. All I have to do is milk. I'm letting him milk Julie in the morning so he can learn.

April 26, 1977: Another successful milk run—picked up just a few new customers. Anyone who tries the milk thinks it's great. They like to see that rich cream on the top.

Indeed it's spring and another gal has joined us. Marilyn is a little spindly, long brown hair pulled back, mischievous eyes. She and Virginia learned the milk-room washing procedure. Virginia cooked Jim and me French toast this morning in appreciation of our morning milk chores.

Adrienne moved out here today too. I feel pretty good about it; we did the right thing. We are for people caring for each other. Many people become terribly alone in this world. Adrienne comes to us from the Taos Pueblo. After the death of Little Joe Gomez, her husband, she, an Anglo, had to search out another home. A large woman, she has an awkward walk. Her smile shows bad teeth, but her eyes are very caring.

She is part of a classic story. Little Joe Gomez was a venerated elder of the pueblo. He was magnificent in his traditional dress with feathers and bells and is famous for his birdlike dance moves. Adrienne, who is not a pretty woman, became a devotee of the Peyote Road Way, married Little Joe, and was very devoted to him.

April 29: Friday Larry did the milk run in good time. Made our record amount of $150! When he returned, a bunch of us seeded the oat field: 250 pounds of oats and 40 pounds of field peas. Then Larry disked in the seed. I checked the water; it was off.

Young Jon, who's been here several times before, arrived yesterday. He took to the greenhouse excavation with tremendous force and has the job nearly done!

May 1, 1977: Yesterday, with the red flatbed truck, I moved Virginia over here with her two kids and one walking baby. Marilyn came along and helped. Virginia was all packed and ready. We just about filled the truck—an incredible amount of stuff. That night we had a few beers, some smoke, and sat up late with songs and guitar.

Mike and Jon are milking together. Jon, a strapping young lad, is learning. So he might become a real steady here. He seems to want that. He's only twenty years old, but he's been looking to settle into this home. He's tried twice before. This time Mike is rewarding his persistence by showing him one of our central tasks, milking.

Mike, Jon, and College Jim took the fireplace out of Virginia's new room, a big job they did in one day. It had tremendous stones and burned extreme quantities of wood but threw off little heat. This gives them a lot more space. Busy, busy.

15. *Family moment: Back left: Jon, college Jim, Virginia, Rom.*
Front left: Sandy, Arty, Emil, Heaven

Tuesday Virginia, daughter, and baby came along on the milk run. Virginia's a very lively gal—open—once was a bar dancer. She's got a lot of good attitudes. Her two oldest are going to school with Jason. Spirit is in the new bed we just made in the boys' room.

Emil got stung today—only cried for ten seconds. His little lip is swollen. Our bee trip is a little uncool though, because we keep attracting angry bees to the pueblo. Mike is recovering from bee stings—his eyes just slits, puffy in his newly expanded face.

Nelly cow is being a problem as usual. I have to lasso her and then she leads in easily. Sometimes she jumps. Big Beth, our Brown Swiss, is more cooperative and quite relaxed. Nelly bolts from the lead stall; Beth is really slow and easy.

Sandy took a good hard cheese out after aging. I'm very impressed.

May 5: So many men willing to go on our first 1977 wood run that I bowed out. Mike and I corralled the steer Carnegie and put Nelly to pasture. I've never seen it before; our neurotic Nelly and her calf are so attracted to each other that he humps her all the time. After they've been apart, he jumps on her in a minute, and she goes for it! As he is a bull, maybe we missed one testicle. A more normal cow probably won't go for his horny actions, but she always does something wild.

"We're down to two good beehives," says Mike. The dividing last year was a failure. We had five hives; after the dividing, we've got two. Mike says it's not a bad level to have until we get better facilities, like a tight shop with a bee room for all the supplies.

We came up with a good new idea to put more gardens right near the house. There's a ditch that passes by the arch in back of Sandy's room for water, and it should be much easier to care for. How long it takes to figure out a simple thing like keeping the garden near the kitchen. Adrienne planted onions in the lower garden. Tomatoes in the four greenhouses are doing fine.

Jon milks the seven goats every night and Mike watches. Jim milks Julie and a good job he does.

May 6: Jim and Jon tried to pasture our 600-pound steer with the goats. I knew it would be unsuccessful, but they had fun learning how tough he is. Eventually they did rope him and bring him in. Nelly was better tonight; she did break the headstall some, but for most of the time she stood still.

Feels good here. Everyone can dig a happening scene where a lot has to be done. Marilyn is sticking with us. She made granola, biscuits, and gravy for breakfast. She's definitely determined to be very useful, undemanding, and an asset to her friends. She's a country girl too—not too country—shaves her legs in the washroom sink.

A new day: Continued clear, hot days. We're cut off from the irrigation water now. To get water here we need cooperation from Valdez and Cañoncito ditches and from Atalaya ditch, all upstream of our main ditch. They take all the water. Easier to pray for rain—we're not desperate yet. When they do install a state supervised system we should be able to get more water.

I was offered the job of mayordomo for this year. I've been thinking I'd take it. The commissioners suggest one head of water; pass it around every twelve hours—twenty-four hours for bigger spreads. We have to organize it some way—a lot less water this year. With some rains we might luck out. It's amazing how many years we can fill our holding pond—water the crested wheat for days, flood unplanted sections of the garden, and run water to the meadow. Not this year. I'll have to make up a tentative schedule and talk to some people.

I watered a bunch of trees. Several cherries are doing very well. The plums are showing life too. Most of the Russian olives are coming out, and the Chinese elm shows their superiority, looking very green and hardy.

May 15, 1977: For the last three days we've had a terrific storm—snow for the mountains and a near drenching down here, quite as though the Heavenly Father is really looking out for us. I am again mayordomo. Hope it won't be too much trouble.

Mr. Proctor and his assistant from dairy division of the Health Department will come up Tuesday to make a final decision on the barn site. I've been reviewing our plans and drawing up a few new diagrams to scale.

Tuesday: The inspectors arrived and spent much time with us in the milk room, while I hit them with questions. They saw Mike's greenhouse and our kitchen and circle. It is spectacular to open the simple circle door and walk down into the earthen meeting room, built by the ancient hippies. The place was tidied up the day before. Virginia did an excellent job cleaning the milk room. Proctor said he could see we're making a good effort to stay clean.

Jon cut his finger pretty badly; he can't milk. Lena's friend Dee is staying down there with him in the candle shop—my old room. Seems rather nice for Jon, a gorgeous mature woman with the young stud. Marilyn and Larry are staying together too. More like normal, wonderful life.

May 20: This morning before sunup, I helped Adrienne plant white and blue corn; it is a religious exercise with her that she learned at the Taos Pueblo. I volunteered to help when she requested someone to drive the tractor and plow. She then follows behind and drops seeds in the trench behind the plow.

As a guest we've got Morry, a tattooed mechanic who was through here many years ago. He worked on our Dodge brakes yesterday and bought parts to fix it. Seems quite nice, a nervous laugh and the usual mechanic's beat-up car.

I examined Lama's milk cow; she's in very bad condition—mastitis—bag is very hard and milk is so bad, I've never seen anything remotely like it. Get a vet and antibiotics. Seriously! I kind of doubt a cow like that can recover. They didn't know to get the cow thoroughly milked out! Our own cows are doing great.

Sunday: I spent some time on the ditch yesterday and with College Jim watered at Leo's. Jim is a great help. I took off to do the milk run and still the job got done.

Mike has started on the circle and kitchen retainer wall—first mud then cement. Jim and Morry are helping him. Dee's baking bread and Marilyn's making granola; the air is thick with aroma from rich delights. Larry is fixing up his solar heater to be a greenhouse growing area.

Ron is away. The last few days, he put in a glass door to go into the projected solar collector.

May 23, 1977: Larry, Marilyn, Jim, and I went on the fence-post run. We worked really hard but felt very good when we returned. But we're not going to make a regular thing of such runs; we don't like cutting the live trees. We are mostly getting good corral posts. We'll buy fence posts for pasture fencing.

Busy! Last night, I sent Jim to get the water. I described where it was, and he turned it to us—a good flow. The water came down here quickly from nearly one mile away. We irrigated in the dark until 11:30 and then turned the water to our neighbors Al and Judy. The ranchers get a big head start if the water travels at night and is already spreading on the fields when they arrive in the early morning light.

Friday: I did the milk run. Larry went in too and bought baby chicks: 100 pullets—white and gray leghorns. The kids are fascinated with the little peepers. He also took our new chain saw to a repair shop.

Sold out of milk, did errands, earned money, came home, and went right to milking with about thirty minutes off for a little exercise. Shared a joint with Jim and listened to a few new records on our new stereo.

Uh-oh, I had to go to the Corriara head gate twice! My plans for the ditch just didn't come off like precision. I had two commissioners over to see what was going on. Meeting tomorrow of ditch officers.

Saturday: Hot dry days. Reports of drought in the southeast and even in the northeast. Dry weather continues in California.

Meeting with ditch commissioners went well; our group is able to make decisions, and we are discussing the issues. Manuel Ortiz is spending a lot of time and effort on this.

Sunday: From the Morningstar mesa came Rebel in his white, shiny, late-model Buick convertible with tape deck. I had him chauffer me on the ditch and at the same time got to spend some time with him. Like Pepe and I, Rebel and I have been close and gone through some hairy stuff; hand of God helped us out in the heavy gun standoff we had with Indio and Geronimo. I'm a good friend of Reb's, and I appreciate how hard he's worked for a lot of different causes: his dad, Uncle Sam, us, and Goat John, to name a few.

We talked a bit about the old commune days, when big tough guys like Joe Cota, Jerry Murry, Chuck, Paul, Tucker, and Wayman would lean on everyone heavy for booze money. Max was into it too, and these are big guys. The scene was like that here when the dominant force was how to get wine for the day. Sold the only cow and a good tractor for money. Kim even got into it, really chummy. We have come a long ways from that.

Speaking of parties, well, that stuff has left a very bitter taste. New Buffalo had one of the all-time heavy party boozers—Bob Wertz—he even died here. He had tuberculosis, and, I heard, just drank and entertained— not an ounce of trying to build something. But we yet bless him as one of God's children.

So, enough history. Rebel and I never were too impressed with that scene, though we were and are good friends with those pioneers in our commune way, which most people have long left. I had word of Joe Cota today. Joe has become a really great piano player and entertainer.

Another day: Jon's finger is just about healed. He's back milking goats and is anxious to milk our wonderful Guernsey when she has her calf in a few weeks. Jon starts by putting her in the headstall and feeding her a little grain to get her trained.

I bought sixteen more excellent bales. Made $193 on the milk run.

June 7, 1977: From Taiwan come Dee's kids: Steve, thirteen, and Matthew, age nine. Nice kids, they like the farm. Older one is working with Mike; younger one has fallen in with Jason and the gang. Mike sure can put in hours after hours of pretty intense work: mixing mud, hauling dirt, applying mud and concrete. It's gonna make the place look great.

Wednesday: Virginia helps with the cows; she brings them up and down, to and from the barn, waters, and is learning to feed. She also did our Mr. Pots a big favor and took him to bed. He's so new that he has temporarily fallen in love with her. She didn't mean for that to happen.

We got the water at night and in the morning. We did the entire garden, much of which looks excellent. The kids and I planted some empty spaces: acorn and Hubbard squash. Sandy has a patch of summer squash planted near the house.

Our savings is down to $100. We bought three pairs of boots last week, hay, and chicken wire.

Bricks: Once we have the bricks, the rest of the milking barn could more easily fall in place. Seems what we should do to make the barn a reality is to make adobe bricks, with stream or well water right on the site. I'm not especially enthusiastic about the work, but I sure want the barn. *Ha, ha, ha, Artie. You're funny!*—Writer unknown.

Here we are in the richest society in the world, a few humble people who have been given a piece of land, and we will use it to get to the point where we are not poor. And here we are with a new crop of people at New Buffalo. We do not attract professional people or people with any kind of money or more than very minor skills.

Adrienne cleans houses and takes care of invalids. She earns enough to buy gas and keep her car going so she can continue to go to work. Her earning ability is very minor. She has given me about $25.

In town, my partner Pepe is a successful jeweler. Not all jewelers are successful; most just get by. We've got one, Lena. She has a decent little shop and does nice enough work. But she's been here nearly a year and is still not able to contribute money. Does help buy food but nothing at all dynamic. She drives a fairly fancy car, which she's had in two accidents. No buyers for the car yet.

Larry, unlike some of us here, is a skilled worker—a good cabinetmaker. He specializes in inlaid boxes. But his earning ability isn't any better than most here. He doesn't make things to sell. He has a place in the dairy though as deliveryman, mechanic, and general idea man. Now with the dairy in operation, he is contributing financially by being part of the business. He is also in charge of the chickens, which do make a little cash for us.

Jon, who is working in the dairy, is an unskilled laborer at twenty years old, not yet especially handy with tools. He's willing to work for the dairy.

Virginia was a bar dancer; now she's a welfare mother. She, too, would like to work for the dairy. Dee has a little money, no tools, and no craft; she has a car and it's a rather good running one. She has had jobs. Now the jobs are over, and she's back to poverty. Marilyn had a responsible job in a big city. No job now and back to poverty. She, too, works for the dairy. She and Dee are potential drivers for the milk delivery route.

We've got Ron, who had a series of mining jobs. Now the jobs are over, and he has no craft. He has picked up on the candle trip and is a good taper maker. He's also getting knowledgeable about installing windows in adobe walls.

Mike has developed some woodworking skills. He works doggedly in town as a laborer to earn a little money for pet projects like the bees or capping the pueblo. He has found a major role in the dairy and would just love to see it give us some earning power.

Then there's Sandy, another welfare mother, excellent homemaker and also some skill as a seamstress. She, too, is given a new role by the dairy as our #1 cheese, yogurt, and butter maker. Me, I came with a lot of education, and am just learning to be handy around the farm myself.

So we want to build the business where people can do some real work, and there can be more return to support them all. So what does it add up to? We'd best make adobe bricks so we can have this dairy barn. Mike suggests we pour adobe to create the walls, using a form like our neighbors Al and Judy did. I'll have to ask around about this. Most people, by far, use bricks. Why, I don't know.

A new day: Dee and I did the milk run. It was rather bewildering for a newcomer. She drove well and understands our bookkeeping system is quite efficient. Dee has an Afro of light brown hair and a voluptuous body. She was the sophisticated wife of a businessman who is in Taiwan; now she's riding with us on the desert mesas of New Mexico.

Jenny dropped a bull calf. Jon started milking, but I had to take over and call in a vet, because she hasn't let down the milk. She's being very cooperative in handling but is having difficulty in getting milk to flow.

Larry's half brother Brian is wanting to spend the summer, and he'd be interested in adobe brick making! Rebel told me to get some straw and the lumber for the forms. He's been here quite often. That's good. He's got several money scams in mind: to sell his fancy car and do an engine installation job. He likes Lena.

I felt good today. Did some running and talked to some neighbors about getting the water down here and away from other communities that have done much more irrigating than Arroyo Hondo; I'm pushing for it. It is dry, but few people are hit as bad as we are. Our neighborhood is too asleep and lets the other communities monopolize the water. I'm trying to get some action.

Mike is doing a tremendous job, sometimes with thirteen-year-old Steve's help, concrete-capping the retainer walls of our pueblo. He color-coated the stuff last week. Now he is into another round of mudding.

June 20, 1977: Manuel Martinez came to get me for a ditch meeting. I left just after milking on the rush. We got some more water going to five head gates.

We went for hay—brought back sixty bales. On returning we could see the pickup truck raking hay in the far field, pulling the buck rake. The farm, overall, has a captivating beauty. There's not even two inches between where wheat fields start and alfalfa and grasses end.

Ron made candles and colored them for money for the upcoming peyote meeting, a very nice way to honor New Buffalo and remember all the people who have helped create it. Thus we resolved how to celebrate the birthday.

The next day: I have introduced Jon to Big Beth, our Brown Swiss, and he is going to quickly take over milking her—big man—big cow. The new calf lives in the courtyard. Virginia and Marilyn take him out for walks. The calves are looking good.

Rebel helped Larry rake the hay. He's impressed with how the scene has grown in a fairly short time. He likes the direction, and I think he'd like to play a role. He's a real Morningstar veteran and, underneath a tough exterior, a nice guy. Actually, it was Kemal who blocked him from moving back once. And then some people were a little leery of his temper. But Reb has a good understanding of the commune idea, and he keeps bouncing back to it.

Rebel is getting interested in the barn and so is Brian, Larry's brother. So here is a new situation: more people to build the barn. Ron has only recently gotten the idea he could help with the foundation. My thinking was that if it's communal, it should be able to come together through people helping out. And now it's happening! Makes me feel great.

Here it is. When we go to milk and see those beautiful cows and know how to handle them, we feel proud. How really good we'll feel when there's a neat little barn and delivery truck! So up early for milk run tomorrow. Need to get Rebel to cut more hay before he leaves with the big Case tractor, which we borrowed. He's quite good with it.

June 28: Off and on rain for the last two days. We have a good head of water; I turned up our ditch the night before. Worked hard moving water, mainly just me irrigating. I wear my big clumsy boots, which irritate my feet, so I'm limping around in and out from the fields.

Sold out of milk.

June 30, 1977: As soon as we got the tractor back, Sandy and I mowed. Then Sandy and Jon mowed, and next Brian and I finished cutting the alfalfa. It's very hard to pick a hole in the weather—thunderstorm to the northeast— such a dry place; then you mow, and it acts like a magnet for these little storms that swirl around.

A neighbor Jeff came and trenched the line to the new corrals, and we put the pipe in. That simple.

July 4, 1977: In the "good news" department, our milk passes the test! Standard plate count of bacteria can be 20,000 or lower. Our cow tested at 200—very low, and goats at 6,500—not as clean but still good. Under mastitis heading, need a somatic cell count fewer than 1,000,000. Our cow had 550,000 SCC, which is fine, and goats had a count of 6,500. We do have clean milk, just as we suspected.

Back in style: Dee got some money from a friend and gave me $50. Ron contributed $20, and there's a milk run coming up tomorrow. Rebel sold his car and got $700 for it. So we ridded ourselves of another vehicle, which is progress. Now, how well will Reb make that money count?

Rebel and I installed the faucet at the new corrals. We put it in during some lucid moments after a very enjoyable smoke up on the barn roof. Only made ten trips back to the shed for tools.

July 10: Lots of guests: three young ladies and one baby, two guys, a colorful couple from the Rainbow festival, Jonathon's cousin Peter, and Virginia's big boyfriend, Earl. Pepe was here, too, and Goat John came down for some volleyball. He's here most every day at some time.

Pepe proudly spread out a copy of the July 7 *Taos News*, which has a feature article on us: "New Buffalo, Ten Years Old, Still Follows Vision," by Merilee Dannemann, who was out here recently taking photos and doing interviews. Wow, they did a great job.

Monday morning: Sandy beautifully cares for the new greenhouse sun porch. There are lots of tomatoes developing, sweet peas, nasturtiums, California poppies, peppers, marigolds, and alyssums flowering. It is truly an attractive and productive area. And more greenhouse space planned to join Adrienne's. I'm anxious to see the new one dug out dramatically more, so we get a big collector and a livable space.

Tuesday: I did the milk run and took Jason along. I always try to take a kid if it's convenient. Takes a little pressure away from the house, and they enjoy it and can be a bit of help.

It should be noted, before I forget, that we had an unusual occurrence. Mainly four attractive young ladies camped in Holy Ron's neat little room for several days. This is certainly a positive point about our lifestyle. Ron came back from the Rainbow gathering with good feelings to find them there. It is part of the cosmic balance that someone from here felt free and Aquarian enough to take off and join the happening. Ron got the message that his inspiration to go was the right thing.

Neal, young New York textiles businessman who stayed here during the winter, was up to see us. Eddie Cat Godet came by—tough rebel boxer—cool, cool—been in New Orleans, Miami, Denver, Montreal, and Houston, living life as it comes.

Peter Rabbit poem quote: "How long will it take for us to rid the earth of this legacy of waste and greed. A strange generation—gobblers of the earth's resources—burning it all in a few short years—reflecting consciousness of our world."—From Libre commune.

Consciousness from our local Amigos de Salud Co-op. Some figures (they don't say where they came from) might be near true. Only seven out of a thousand of the earth's humans have a university education. Over half suffer from malnutrition. Over eighty percent live in substandard housing. Americans are only six percent of the world, but they have half the world's income. "How can the wealthy six percent live in peace with their neighbors?" they ask. They are driven to arm themselves, spending more on military defense than the rest spend on everything.

Our hay coming off the stack looks very good.

16. *Hot springs on the Rio Grande. Photo by Clarice Kopecky*

July 14, 1977: Beautiful cloud formations in the changing sky. The four girls from the west coast left. Two more young ladies take their place: Two Songs, who was here before, and Stacy. Two Songs was showing off her fine, thin, brown legs this morning—Stacy laboring in the adobe brickfields.

Three guys here for the night. And Dee's parents and sister are visiting! They've never seen anything like this. Ron helped prepare fantastic pork-and-rice dinner—plenty for everyone served at the great table in the circle room. Her folks put a bottle of Kahlua on the table, I brought out the guitar as usual, and we're rocking to some Rolling Stones numbers, keeping up our reputation for hospitality.

Little Emil's really getting around now, crawling and getting in and out of rooms. He even climbed three steps into the kitchen from the circle. Still with his famous smile. Little Rom is down in Santa Fe with his mother, Virginia, for an operation on his little hand. One finger was damaged in an accident, and some doctors think they can repair it better.

Disturbing story told by two girls of masked, armed vigilante types threatening to clear the hot springs of hippies! Reminder of the hostility in the world, the sort of feeling we'd like to see disappear.

Wednesday: I organized a wood run. Reb, Ron, Mike, Jim, and I gathered things today and took off, found a good spot, and gathered a full load of cedar wood, long dead and very dry. We went over one hundred miles round trip. We explore the territory as we cruise the wide-open spaces.

This is a tremendous effort for no solution to our problem, except for the moment. Wherever we go cancels out one more place for us or anyone else to get wood. By the time Emil is grown, burning cedar constantly every day will be just an incomprehensible legend. Propane is an alternative, as a supplement. If we had a regular income, this would be one of the best things for us to purchase. How many more years of searching for scarce wood can I face? When we got back, I felt good. I love to see a growing stack for our immediate security. This is the same problem our society will soon face vis-à-vis petroleum. Most people can't see two minutes past their nose.

A new day: Adrienne lives in a mess. It's very unappealing, and it is too bad she ignores her adjoining greenhouse. I saw it was closed and opened it—the tomatoes that had been so meticulously cared for were withering in the motionless heat. I secured hoses and then got Dee's sister Judy, a Jersey City public defender, to water.

Jon and I went out to pick up the hay we had cut yesterday morning. Jon was left in charge of raking, and Sandy did the tractor driving. Jon judged it well. It was plenty ready when we gathered and stacked it. Always handy to have company to pick up the hay with pitchforks, and people love the experience.

July 21: Larry and Mike to the rescue to fix the cook stove! Sandy was quitting—can't blame her. She cleaned it, but it's still smoking all the time. Terrible. Larry sealed some holes and greatly improved the connection between the smoke jacket and the above-roof stove pipe. Sandy then cooked soup; our last potato and last onion went into it.

Friday: Rainy season continues. I did the milk run. Didn't sell all the goat's milk but didn't have enough cow's milk. I sold $48 of candles so I could pay the income tax. I've got to become better educated about these taxes.

I went and talked to a lawyer friend, Larry Taub, who buys milk from us. He helped me fill out a new form. We won't have to pay corporation income taxes, and we should be able to get our money back.

July 24: Back in the swing, Larry and Marilyn went to two consecutive peyote meetings. With this gal on his arm, Larry is rewarded for his dedication. They are living together in his room. Jim went along for a true Indian religious ceremony, the likes of which he'd never imagined in college.

Jim and Mary Kehoe returned with their bus and have moved back up here! Rebel and Ron moved Ron's new teepee to prairie dog hill. This high point looks dramatic with the entrance facing east. Buses and teepees—plenty of people willing to live simply if they have some help.

Adrienne is away, as usual. She almost invariably leaves here all day. She's sort of a recluse when home. She doesn't like anyone in her room. She keeps it in chaos so no one would feel comfortable going in there. Sandy fertilized, cultivated, and watered that greenhouse yesterday. It's got a good crop of tomatoes.

Reb, College Jim, Red Jim, and I made one hundred more bricks and stacked what we had. Then the new bricks got rained on! Most will still be fine, I think.

Tuesday: From the inspector Proctor we got notice of a dairy selling its equipment! So Yesterday Red Jim, Jon, and I went to see the Rizzo Dairy in Albuquerque. Rizzo is one tough man—short and thick. He's quit selling bottled milk because he couldn't get good enough help that he could afford. He's milking ninety-five cows, housed in fairly small pens. There's a lot of old equipment around, kind of a junky scene. Barren land surrounds Albuquerque for fifty miles or so; most trees gone, not even many little sage bushes. Just parched, short grass here and there.

We certainly learn a lot from seeing these places. He has a load of stuff for sale, among which is a refrigerated truck for $500 and a simple, small bottling machine for $300! Having this is a must for a license. And here it is!

Another insight: no shelves for bottles at all. Use metal cases to hold them—clean, dirty, or full. He gave us four cases for half-gallons and twenty-four bottles for free.

While we were talking, a cow was wandering in the yard, loose. Rizzo said, "Open that gate." He has a lot of electric fences around. So I go to open one metal latch. ZAM! I'm zapped! My hand involuntarily jerked away. "Come on, open the gate!" I can't appear the wimp; I steel myself—try to move the latch quick. ZAP! He's got 120 volts in that gate loose all over the place! On my forth attempt I got it open. "Nice electrical work there, Rizzo." But we can't complain; this is the "mother lode" for us.

Back in our native mountains, we finally got irrigation water for the

17. *Heaven, Jason,*
and Spirit

garden. I was up first thing, one hour before sunup, and put the water toward the garden before sunrise milking. How can most people be content to be in cars on crowded freeways, looking at concrete and cold steel buildings? The fresh air, the fresh smells, the water, the soil, the greenery, and companionship, too—these are treasures to me.

Dee has moved into her new room. It looks very nice. Virginia has left her kids Spirit and Heaven here but has started staying in town. She quit feeding Crystal, calves, and everything else. She wasn't doing much else. Her main thing, it seems, is boyfriends, and it's just too awkward and inconvenient to live here and have fun with guys in town. Rumor is she'll rent a new place and is moving out in four days.

So there is a room for Jim and Mary if they like. And there is the possibility Jim will sell their bus, again. If people join and contribute something substantial, that would really help us make an advance toward supporting our big family. That'd be dramatic if we could get those things we want from Rizzo.

Wednesday: Today the dairy contributed one of its proud sons, Carnegie. We'll butcher him next week. This is the first year we've had more than one steer.

Cooperation: Mike pitched in and helped Larry finish putting in an electric line to the pueblo from the pump house where the electricity comes on the property. Red Jim helped, filling in the trench. Those projects can drag, but with some people helping out, it gets done.

July 28: Today Brian and I plowed the new garden site to the west of the pueblo, back of the kitchen. The ground was so wet from the rain that plowing was easy. It is such a good idea, and we'll have much more reliable production, since the seedlings will be near the hose. Good move.

Larry got the wheat grinder hooked up to its new circuit. Now we won't be blowing out the fuse because the grinder and washing machine are both running. A great help to the cooks who work so hard for us. It's a pain to be in the depths of the back pantry and have the power keep going out. We grind a lot of wheat. Make a lot tortillas. That's our secret for feeding a lot of people.

O. G. Martinez, one of the elders of the community, and I went up the ditch this evening. He was talking of rising prices. "Still," I said, "people must be better off than years ago. They have more." I see lots of people building houses. "Yes, yes," he said certainly. He recalled in his childhood, his family had servants—people to do laundry—cut the wood. His parents owned a lot of land, and his granddad had a store, as did most of the haciendas. Most of the poor people's land was mortgaged to the store so they had credit for food. "Everyone used to work for us," he says. Then his granddad tore up the mortgages and gave back the land. His family had Indian slaves who stayed with the family after they were freed. It's a very different world now: more prosperity, more freedom, more equality.

Back then, the poor workers were getting one dollar a day. Now the descendents of these people go to bars and spend money, go home in their clean cars, and eat well every day.

Jim Preston and Brian are both leaving Friday—very nice, sensible, helpful, courteous people. They are getting ready for college this fall. Both will be truly missed.

July 30, 1977: Saturday I went with Paul Rotman to gather vigas for his house. Paul was a close compatriot for several years. We traveled way up in the woods on narrow dirt roads. Saw a bear and a doe. We had to climb over downed logs, strewn like pickup sticks, and slide the vigas over the fallen timber to get them to the truck. It was a very dusty ride, lots of driving (nearly six hours), and plenty of chance to get hurt. But we had a good day. I expect $50 for the work done. I have $85 put away. So I'm thinking I'll be able to make that $300 pretty quickly for the bottling machine—my immediate objective. At the same time we get the bottler, we should get that milk truck together.

Red Jim is in on milk-room cleanup. Our other Jim is gone; he's off with a tear in his eye. Already people are beginning to work in the new garden; it's so handy being close to the house.

Larry installed a circuit for the grinder and a new one to the kitchen and one to the milk room. Jason often follows Larry around and fetches tools and things for him. Mom says, "Thank God for Larry."

The wheat needs to be combined. Local rancher Manuel was over yesterday; he talked to Rebel and offered us the use of his combine again in return for past help to him. Today Manuel brought it over. Sky very clear all day. The hay we cut is going to cure fast.

Reb got a lapidary stonecutter for $160, plus a grinder for setting stones. He is working with Lena. Yes, it appears romance has indeed sprung again!

August 1, 1977—Monday: A busy week ahead. We'll be butchering starting Wednesday. And we're into a big hay mow.

Had two fellas here, Charlie and George from California in a short, white school bus. Charlie installed a new water pump. We lent him a car so he could get to town. He had to go twice but finally got the right part. One of our functions is helping people on the road.

Plus, we're hosting two fellas, twin brothers John and George, who are with the Boarding House Reach Band from San Francisco. They've been staying at the Mabel Dodge House. These brothers wanted to get out in the country for a bit and asked if they could help out. You bet!

Good timing, I say, because we've got this big hay harvest to do. And while we wait for the hay to cure, we can make adobe bricks. While Reb and Jim cut hay, that's exactly what we did. Another 125 made.

Tuesday: Quite a busy day and hot. Picked up the oat hay—two truckloads of excellent quality. In the morning hours, Reb and Lena cut another field.

Sandy and visitor George mowed hay in the afternoon. Sandy drove the tractor, which takes some practice. George just had to learn how to pick the mower blade up and set it down for the next pass. Anyone riding the mower also has to learn how to hold on.

Wednesday: Mike took out the goats and looked at the hay. He got the truck ready and said, "Let's bring it in." I looked at the hay and thought it was too fresh. Reb agreed and so did Ron. Then we waited too long! I can hardly believe I misjudged, but I did. We missed. The sky had been a little hazy, and I thought it would take longer. I got involved in dairy cleanup and this and that, and felt confident it needed several hours—ugh—I apologize. That hay came in too stemmy. The rest of the hay we better get right—too wet and it molds—too dry and it crumbles.

Larry and Marilyn hauled in half our meat and then they butchered on the kitchen table. Fabulous. O. G. says hang beef meat in cool place for thirty to sixty days.

Saturday: Jon gave me $10. Now we have the $300 for the bottling machine. Still we need gas money for the trip. And more great news: Crystal the Jersey had a heifer! Born on Rick Klein's birthday—little "Rikki" is her name.

We took in one more big truckload of hay—perfect—we did it right. Stack it and don't cover but do always salt it. I think we'll get this haying down correctly. Over the last two years, we have been doing a good job; just blew it with about four acres worth. It's still hay, but not grade A. On another aspect, I was cautioned by several farmers' astonishment at our using plastic tarps! The hay can't breathe; it gets hot—sweats the hay. Keep the hay uncovered for five to fifteen days to dry out in the stack.

Red Jim went to another day of work in Taos and put up notices about selling the bus. He just got the title in the mail, too; I'm holding it. Very communal, people come and throw in what they can contribute. That's as it should be.

We had a wonderful party Thursday night. George and John, part of the San Francisco band, have been working here. They got their band together (Boardinghouse Reach) and played for New Buffalo. People danced until 1:30 a.m. About 150 people were here and no real damage. Except maybe we danced too much; the circle roof is caving in on a split beam!

—Writer unknown.

Sunday: Another hot day. Stormy clouds in the evening. Yesterday I had to go out on the ditch early and set up for the weekend. Hard to get through the ditches these days, they are very overgrown. The plants are at their maturity—flowering—tall to reach the sun. Season is drawing to a close. Here's the last chance at making hay if we can get the water. We shouldn't be denied, but the system is unequal, and we, at the extremity of the 3,000-acre system are cut short.

Seems Marilyn, Jon, and Jim might all really stick with the dairy and thus the commune. Far from wanting a scene I dominate, I want one I can step in and out of. We have a good staff. Only six months ago, on the cow side, it was just me.

Both Marilyn and Dee have found new customers. To sell forty gallons of milk, you need about forty-five orders. Our business grows easily. In this season, goat's milk tends to get stronger tasting. Goat-milk sales have fallen off.

I made arrangements with Mr. Rizzo to meet us at his farm tomorrow. Larry and Red Jim are going to go. Larry is excited to hear about our discovery of a refrigerator truck. He's going to go see it. He and Jim are both pretty sharp about vehicles—a dynamite team.

Mr. Proctor from the state health department said we can use stainless steel, five-gallon cans to cool milk as long as we agitate them. And we can agitate by hand.

August 9, 1977: Larry and Jim made the long haul to Albuquerque. They worked all day on the truck and got back at 10:30 at night. Yes, we want it! They did not pick up the bottler. Guess we'll get both, at once, when we raise the total $800.

At New Buffalo canning has started—tomatoes and apricots first. Sandy gets real excited about this very important aspect of country living. She also froze some peas. And Sandy is very happy to have Mary back here with us—a real friend. Mary keeps her blond hair chin length, sometimes in a ponytail. Tidy, cute, and slight, she's right back by Sandy's side, who hasn't had a close pal since Miss Carol left.

Ron butchered the second half of the steer the other day and a good job he did. It took four or five hours. Ron keeps his teepee very nice and simple, right out by our fields. It's almost like a little spacecraft—so foreign to come upon on the side of a nice hill. We've planted some pretty pastureland in that area.

August 12: I shot down to Albuquerque and picked up the capper-and-filler bottling machine and shot back up. This is a solid step toward greater volume and Grade A. The bottler is a compact machine with stainless steel precision parts and brass parts on the cappers. Rizzo gave me a quick lesson. We loaded the machine easily enough.

I spoke to two dairymen today. Rizzo says if a farm fails, it's poor management. He can make money at it. Mr. Simms said he and his wife worked real hard, and they did make some money at it.

I talk with everyone I know. We're gaining steam. Let's keep it up. A few friends say they will lend us some money. We aim to get the truck; seven days from now, it should be here.

News about Art: Art (that's me) has been living with a hernia for months. It has gradually gotten worse, so I am constantly tucking my guts back inside. On wood runs, making bricks, whatever, I haven't been my best. I've made arrangements for an operation on Monday. I go in tomorrow. I'll have to be real cautious, at first, after the operation, but then I should be better than ever. Sandy is concerned; in typical male fashion I never told her of this weakness.

The ladies canned sauerkraut with homegrown cabbage. Sandy started them, transplanted them, watered, cultivated, mulched them, and saw the trip right through.

Marilyn went to another peyote meeting with Larry. They get dressed in their Sunday best. Larry carries his handmade rattle with delicate beading in one of his custom boxes. They wear beaded moccasins in the teepee and give thanks to Mother Earth, Father Sky, and also Jesus for a good life. They pass the drum all night and sing traditional songs the Indians teach. The fireman keeps the central fire just right with the proper-length cottonwood sticks, and the Roadman slowly builds the Peyote Road in sand as the ceremony continues.

Tuesday: I'm home. I had a major operation done on Monday morning. They put me out completely. And I bounced back quite well. They are quick and very skilled, and there is really little shock to the body. I'm grateful such a good hospital exists here, and that they take care of me and only then try to make arrangements for payment. As a hardworking mayordomo, I have a reputation in the community. I am going to pay the surgeon and his wife, also a doctor, with milk.

Larry has picked up my eagerness and raised over $545 for Rizzo's refrigerator truck, a lot of it borrowed. My surgery was on credit too, and I'd very much like to be able to support the hospital and doctors who did such a professional job on my behalf. That's why we are trying to build a business. We can help out and participate in our society and make improvements too.

The dairy has continued easily without me. But then tonight, Jon had to fill in for Jim and finish Beth. He also milked all the others. Marilyn didn't feel right or something, and she has been missing many milkings, not the mark of dependability. Jon, however, is very dependable, eager, and loves the cows and is quite willing to milk them all, which three days after I quit he ended up doing. We do have to grow slowly until we know what each member is willing and able to do.

In the wings we have Rebel and Lena. They have a silver shop at the commune and spend considerable time working there and have put hundreds of dollars of investment into it, $700 or more, I believe. They both sound anxious to make a substantial contribution to the commune treasury. The idea of individuals having crafts is sound. Whether they picked the right one should be reflected in whether they can earn some income at it for their family. So far they have not.

Electric bill needs paying. Flashlights need batteries. Dee's car needs a tune-up, combine needs a belt, and Wetzel's needs four dollars for storing our meat. Plus we need the vet to examine our cows. I believe Mike and Rebel are hiring out to get vigas with the red flatbed truck. I have to stay in bed or just can walk around a little.

Rizzo still has the truck; Larry plans to go get it tomorrow with Marilyn. Amid all the bustle, that will be a great accomplishment. If we just keep the dairy producing and growing, we can cover everything. Now, will Jim really sell his bus and buy two more cows?

It's exciting. I can feel proud and confident at the hospital. I'm not a derelict; I'm part of a happening scene. If we pull it together, we'll play our part in the community as the doctors and hospitals play theirs.

Next day: Early this morning, Larry and Marilyn took off to fetch the truck. It will be an adventure; that truck hasn't run for over a year. Larry knows his stuff and should be able to get it going. Go get it.

Jim and Mike are off on the vigas job. Mary and Sandy busy taking in our big crop of sweet corn and freezing most of it after cutting it off the cob. Lena is real involved getting the silver business together and getting ready for a long trip to the Northeast. Adrienne is away, of course. She is not to be counted on as one to help with the daily tasks.

Ron filled in by cooking dinner last night. Today I hear he took the delivery pickup truck for a wood run as a favor for someone. If anything happens to that pickup, we're out of business. I sure wouldn't recommend it for wood runs.

August 18, 1977: Just near dark, last evening, the kids start yelling, "Milk truck! The milk truck!" I hear a rumbling, which I've been listening for, for hours. I get up, people come out, and sure enough, up she comes—headlights bobbing up our rutted road—Larry at the wheel of a genuine refrigerated milk-delivery truck! We did it! This is a hell of a big step for us. Good man Larry; he carried it through with help of his gal Marilyn and a lot of our friends. Wow!

Dee is off to town to take care of some business and talk to the vet at the same time. Vet says if temperature is normal, around 102°, you can eat her. Nelly was down all day yesterday. Once a cow can't get up they will just decline quickly.

Jon comes in frequently to tell me what's happening with the cows and the irrigation. Nelly is a big worry. She threw some intestines out her rear. Marilyn is calling the vet. If he thinks it is advisable, we'll make hamburger.

This morning Jenny gave thirteen pounds of milk. That's down. So what's happening? Will our little herd be decimated? Nelly we can lose, but anymore and our business is really set back. We have a great deal to learn yet. We got the truck, but we have another crisis right on hand to divert our attention. *IT'S NO GOOD!*—Writer unknown. Amidst this, Dee scored a lot of apricots, and they're being prepared for canning and drying. Their color and perfume—an uplifting tonic.

Every organization that's big and tough has its crises and problems. We have a big success getting some essential equipment, and now an epidemic starts in our cow herd. Vet Charles Kelsey just came by and gave Jenny 20cc penicillin and three sulfur boluses and is suspecting we've got dysentery in our herd! It's tough. Our dairy is hit by its worst crisis. Just when we borrowed money and now our sales will be way down.

Friday: Jon went to the vet, who has been helpful. He gave Jon a one-page bulletin describing winter dysentery, and said he believes that's what we've got; that was his tentative diagnosis last night. He said he believed Nelly would recover. Beth's milk is up. Jenny is up. She's eating, so she seems better. Nelly is alive.

Ron is working away to pay for his teepee. He talked to me about water, but he had no time to take responsibility to help us get or use it. He wasn't even aware we could use the water.

Reb working on jewelry. He and Lena may have a ride with Alfred Hobbs going east and coming back. Rebel comes in and sees me quite often. So does everyone.

Saturday: Nelly is up and around and dry—no milk. So we look to be pulling out of this sudden crisis—to be able to get back to the excitement of creating our dairy. I'm absorbed in the commune, and I love it. I've been able to stop my chores and still everything gets done. Our commune is happening and getting stronger.

Sunday: Clear blue skies again this morning. Dee has taken main responsibility at the candle shop. We have lots of orders. She got Adrienne, on a rare day here, to help dip. I did the straightening at the end. The candles never dry straight but have a little banana curve. I have the eye and feel to bend them just a little.

Rebel and Lena got the prize belt together. Estimates of possible money they can earn from it from $800 to $1800! There are silver earrings, a bunch of rings, and a few other pieces. But no sales that I know of.

We have too many flies. After a few days, they are dripping off the flypaper. We could use perhaps fifteen screen doors. I've got a good basic design. I saw Jim making one the other day. His bus is in town at a good location for selling. Me, every day I get better.

August 23, 1977: Tonight we did some singing in the kitchen: Rebel, Lena, Jon, Larry, Marilyn, Dee, Sandy, Jim and Mary, and I. Very nice to be here with these people. Sure feel we're getting there.

Yesterday, I went out with Jon and examined the irrigation. This morning we went out to gather the water and discuss how to get different places irrigated. Me, I can only advise; Jon does the work.

Dee making bread. Sandy colored candles, and then she went to canning tomatoes. Larry has a job lined up with the truck this week hauling vigas. We've got more candle orders.

Today was Red Jim's thirty-first birthday. To celebrate we just happened to have some LSD on hand. Jim and several others took some for a pleasant sunny day. Through all time people have discovered what all the herbs and plants can do. There are many psychedelics in nature. And from all time, most, even all people, through alcohol or other things, have sought a periodic change of consciousness. The hills dance, the colors become more alive, the oneness with nature becomes more pronounced. "And all the earth is love."

We confidently raked the hay. Tomorrow we pick it up before the afternoon storms can play with us. Rebel keeps an eye to the weather. Larry, too, and then we decided to go on. I'm happy with our collective consciousness about hay. We're doing pretty well and should get better.

Tahiti showed up and is fixing a truck he left, finally. Tahiti lived here for years. He can vie for most colorful of the lot of us. He has a black patch over his blind left eye, which he lost in the merchant marines. He wears a sort of turban headscarf usually; the rest of his clothes are homemade with plenty of leather and beads. Even the sheepskin boots are frontier made. He usually has two very heavy-boned horses somewhere.

Tamale pie again for dinner with green beans, lots of sweet corn from the garden, and a super good cake baked by Mary for Jim's birthday.

We discovered Julie had dropped a bull calf. She's going to give four gallons a day, at least, maybe five. Jenny cow is right back to normal. We'll be at our maximum milk next week. Oh boy, I just love it, having a good little dairy. Julie, the Guernsey, looks great. I can just look and look—happy to see a good quality animal, and she's ours.

Jim made a deal for his bus. A friend Byrd wants it. He got a little down payment and bought some concrete bricks for the new collector foundation. Jim and Mary are in a new room. They like it more than the one Virginia moved out of, which is now empty.

Some things need to be taken care of. There's our sinking circle roof and plans for a clean, shiny, vinyl kitchen floor, and the seepage drainage pit needs the lid taken off, again, so we can see why the overflow pipe isn't working. Combining the wheat has to wait for a new belt.

Friday: Change in the weather—cool and windy—autumn. Last night Julie was full, but the calf was at the pen, and she held her milk and was jumpy. Jon got frustrated with the new cow and broke several bones in his hand with a punch to the big Holstein! I had just come up to the barn; I finished Julie. I reverted to the old rope and got some milk.

Sweet Dee took Jon to the hospital—a costly error. Jon cut his hand a few months ago; now he has broken some bones. So I am back to milking, and I feel fine. Saw the doctor yesterday. It is ten days since the operation, and now comes the holding back, since I'm feeling quite better. But milking I can do. Lucky because Jon is out for six to eight weeks starting right now.

18. *Big Jon*

Armando, who has a backhoe, came up to look over the greenhouse digging. Larry bought a special plug we need to make the refrigerator truck work. We sent off our dairy test results to the State Health Department.

Jon has to have his hand operated on to be fixed as best as possible. One more big bill for us. It'll be a while before we can give them much, but we'll try to give our local medical corporation something. They do take care of us.

Five young people here passing through. Jason from Oklahoma is fixing some shrubbery guards. Carol's friend Yvonne is here for a day. She helped dip candles. Pepe drops by quite frequently. He's going to go stay with Henry Grotto at the farm in Wisconsin with Jenny and new baby coming up. Sounds like a good move for the winter. Pepe keeps on coming up with things to make life interesting. I hear I was mentioned several times in a *New York Times* article, and Tahiti got his picture in.

Lena bought an acre of land across the Hondo River from us. That was how she originally met New Buffalo. Then she bought some bricks to build a house. But the house is not happening now; we have captured her interest. She likes it here—living here and with Reb—being part of our big house. So she got Reb and Jim to go get those adobe bricks, about 1,000 of them.

Saturday: Jon came back last night. He is getting excellent care. Today he irrigated with one arm and hand-shoveled manure, unloaded adobe bricks, tossed the hay, brought up the cows, found me some bolts too, for the mower. He's determined to stay in there with us.

Larry finished the electrical work on the new milk truck. And he spent a lot of time on the brakes. Larry pulled the truck over and plugged it in. The cooler is run by a heavy extension cord from the house. As long as the doors aren't left open long, it stays cool during the delivery. The box, which can carry nearly 300 gallons, cooled all afternoon, brought its temperature down to below 35°, and then cut off. First time we've seen it get cold. Very impressive. Goat John was here, checking it over—inside and out.

So now we're back in the milk after losing one cow and having another out of production for eight or nine days. Next problem: our pickup delivery truck is out because the rod-and-ball joints are extremely worn, and the one side just fell apart. Lucky it happened here. So we'll have to replace that soon as possible. We might just use the new milk truck for a town run. I think Larry would like to try it out. I'd like to get the writing off the truck. Don't want to attract attention.

Throw-out bearing on Lena's truck is wearing out fast—a bit comic. We did sell one vehicle, thank God. Adrienne's car is junked here. She's broke. She works but she never has money. She was just in the hospital three days having her tumor analyzed. She's taking teas. In October she'll try the doctor's advice.

Armando came and dug for several hours with the backhoe. That's a major step. I think we've done the right thing there—to get a decent size collector and greenhouse.

Milk is piling up—sixteen gallons a day of cow's milk. It's really happening.

We don't have to just hope for "some pie in the sky" handout, though it would be nice. Still, it's not necessary. We can earn what we need.

Mike took some dirt off the circle roof where it is slowly caving in. Do need some immediate plan of action though. Weight off is the first step.

Sunday: (Written on yellow slips of paper inserted in the journal): *From the Crowd Rouser Press: All The News that Fits We Print! Caution—Volatile Area—Enter At Your Own Risk! Hot and cloudy, light precipitation with particles flying. Overwhelming Stupid Riot Erupts! Ai, Chihuahua-a!!!*

At 5:45 in the afternoon, dinnertime at the Buff! Wild woman walks in looking for ACTION. Reason? Tomato giveaway! Tired of canning lately? No! The Buffalos can never can enough! One punch deserves another—you get what you ask for. Has your face been punched in lately or your arm bit off? Come and visit anytime, Miss Carol! Don't ask for something twice and expect to get the same answer. It could cost a lot; maybe your wig loosened! So don't hesitate, don't wait, lets communicate; lets get down at the Buffalo Arena!

It must always be remembered, that anytime things appear to be going better, you have overlooked something! Next week don't miss, "Flying Apples!"
Signed, The Buffalo Underground Herald Tribune Times.

August 30: Riding tall and proud, Larry and I took the new milk truck on the milk run—sold out on cow—did the entire route. The truck did very well.

Sandy, this morning got upset with Marilyn and Lena. Other day she was angry about the missing tomatoes. Marilyn took a bushel of fine red tomatoes that Sandra had cared for and just gave them away to Micky Long across the valley without a word. That's very wrong, but gee, its been getting to feel like Sandy's going from one crisis to the next. It's the sewer to be upset over or this or that. Next she says to Marilyn, "Go ahead and hit me if it makes you feel better!" Big mistake—she hits the floor—Larry helps her up.

We live in a somewhat poor and wild state, and everyone has his or her personal problems. I think most people make a conscious effort to be pleasant around the family. This is a consciousness to develop. Remember to be pleasant. Direct the uptight energy—the feeling others are lackadaisical—toward heightening our own ability to do more so these problems get taken care of. "Raw" is what Adrienne said our social life is. And we do examine deep. We want a lot from each other.

And we do have to improve our scene. Consciousness can be higher of what needs to be done. We want to make this commune work. It's our hope for a place in this greedy, confusing world. We have to know people can get along: trust one's friends in daily life, share their good fortune, make it together.

But a lot is happening. Jim got lumber for the new greenhouse. That's essential and great. Also got some lumber for some brainstorm of Rebel's—a front porch. Now, building a greenhouse is already a lot of work, especially when you are supposed to be doing wood runs and even making adobe bricks.

Then there is need for someone to do the sewer repair. I'm out of digging for a while, and Reb is leaving, and also he's supposed to go into the hospital because of a bad back. We're spread out a little thin.

August 31, 1977: Larry's birthday! We had a nice party. Marilyn worked all day preparing a big feast: three little pigs, cake, a very good sauce, and rice. A bunch of Larry's church friends came over, and so did John Pedro and Joseph from across the valley.

Today we started, Mike and I, to unclog our sewer line. Gee, it's really plugged! We've almost got it unstuck. We're using a twenty-foot-long piece of cable with a loop at the far end to go down the pipe. He had to get down in the pit to do the work.

Jim says, "Let's go for the bottle washer." So I called up Leo Rizzo, and he said come Sunday. Hasn't been run in four years, so we'll see down there. For $100 it could be just right. It has got to get the bottles clean.

From the depth of our kiva, the "Peyotes" of the Native American Church are in their element. With rattles in hand, they're up late singing and drumming. I like the music myself—the people and consciousness—like it very much.

Tomorrow we try to get my mother moved.

Next day: Clarice got moved quickly. Mike, Reb, Jim, and visitor Paul helped her. She gave a $25 contribution to the treasury. It was too cold in her former house.

On a little cul-de-sac in town, five houses recently were built for low-income housing. Clarice applied several years ago and now is going to rent a very pleasant little house. My parents were great believers in President Franklin D. Roosevelt; their hearts stopped when he died. This is the sort of program he introduced to American society.

Sunday: Jim, Jon, and I got up while the world was still quite dark. We milked, checked the truck, and took off for Albuquerque, again.

Hours later, we returned with a small, heavy bottle washer. Looks like it will do a good job. It needs some minor repair, plus a two-horsepower electric motor. Also brought home 40 one-gallon bottles in ten cases and 20,000 bottle caps. But our prize is the baby Holstein heifer for ten dollars! Hope the calf does well. That's a rough ride.

To add to the excitement, the radiator blew a leak, where Larry fixed it just several days ago. Mr. Handy had a lot of trouble fixing it, and then it blew again. Took us over half an hour to figure out that we had bottles. Jim and Jon filled them, and we limped home, refilling the radiator every fifteen miles.

A new day: Larry and I combined—worked pretty well—makes a racket. I always expect to look behind and see a thousand vibrating pieces lying in the field. So far we got maybe 700 pounds of wheat with lots of weeds in it, a romantic effort but a poor crop. The other field will give us nearly 1,000 pounds of fairly clean wheat.

Jon switched the water to first and second gates—get water away from where we're working with the combine. He is really learning the system, one of the few to come along who really tries. It takes a deep involvement and a consciousness that sees, day to day, that moving that water is absolutely essential to farming this land.

September 9: Larry did a sellout milk run. That's a little over $100. We're getting fourteen gallons of cow's milk a day. Jim and I finished the wheat.

Sandy's baby is doing much better—a very good boy. Keeps himself amused and out of mischief for long periods. Sandy cleaned the washroom in the thorough manner no one else gives to it. Also she's been cleaning in the kitchen and cooking: chocolate pudding last night and pot roast, potatoes, and garden string beans tonight—real country fare for our little family. Sure good.

So we've got reduced population. Dee, Lena, and Rebel gone for a bit. Adrienne is rarely here. Word is she will vacate. Expected. Also Ron is rarely here, and rumor is he will move his teepee. So for the steady farm work, there are Jim, Larry, Mike, Jon, and I. We're open for new energy.

Mary got ill for nearly a week. She is thin; it really got her. Others have had a taste of the bug, but Mary is the only one to get so knocked out; it's hard to see her down. A happy, sincere gal, she keeps in touch with her inner child; she skips across the courtyard.

Mike burned horns off the three youngest calves. He next castrated little Simon, about three weeks old. The calf recovered very quickly and is doing well. Little Abby, the new heifer, has a little of the scours (bacterial diarrhea) but not too bad. She's lively and very pretty. Raised with people feeding and petting them, our herd will be easy to manage when mature.

Peter and Elaine here from Ortiviz farm. Their commune is doing pretty well: big garden—sold $1,400 of hay—four ladies and ten or so guys.

September 13: Sandy bought juicy and delicious peaches to eat and a bunch for canning. Larry is replacing his floor. He dug up three inches of floor, made it into mud and then leveled and flattened it. Tomorrow he'll buy vinyl flooring to cover it. Home improvements.

Red Jim bought a used Homelite chainsaw the other day. Good. Today with a new spark plug, he got it going and cut up kitchen wood. We are never very far ahead on cut wood. And it is no good when the cook has to cut wood first. Plus the dishes don't get washed because of no hot water. Ron made the massive effort for a while. Mike once did it for well over a year. Sandy cuts plenty of wood. Now Mike is back to doing it again.

Mike's stopped doing the concrete retainer, thinking that the ideal roof is wood frame pitch roof. He did do a great deal: kitchen, two pantries, washroom, three-room east wing, plus much of the circle. Seven of these rooms have functional dirt roofs. The view coming up the road is of a well-cared-for house.

Our oldest cow, Nelly, is gone. Goodbye. After five years of serving us, she sold for $100. If you need a story about an ornery cow, she's your gal. We never broke her in—she broke us in—to the dairy trade. Thanks, old girl.

Very quiet and peaceful here at New Buffalo. Wood runs seem to be waiting on me to recover to lead them out. And I'm ready for a big effort.

Another day: Jon and I cut hay under very clear skies. We got a freeze last night.

We are preparing candles for a Renaissance faire next week that Pepe invited us to. Three friends from Germany—Axel, Harold, and a pretty girl named Elke—are helping us.

Today Ron moved his teepee out. He is gone, sort of bitterly too. Just the way he is somehow—angry—resentful. Probably it will be relaxing for him not to "sort of" be here as he's sort of been.

Lena, Reb, and Dee returned—glad to be here. Lena's son came too. They sold out, except for the expensive belt. Marilyn has her son here, too. That's six boys living here now: two babies and four older ones, a lot of people to support. Lena and Reb getting their silver craft together so they can help support the big group, I hope. They took orders for beaded earrings, so maybe now someone here could learn to make them.

A new day: A little breeze blowing as we picked the last sweet corn out of the garden. Jon and I mowed the last of this year's alfalfa. I could almost cry. That's it for this year. Our stacks are awesome—huge. Plenty of cherry tomatoes coming in, which are very good in hand-made tortilla sandwiches.

Out behind the pueblo, to the west, are all the plants we've got started, lots of emerald green grass, and irises nicely weeded. Still some color from the phlox, about six pale-green Russian olive trees, four dark-green Chinese elms, three cherry trees; one lilac looks good, too.

In the courtyard, near the one big olive tree, Sandy has a lush growth of bright orange California poppies, hollyhocks, and a special large violet phlox that is in full bloom. Right where I'm sitting are our dozen Hubbard squash—deep orange—curing in the sun.

Sandy: She has an instinct to put away food. Some people really get it together, and she likes us to be among them. She canned tomatoes again yesterday. Still lots more to ripen.

We took three truckloads of very excellent hay off three acres of fields. So very beautiful out here—blue sky, a few puffy white clouds, rugged rock terrain, and desert country, plus our own patchwork of fields in different stages of being harvested. Along the ditches, lots of healthy grasses and alfalfa and clover grow, a real richness for grazing. On the other side of the fence—desolate, fairly barren sage and chamisa bush country.

Sept 22, 1977: Next day Reb cut some stout vigas for the circle-room support system. He, Jim, and Larry hauled them in and started jacking up the roof. Bit by bit—breath by breath—they raised the ceiling about twelve inches, blocked up the top of the sunken support and put the two new supports in place. Now three uprights hold up what one was not holding up. The ceiling is a masterwork of a thousand, crisscrossing small and large logs. We watch in anticipation as everything moves slightly in adjustment. There were a few scary moments when—in a flash—the jack and its log snapped out from under the weight! But the fellas just kept right on and got the job done. Magnificent. That was really necessary.

Another day: We now can let the cows loose on the fields. First Jon and I picked a few hundred ears of blue and white corn and put them in the red truck. As we worked, the storm built up.

Lots of things in the works. Talk of how to do kitchen floor. We must figure out how we'll cook and wash without the kitchen. Mel contributed $30 specifically for regulators and propane tanks. But we already bought cement and lumber for greenhouse, so let's do that. Plus, it is getting cold; none too soon to get solar heat together. Where does the front porch come in? That was hastily started. Rather than just say, "Okay, greenhouse let's go," those guys thought greenhouse and porch, but they can't be done simultaneously. Reb sneers at my opinion; he'll do what he wants.

Here I miss Kim. He and Peggi Sue never returned. I got so close with them. Then I really stuck my neck out confronting my partner Pepe in support of Kim, and he leaves everything we started. That leaves an uneasy feeling.

Also abandoned is Ron's unfinished outhouse. Without getting anyone else interested, he did a quarter of the work and left. Just like the wood runs he called that never left the house. As far as I'm concerned, the other outhouse will do very well this winter. And I'm sure it will have to, because it is a big job to completely move the outhouse, brick by brick, from one place to another. Just like fall planting, it's not happening. The hole will keep, and we will need one at some time.

I'm learning. We have a house poorly laid out for solar heat but one that can have many added solar features. There's a too-small sewer system that does seem to just make it, a ceiling that is coming down but that we've got propped up. We've got floors that are a step above the cave type, but we're adding better and better ones as we gain experience.

On the outside some mud is falling away, but Mike made a big step this summer by creating that permanent and attractive concrete retainer cap on maybe two hundred feet of wall—quite a bit—less than half the pueblo to go.

"Concentrated energy," that's one of my catch phrases. Do too much and nothing gets done to completion. Keep too many vehicles and none is in good condition.

Part of the communal spirit, I feel, is the willingness to contribute to other people's ideas and efforts—to continue what other people started—join other people's projects. This has been a motto with me since Pepe and I started out to live with communal families. I've gone along with a few zany scams and projects.

A new day: Getting costumes together for the Sunday Renaissance faire. I gave Jim use of my wizard's outfit, complete with black, conical, two-foot-tall cap.

Jim's got more money from the bus to cover the rest of the greenhouse.

Let's get on that project! And wood runs. Kitchen floor must wait a few weeks. Reb has got savings stashed for it. Now he just needs to hold on to it.

Tonight we dipped more candles—a group effort. Sandy colored a batch yesterday. We're really getting a stash together.

September 25, 1977: Jim looked fine as the wizard. Reb, with rags around his feet and Sandy's big, hooded robe, made a very good monk. Dee looked fabulous as a lady of the court. Lena wore a simple one-piece robe-type dress, using the five-foot cross Jon made. They sold $75 worth of candles.

In the circle, Reb and Larry fixed up the one post so it will hold alone, again, then took away the two extra supports. Good idea of Larry's.

Reb has been busy putting in a floor in the room Adrienne moved out of. Years ago, Louisa had that room, and we used to have some fun in there. Reb dug it out and then brought lumber for the joists and particle board. The previous floor was just uneven dirt.

Another day: Full moon giving a dull light through the clouds—the world luminescent.

Mr. Ron has moved on. Ron was here for quite a bit of five years. Sometimes happy, sometimes blue, a strain of frustration running through his life—contradiction between revolutionary ideals and the everyday reality of the work.

Ron contributed several thousand dollars when he dropped out and joined New Buffalo. He leaves with a nice teepee and a bunch of very fine blankets and rugs—always kept his little home fire neat. He got a fair share of female company.

Ron put in a pasture fence for us, which is very important. He helped a great deal to make the first solar addition to the pueblo, a work that will be here for many years. Ron was a hard worker on the wood runs and cut a good deal of firewood at home. He herded cows and goats and did a bunch of irrigating. He never used the vehicles. He put big windows in two south-wing rooms. He helped cut and pick up hay and haul gravel for the road. He sold candles and knew how to make them. Yet he did not leave entirely at peace with us. Too bad he didn't.

A different day: Good day today, though I did forget to feed the chickens in Larry's absence. Larry went out for the evening after the milk run.

Jim and I took the truck out to the wheat field and gathered rocks. Then we got together and poured the concrete foundation for the new greenhouse, working very well together. Jim had gotten the supplies several weeks ago. Now we have something to build on.

Jon got the pin out of his hand that was holding the little bones in place. Pretty soon he'll be back to normal.

October 2, 1977—Sunday: I got Larry to go on a wood run, and he got Mike Pots to come along. Under a bright-blue clear sky the aspen leaves are turning yellow. There's a cool, extremely fresh wind blowing.

We go into this winter with a sixteen-ton-or-so stack of wood to add on to, a far cry from the time I came here in September of '71, and the woodpile had been cleared of twigs. It took three years before we started to get ahead. Partly this is because we burned less fuel in recent years.

Jim took Mary and kids to the airport so they can go stay with Mary's grandma for a bit—nice to have a change once in a while. Sandy is planning a trip too.

Reb is going to let Pepe have his short flatbed truck in return for some cash and some trade items. Sounds good. Pepe wants it so he can move to Wisconsin for the winter. He's going to live at the farm near Ettrick where we were camped before we came accidentally to New Buffalo.

Next day: Jim returned from Albuquerque with six cases of half-gallon bottles and four cases of whole gallons. He also brought news of a possible source of cows. We have to call Rizzo next week.

Jim also brought news of his leaving! That was unexpected. Sandy felt her heart sink. Only two days ago Mary said to her how she was glad she was no longer living in a bus. And now they plan to travel again. So Mary is gone, and Jim is planning to leave in three weeks. No, we don't have so much of a solid crew.

That leaves Reb, Larry, Jon, and me for the men, and Dee, Sandy, Lena, and Marilyn for the gals. Mike is still with us, but he seems serious about leaving too!

So will we get some wonderful people to live here with us? Are there people actually interested in living in an up-and-coming commune? I suppose there are. I certainly prefer resourceful people.

Dee and I did a milk run together. We managed to take forty gallons of milk in. Emil is having a wonderful time crawling around the house, laughing, laughing. He's a real doll, and his little sounds and chatter I like.

Wednesday: I did a wood run with Jon, Larry, and Marilyn. I took them to a place they'd never been, in a beautiful forest across a lively little creek. The road is rough through piñon forest, where the dry ground is rocky and gravelly. Down a steep hill and across the brook, we go up a sharp incline into tall pine forest. The ground here is covered with grass and bushes. We found lots of dry dead wood. All alone in the woods we worked. Every place, before you get that far away from people, no dead wood is to be found.

October 7: Jenny cow was in heat, and Tieder did his best to breed her. Larry took the milk run. Forty-one gallons went in. Larry had to skip a bunch of customers because we didn't have enough milk.

Goat John brought down a bunch of apples for pressing. We got some good ones for eating out of them. He was over, checking out the Rizzo truck.

Jon is back milking goats and milking Jenny.

October 8: Dee took the Saturday milk run. Mike and Jon killed and butchered two goats and put them in the Rizzo truck cooler. That's a little more meat and fewer goats to feed.

Monday: Heavy frost in the morning. Clear day—warm in the sun. Jim takes Reb to Veteran's hospital in Albuquerque. Reb's got some back problem—a crack in a bone and a cyst or something. Finally he makes a move to get it fixed.

Sandy and Dee sorted and wrapped apples. Carol came down from the Morningstar mesa with friend Debbie, and they are making apple cider, visiting Deek helping. Mike and Jon butchered the goats on the kitchen table. We'll have a rib feast tonight. Good tasting, like mutton.

October 11: I listened to a little of the World Series' first game—Yankees versus the Dodgers. In our own play-by-play, Larry took the milk run. Could only bring back $3 because we bought a $30-part for our Dodge truck, our family vehicle.

Jon and I finished putting on the concrete blocks, a first for me. Jim was going to help, but he got out quickly. He said farewell—a nice mild-tempered man. No ill feelings. Says he finds it difficult dealing with people—doesn't hold jobs either—wants to keep moving. He definitely helped us greatly while he was here.

Dee and new man Deek went after pears and came home with apples. We still have the fantastic solar dryer that Mike made; it's loaded with apples. We could make a scam out of that and sell some. They are terrific.

Marilyn is out sick for a second day. She says she will be back tomorrow. She has been off milking at least fifteen times, I'd say, since she started. Still, we go for having a woman learn milking and give slack if the constant two-times-a-day pace is harsh.

Jon is about recovered completely. He wants the dairy like I do. If we can get to that point of professional production, he'll sure be proud to be taking care of "them cows."

Sandy canned tomatoes and applesauce. Applesauce is a big effort to make. I know she misses Mary. And now she won't be back.

October 13: Clear days and nights—hoses are frozen in the morning. The water troughs are frozen over. The aspens in the mountains are past the bright-yellow stage. The greenhouses with one layer are starting to get frost. The rooms with solar collectors really are warmer than the ones without.

Rebel made a go-cart for the kids; big kids can use it too. They've been out on the road to the fields having a lot of fun.

It's late but I'm still up. I enjoy the solitude now in this rustic house. Apple butter, pushed over to the side of the wood stove, slowly erupts a bursting sticky bubble. Soon the fire will be out, and tomorrow will bring us the adventure of a new day.

October 15, 1977: Jon, Dee, and Sandy sorted apples. Reb and Lena moved their shop to the south wing in anticipation of solar heating. Lena is pregnant and looking very good in that state.

Mike is planning on leaving! One of our main men feels it's time to seek out another way. But, terrific guy that he is, it hasn't stopped him from still helping out a lot. He's been cutting firewood and cleaning in the kitchen. Seems pretty considerate actually. He's ready for all the wood runs too, and milks goats in the morning. Maybe he wants to join the Army.

October 16: I set up a deal to see the Guernseys next Sunday—$500 apiece. He's got eighty heifers for sale with some ready to freshen.

Jerry and I brought in a load of rocks from the furthest field. Yes, Jerry, my old peculiar friend from Bolinas has showed up. Reb has asked him not to make it a long stay. Jerry, Jerry. . . . I've been thinking of getting those rocks for about one week. They're for the new barn site.

19. *Lion buckle. Courtesy of Dan Cohn*

Reb and I spent a little time with Pepe—far-out discussion about revolution, America, and our brother Willy Chaplin. Pepe gets animated, frequently punctuating his remarks with "Ain't it, hey?" Among all the fast-flowing imagery are some very essential things about the evolution of our consciousness—our world consciousness.

As technology has changed and communications developed and psychedelics introduced, people in one lifetime can evolve through many stages. Pepe was very prejudiced and defensive as a youth. I always saw that in him. How far he and millions of others have come in their world outlook. And he's still excited about our changing world, and the part we can play.

Pepe is now making another engraved belt with eight different lions as portrayed in different symbols: the lion Leo constellation, the lion in King Arthur's shield, the Sphinx. The engravings are intricate and involved, with lots of detail, and each symbol has a little history of where it comes from and what it represents. Pepe knows so much; his work is getting more exceptional. He's been showing Rebel techniques and giving him some tools. Reb's impressed with Pepe; so am I.

Dynamic: We're connected with some dynamic people. I feel my incorporation with Pepe. We put our lives together, which helped us both to step into a better path. We created something more exceptional by complimenting each other. It propelled us toward Cro Farm and the Minnesota Farm with Henry Grotto, Willy, Mike Torgeson, and Curly Jim—big strong lumberjack types—legendary folk heroes of the Cro Farm commune. I always loved the message painted on the rear of their bus: "Price of Freedom."

A different day: I did the milk run, and at the end, in Bill Betz's driveway, a front wheel sheared off the spindle that holds the bearing that holds the wheel. So Saturday Larry, Marilyn, and I will go after a front end in the Albuquerque salvage yards, then pick up the cow Sunday and come home. We do have just enough money to operate with.

At night in my bed I am thankful for a place to put my head; a warm little place where I relax and feel good. Of course many nights I spend with Sandy. Some nights when the baby cries I take him into my cold room, and we hold close under the covers for warmth, and he is quiet.

In the mornings, back to the struggle to put our scene really together.

October 24: The cooler's getting full of jugs of milk. Jon has been doing well with the cows. He did three milkings alone. Now we have returned with a new Guernsey heifer near to freshening, and a replacement for the part that broke on the milk truck. We also bought a stabilizer bar for the Dodge. Good trip.

Our new cow comes from Jordan Pareo, a big, clean, very nice fellow about my age. He has lots of Guernsey heifers. He was interested in our scene. He's not impressed with the "system" he's been working in. He brought us in to a kid's birthday party.

We enjoyed hospitality with Larry's brothers Bobby and Brian. I spent several night hours walking, running, and touring the ultramodern and gigantic University of New Mexico. The running was very easy at the lower altitude.

Right after returning from the trip, we took the cow out and put her in a pen. She went for some hay right away. It took four of us to maneuver her up to the corral in the moonlight. The morning after we delivered the cow, we took the borrowed stock rack back to Carlos's farm where we talked with Mrs. Trujillo for a bit. Then right back to fixing the milk truck.

Meanwhile, to complicate matters, the Rizzo delivery truck needs some investment; it was to be expected. Within a week or so, I expect we will be able to pay the taxes. That will feel good.

At a meeting, we decided we're going to have more frequent meetings and more open financial discussions. It is difficult deciding among a big group how to spend just a little money. At least we do have something to talk about now.

And the milk keeps flowing—the customers want more milk.

Wednesday: October draws to a close with continued clear skies. The leaves are dropping off deciduous trees. The landscape has turned to browns and pale straw yellows. Still there is green graze. Larry and Reb, returning from town, found me trying to get the tractor out of a deep hole. I had just started to plow and got very stuck.

Dee got some money from the treasury to go shopping. We have established, now, that I must fork over some allowance for the kitchen every week. I just hope we can gather enough money to cover all the angles. I think we will.

Reb announced he's going to build over at Lena's land! He went over there to survey a site.

October 30, 1977: Changes: Marilyn, our Oklahoma cowgirl, told Larry, then me, that she was leaving. Whoa! She called up her husband in Oklahoma. Whoa! So much for this fling. Sort of peculiar—just yesterday she was swaggering down to the chickens with Larry, holding his arm. They would go on the milk runs together. And she got pregnant right away—on purpose no less, it seems. Now, happy trails to you—Good-bye!

Well, be thankful for what love we get to share and be happy in yourself the best you can. We do like to trust each other and be able to depend on some people. Now Larry say's he'll take off, at least for a while. It's a heavy blow for him.

Getting really trim for the winter, which has certain advantages, of course. It is some more work, too, for the dairy crew to lose three helpers. But we surely can manage. New cow is doing well though she is very hard to lead.

I've been working on the solar collector. Reb and Larry have lent a hand and some of the frame is up. The baby comes to the construction site with me. He's playing quietly and talking baby talk, as I put another roof section together.

Miss Dee got busted for shoplifting a pair of scissors! I gave Carol $50 (that hurts) to bail her out. Still, we saved up to $90 because of good milk run.

Jon's parents are here. They are very friendly and seemed to like the place. They did buy us a super stash of toilet paper for the outhouse—couldn't quite manage with the newspaper.

It was a nice quiet Sunday with the wind blowing that fresh, fresh air—white clouds gusting across the blue sky—new snow on the mountains. Mike cooked dinner for us: pea soup, roast goat, and biscuits.

Joe Novacavich was by for the night. We sang some songs and had a nice evening. Joe was part of the early Grateful Dead family and has helped us out financially before. Interestingly, he was born to missionary parents in China. His deformed hands make it difficult for him to do many things. And like so many people, he at times has a problem with alcohol. Dear God, it's not easy to be human.

November 2, 1977: Cold weather has set in. One day of overcast really cooled things off. I had to abandon the Dodge pickup truck after the Tuesday run. The clutch wouldn't work.

Dee and Jon drove Sandy and kids to the Albuquerque airport. I took care of the farm. At night, Reb and I towed the Dodge back to Buffalo.

On the Albuquerque trip, we didn't buy soap or any bottles. We had a slight financial meeting and decided to buy that engine part for the Rizzo truck instead.

Larry is going to go to Oklahoma when he gets some money together. He's been working for Bruce, a neighbor across the valley who works on the Alaskan pipeline. I think Larry's going to see Marilyn. He doesn't mean to be just put off like that. She had to go and get pregnant—really crazy. To me it seems she did it to torment her husband and to string Larry along. Rotten thing to do to such a decent guy as Larry. He doesn't want a little McInteer running around that he never sees or knows or can be responsible for. So our farm has to lose another member.

The calves look good. Rikki is growing fast and looks excellent. She has a very small udder, of sorts, already. The Holstein calf is a bit odd looking. Her teeth are set a bit funny, giving her a grin. She also has a sort of gorilla look to her. She carries her tail up a lot. But she may make a good milk cow.

Whatever the perturbations, I enjoy the simple things: drinking clear fresh water and breathing in the breeze. These things I love.

Our fabulous Mike Pots is gone. Before he left, Mike split a lot of kitchen wood. Each time we use the red truck, we benefit from the job he did bolting down the bed and fixing the cab roof. And when we drive up the road, we go over many truckloads of gravel, much of which he helped load and unload. He put a hell of a lot in. Then he wonders what he got out of it.

It's rough being a cynic, like Mike. I'm more the optimist. I believe my work, combining with that of other people of different times and places, is spreading sharing—love—brotherliness. The effort gives good karma, a place in the world, a life of significance. I sure wish him luck and happiness. A terrific guy. This hurts.

Lena cooked up a last-minute, delicious dinner for us. She and Reb are quite excited about building a house over on the land, directly across the Hondo River, across from the buffalo fields. Reb is trying to scam bricks to build with by finding houses that can be taken apart. Now they may regret having contributed bricks to New Buffalo.

November 3: Yesterday Sandy went to California. She made the big effort to get herself and two kids there. Good for her to have a change and see other people.

Larry got off work early and ended up examining the Dodge clutch. He reasoned from various wear marks that perhaps the fulcrum for part of the linkage was too low. He manufactured a shim and now the clutch seems to work. We'll see on tomorrow's run if it's fixed. Reb picked up the rebuilt Chevrolet engine head, gasket, and spark plugs. So we're continuing our fast comeback on the vehicle front. Lots of cooperation.

Eric, the bee man, left two goats with us to be bred.

Friday: The sky is so blue—the sun warm. I did the milk run. The Dodge ran very well and I drove nice and gently. I brought home one hundred pounds of potatoes, $12 for the kitchen, feed for chickens and dairy.

Larry worked a long time over the Chevy engine. And the darn thing when he fired it up sounded terrible. He took the head off, and then put it back on. No. Five and six cylinders do not work, and one bolt hole is stripped out. Bad. A tough break on top of several tough breaks.

We certainly don't have just clear sailing. Larry is ready for a break from these vehicle problems. I don't blame him, and we can hardly buy him a $30 battery for all his valuable effort. We're still in the same old pinch. But a core of us will carry through, and we'll work our way out of this poverty yet.

Jon milked the goat being boarded here. He had her up against a fence, holding her hind feet together with one hand while milking her with the other, as he sat on the ground. Then I came along with Candy cow—she leading me, of course—and the steers following almost stampeded Jon in the confusion.

I finished the basic collector frame in front of Dee's wing today and framed in a few roof vents. Still have the door to frame in. I can now think about the cow shelter.

Early to rise—early to bed. We get going when it's quite dark. By eight o'clock we're getting off to bed sometimes. No fire for some—little evening fire for some—that's all our heating. We do have kitchen fire much of the time. The heart of our home is most always warm.

JOURNAL 21

**I'm immersed in the
commune, and I like it.**

November 8, 1977: Three inches of snow on the ground this morning—warm and very messy up at the barn. Rubber boots are a very handy invention.

Headed for another adventure, Dee and I took off in the snow with our precious cargo of thirty-five gallons of milk, twelve dozen eggs, plus 140 pairs of our rainbow taper candles. Each glass bottle of milk is carefully placed in the horizontal refrigerators, and snow and ice are added. I enjoy my conversations with this very levelheaded lady. She is also becoming friends with Sandy.

On the way out we got stuck in our own driveway, but we pushed off quickly and drove to town in a thirty-minute blizzard. Driving at thirty mph, we didn't slide at all. Windshield wiper worked, and defroster and heater, too, a sort of record for us.

Rebel went in with us and worked with Pepe all day learning techniques in silver concho stamping. Rebel seemed a little cold toward me today. He comes from a rather bellicose family in Virginia. He told me a story once of his father in court striding up to the judge and punching him in the face.

Milk run went very well. Then on the last stop we got terribly stuck on a no-gravel dirt road. We did not advance far down the road, but we could not get out. I put on chains—laid down in the mud and water—shoveled mud and jacked up the truck. We drove up and down the road but could not get our tires out of the ditch on the right. Finally a Spanish fellow with a new four-wheel-drive pickup stopped and said, "Let's go get a chain," and we went after one. An hour later we returned with the chain, and he pulled us back to the blacktop highway from which I never should have strayed.

That was close. For almost the third time, I came home without the delivery truck. But thanks to a prosperous Molycorps miner with a fancy truck, we were miraculously saved. He wants me to do some carpentry with him. I said I'd help Saturday.

Friday: It was 18° this morning. Days are balmy again—the ground still muddy. The snow is nearly gone from the fields. The mountains got a big hit and should stay white for quite some time. Yesterday Larry joined me at the corral and woodpile, and together we put up a basic frame for the cow shelter; it has a southern exposure. Friend Alan helped. Then we colored candles after lunch until it was time to put cows away and milk. Today complete exhaustion hit me for a few hours after I cleaned up around in the barn. Larry did the milk run.

Two young ladies are here from Binghamton, New York. They've been hitchhiking and traveling around, seeing what's happening. Outfitted with lots of warm clothes, they've been very helpful—cleaned out the calves' house and put fresh straw down, did lots of dishes, cut apples, chopped wood, and the pretty blond stayed with Larry! He's feeling better. Buffalo working some charm for him to keep him here with us.

Rebel finished his belt, near $200 worth of silver. He worked with Pepe and made his own stamps and learned a lot of technique. He also set up the hammer mill; we still don't have a belt, however.

The chickens, which have been under Larry's care, are doing very well. Gave 77 eggs today! Our largest flock ever is now gearing up to high production.

Saturday: Big storm came in—a cold wind blowing hard. Inside with a fire, it's nice and warm. We had a bit of a scare. Two smaller kids were playing with matches! The mattress in the unoccupied tower smoldered. By the time we found it today, the mattress was gone and the floor was burned too; we put it out. So the loft floor was destroyed, and the vigas holding the floor partly burned. The ceiling got smoked a very beautiful red.

Then Rebel got very angry when he came home. Belt in hand—accusing and threatening Jason—Sandy stepped in between. Rebel in our faces—raging and spitting—Sandy, Larry, and I got yelled at. Built-up frustrations over home, money, and what have you came out. These scenes are not fun, and nobody says the right things.

Getting the communal thing together is not entirely easy. I hear Max will be in town. Be nice if he'd spend some time with us. The wind is howling outside.

November 20: Tonight there is a shroud of clouds making the moonlit night very pleasant. I've been out for hours running and walking, thinking.

Sandy, I believe, has been feeling quite happy. The baby is being very good; he's full of laughs and fun. Sandy has some new clothes she made that are attractive on her slim body. She, Dee, Jon, and Larry have taken this last excitement right in stride. Larry plays with Jason at clever games and laughs plenty. What a good man.

I went up to Lama Mountain and spoke with Rollo and Rick Klein about this idea of Rebel's that he's going to rid New Buffalo of the likes of Larry and myself. He's confused, turning on one of the best friends he's got.

Pepe's been feeding his rage too. Pepe is a bit frustrated, with his young lady having such a hard birth and having to raise a lot of money. The mansion got sold and everyone ordered out! Pepe, though, says a lot of things. If he returns my outspoken love and admiration with hatred, that is sad. With the support of some of our friends, I imagine we won't be terrorized out of our efforts and home here at New Buffalo.

I ran over and saw Ron, because I've been thinking of him. I brought over a coat I thought he wanted, and we talked and listened to music. He showed me an interesting book correlating birth dates with the 52-card deck. He says my card is the eight of diamonds.

Dee washed a great bunch of bottles—very thoughtful of her. Jon is right with me as a good friend.

Opinions are like assholes; everyone has one! So here's mine. You are like a worm eating a perfect apple.—Rebel

November 30, 1977: I haven't written for a little while, waiting until the situation settled. Lena joining in with a bad word about everyone—things not swinging their way. In the need for a separation, Sandy and I were loaned the use of neighbor Ian's house across from Buffalo for nearly a week. We had a very pleasant little family time. I go to work over at the commune each day. We do work hard for our little home.

Reb got a big red bus from Jeff in trade. He and Lena packed in one day and took off as Jon and I were going up to milk. Sandy came back yesterday.

That was a profound shock, having two people against some of the other people. So much of what keeps us together is trust, love, and respect. Well, the situation resolved pretty quickly without any more added bad feeling or violence.

I've never really been depressed here. Now though, I want something to resurge my spirit. Ever since I started in this commune enterprise, I believed in people joining together to create a good and productive home. We could create a place of harmony and peace. Well, I certainly haven't given up—stick with it. We do have a wonderful home.

December 1, 1977: Rebel was here to pick up a few things. We shook hands; he sort of apologized. Said he wants to be remembered for the good things he's done at Buffalo. Said he hope he'll be able to overcome his meanness. Larry said a prayer for them in Circle. The image of Rebel shoving Larry around in the courtyard, though, is burned in my mind.

And now Larry is going to go. So much he has done for us and then to be so unappreciated by Lena and Reb and so roughly handled. Well, Larry takes it very well. He has been thinking of leaving on and off for years. I hope we carry through, so he will see all his efforts have helped create a beautiful and happy home.

Friend George was here for a few hours. He gave us $20; Jon will use it to get a tooth pulled. I've been helping with dinner often. It was encouraged at a monthly meeting that some of us do a bit more.

December 4, 1977: Last evening Kiva and Kemal were over for a nice dinner prepared by Dee. Sandy cleaned the circle, made brownies, and built the first fire in the big circle room stove.

We have had a lot of good people leave, and we've had a terrific lot of volunteer labor building the commune. Always it has been precarious. This year we did get Dee and Jon joining, and they are tops. A few people make all the difference.

We are reorganizing our finances. Dee is general treasurer. Each person should contribute a minimum of $50 to this general treasury. New people should be able to provide this minimum.

The dairy has two workers, Jon and I, and it contributes $100 for them; plus it will contribute more than the minimum. What we don't have to give to the general treasury can stay in the dairy, some to go to the workers and most for capital investment.

Lena and Rebel wanted an end to my personal treasury and a better way to see the organization. The Mabel Dodge commune had a definite system.

Each person had to contribute a minimum every month to cover food and rent. Then each person's business was free to earn anything over that, and the owner could keep it. The plain idealism of just giving all you've got for years on end with a distant goal in mind is too unfulfilling for most people.

Emil has some very nice clothes that Sandy has made for him. The little fellow is a great joy to us.

December 7: From Colorado a young man showed up, a very nice fellow named Keith. He read about us—wanted to see for himself—sounded good to him. He's quiet, clean, and healthy. Actually, we do need the help. He's cutting kitchen wood. A new gal Reesa is here. She fixed up one room very nicely and is feeding pigs and calves.

December 8: Beautiful day, windy—unseasonably warm—hot in the solar collector.

So what is happening in my immediate drama? Ever since I started with these communes, I believed strongly in people joining together to achieve things: to create a home, farm, and workshop as a group.

At this point I have few companions. I've made many friends, but only a very few have joined with me here at this fledgling commune and stayed. I think we'll just keep going. We have a lot going for us now. We'll get some new people.

December 11: The land is quiet and serene in pale gold shades. But did I misjudge this commune business? I always felt that if we saw it through we would eventually see it blossom as an important trend, helping solve some of the dilemmas of modern society.

At this point it can't be said to be attracting too many bright, creative, idealistic people. This could be just a low ebb; a lesson of how difficult it is to achieve what we want—Harmony. Reesa has been very helpful washing bottles and being a cheerful person who thinks we have a good thing started.

Sandy's been feeling good. She sawed and split kitchen wood yesterday and is cleaning the pantry, which really needed it. The new shelves and floor from last winter are a great help.

Dee fixes us a marvelous meal on her turn. She knows a lot about food. She's been working hard at the new job; she gets home late four days a week. Today she drove the red truck for Jon and two friends who are going to try and earn some money selling wood.

December 14: We bred Julie cow again. Candy cow is at her highest of twenty-seven pounds yesterday. We sold the sixteen-day-old calf for $25, and the milk run made a little money. I'm talking to people I know. I feel our future is more uncertain than I have in the past. I really would like to see this be a good home.

December 15, 1977: Jon and I worked on the new collector. He just about finished putting the wood on the roof, and I framed in the doorway and put up some of the west-facing wall. I'm still using wood that Jim Kehoe bought. Thank you. The roof is being built with wood earned by the dairy. Emil was with us for a few hours. He's a very good boy.

Cheering us on is a very nice guest, Louie, a French Canadian with three children. He cut a bunch of wood and fixed the milk-room door very cleverly. He's a professor of literature, looking to drop out. He says many people speak of dissatisfaction. They want new values—an alternative. And he is looking. So he's seen us, and we were as hospitable as we can be. His boys stayed with Jason, and he and his little girl slept in Larry 's room. Sandy had cleaned the room and made it beautiful. Yes, Larry has left. I told him to write to us.

We had another guest—a gentle, thin person, David. He talks a lot to himself. Even building a fire, he had to be taught.

Another day: Jon and I are conscious that we are closing in on a time when expenses come awfully close to earnings. There are maybe fifty days of hay left, but a hundred days yet before Big Beth has her calf. Our milk will continue to decrease little by little. And the killer is that we need hay to continue getting maximum milk.

I am talking to our customers and trying to cut out extended credit. We could butcher our big steer and sell some of the meat. We could sell Julie. We could cut back production and feeding, but we really like to keep the business going at the maximum. A lot of farmers face the same depressing facts; they are working hard for little return.

We must remember to count our blessings—to see our life as a whole; the simple joys of life we have: delicious clean cold water—it is prayer to drink; the air—crisp, clean, and invigorating—the body's constant prayer to the surrounding earth. And having a warm bed inside a solid house with a warm fire is a wonderful thing. Our four adults make for two couples, which is very nice too. The baby is a delight, and the older boy Jason has a great deal of spirit and adds to the home atmosphere that we like.

20. *Jason and Emil*

The mountains, clouds, sunrises, and sunsets give us a stunning world to see each day. In front of Sandy's room we still have flowers. There are purple irises and the cheery red and yellow nasturtiums. Very comforting to see them.

December 18: Reesa, bless her heart, washed a lot of bottles for us. I fed the chickens scraps from the barn. Sandy prepared wicks and wax, and she and I dipped 135 pairs of candles. She also cooked our dinner on a windy, wintry day. Jason and I cut two Christmas trees, and he and Sandy decorated the big one in the circle.

I wrote to Mel in Texas, to Kim and Peggi, to Jim Preston, and to the unknown doctor Ernie in Minneapolis, the contact with the Cro Farm family where Pepe has gone.

I was at the new silversmith's commune. They have rented a beautiful modern house. It's fine how they keep their home so clean and serve a very nice little group. Really wish them the best luck. They, in fact, set a standard of excellence. They said that they had no intention of taking over New Buffalo along with Rebel.

December 21: Finally the shortest day and the official start of winter. There are lights on the Christmas tree in the circle; Jason is very proud he helped bring in the tree and decorate it.

Sandy cleaned up Virginia's old room where Jon lived for a while. Such good karma, I think, to keep these empty rooms in a neat state rather than being messed up and abandoned, looking like some primitive caveman tribe was here. Make them inviting.

We have a new guest, Bill, from near Lake Superior in Wisconsin. He's like most of our guests lately: he's clean and helpful, and he likes our scene. We do have a lot going for us.

Jon cooked a fine dinner with pastry for dessert.

Christmas, 1977: Greetings! A pleasant good feeling this clear Christmas day. Pork cooking, pies already made, and the kids got some presents. Friends expected for dinner.

Our new friend Bill left to go to Lama Foundation. Bill is a fantastic person but maybe wants a more religious commune. He's one of several people, whom we've met recently looking for a good communal situation to live in. This is encouraging. I see our scene as big—international—and an important development in the USA. We got a letter from a young German looking for a commune. I told him to come by in answer. He said he'd be in the States in a month or two.

I feel that as our commune gets more together, it will have more of a religious aspect. For instance, neat gardens and a house harmony reflected in well-cared-for trees and paths and rooms and harmony in the people.

I sold candles on the street the day before Christmas, then went to see Ed Morgan and Lenore, and Billy Whelan and Susan. Billy suggests we could advertise for the right people in *East West Journal* or *Communities*. It's not a bad idea. These are people into helping people—just our thing. We're not out of touch because we've been getting a few letters, and a few people passing through who are just about right.

I filled out this year's Corporate Income Tax Form 1120 with Larry Taub. "Long Live New Buffalo!" we said. We both are making the effort. Larry's going to fill out a new application for nonprofit 501C-3 status. This could be an important step to getting some capital to work with.

December 26: We had a very nice Christmas. Jon slaughtered a pig. We brought out canned goods and made eggnog. To control the urge to go do some work, I had a little brandy in the nog and developed quite a warm and fuzzy feeling. Jay, Donna, and Mom were here, and Carol and John came over. Kachina is like a little fountain of crystals bubbling over with excitement. Zoom! She and Jason are right together as soon as folks walk in the door.

December 28: After milking, Jon and Dee taped plastic on the red truck windows and went to Monte Vista for supplies. I bought Lascolite covering to replace the plastic of the greenhouse sun porch. The frame is up, the stone walkway in, the soil all in place.

The chickens laid a record 103 eggs! Sandy has taken over their care, doing her usual thorough job.

December 30, 1977: Clouds threatened all day, but it was warm and, as though jinxed, no amount of cloudy days and storm clouds seem to be able to make snow.

Found a repair place to help me make a new motor mount for the pickup delivery truck. And I got battery cable clamps. With Larry gone I must do more mechanics. Came home with $88. So we're still in there. And 105 eggs today from the chickens.

As for guests, we now have Ansel, a local fellow who has a place up in the mountains and is down for a few days to get a dose of civilization. He cut more wood for us.

January 2, 1978: Larry Taub came up with some papers to be signed. We're trying for a tax-exempt status. Perhaps it will be the key to the financing we need.

Today Jon and I slaughtered our big cow Julie. She doesn't give much milk, and we are running out of hay. Plus we can sell hamburger for some cash. We carried through and hung the meat, in seven parts, in the refrigerated

21. *Kimmey family photo. 1980.*

truck. That was the biggest animal I've ever helped to slaughter. It was hard work. I was quite a sight by the time I got in the shower.

January 3: We had John and Marie Kimmey, along with their kids, over for dinner. They play a very warm role in the Arroyo Hondo community. Dee fixed a good meal for us all and made terrific hospitality. We learned something about the Taos Learning Centers, and learned we could become affiliated. Marie also has at least one source of grant money that we could apply for. This could be progress, and I got the two necessary signatures on the amendments that may get us tax-exempt status.

January 4: We woke up to a storm and fifteen minutes of snow. Then the weather cleared all day. John Kimmey came over to help butcher, and he also sharpened knives. With the big iron stovetop hot, we keep a pan going with little scraps of meat and fat sizzling away for everyone to enjoy. We are thankful to the animal; it is okay. It is nature's way that humans are meat eaters. We packaged over one hundred pounds of roasts, steaks, and cubes and got nearly as much meat for hamburger. John was a great help.

January 7: Today we bought alfalfa hay, $200 worth. We jump-started the red truck and added water to the leaky radiator. Everett, at the Feed Bin, did us a favor to get us a good price. He appreciates that though I am a poor hippie, so to speak, I never ask for credit but always buy with cash for farmers' produce. We brought home the most marvelous oat hay bales. It was lush and harvested perfectly.

Yesterday Sandy spent all day in the kitchen cooking lasagna and doing a super cleanup. Today she spent a few hours cleaning the dirty chicken house. She keeps quite busy.

There is a possibility that we will have a really dry year coming up. That will add another challenge to our trying to put the dairy together. So we keep plugging away. We accomplish the immediate tasks before us and wonder constantly how we'll make that step to create the barn.

Some people from Lama Foundation will be here tomorrow. They have a school going, and we showed interest in the educational approach because there is possibly some grant money in this area. We are educational, but we don't have a structured program. We may learn some approaches from la Lama.

January 11: We have another fine guest, a world traveler from Germany. He's interested in communities and farming, happy to be able to cut wood and wash bottles. We gave him our best guest room.

I feel quite positive tonight. John Kimmey has been talking about school and his son Sean. Well, I think we'll offer to get Sean in here to learn these country ways. He's a fine young man, and we could offer to have him stay here!

Outside about midnight, still the clouds are very high. We watch the sky as we are enfolded in one of the wonders of our Mother Earth. Far inland of the ocean, pockets of moisture flit around the mountains; some get lucky.

January 12: John Kimmey came back over today to talk about Jane staying here to be administrator. It's really kind of flaky. He's willing to grab anyone for administrator—no experience—no field of training. I'm not especially impressed. One super funky trip added to our halfway trip wouldn't add to the blessed harmony we want. We did mention having his son Sean over as a resident; now that's more like a real idea. Learn through work. We've got plenty of work.

Harold left. Though he'd been looking for some scene like ours, this was the first he's found. He had been at Amanda Foundation in California, but it wasn't the simple country life. This evening we have another guest, Joel, a young fellow traveling with a beat-up car and a trailer.

January 13: I did the milk run today and turned the tail on Friday the 13th. I had two instances of good luck. At Finley's I arrived one minute before the people whom I had come to see arrived. I got to collect $4 that had been five weeks overdue. Then at Bois's I arrived just before Eric and Susan, which was good luck because I then sold them three pieces of meat. Best of all, I ran into Norman in Safeway who has a big belt that is good for driving a hammer mill. With that, we should be able to grind dairy grain and get better use out of it; our cows are shitting out a fortune in grain.

Last night late, the Ortiviz truck sputtered up our road, and three of the Farm lads spent the night on the kitchen floor; warmest room in the house. This morning we had a grand tour, talked, and ate breakfast. The boys looked pretty ragged and unshowered—good lads, though, and our close brothers. Also they are interested in farming and selling to their special market, and they must have felt good to see us making such progress. We load our truck with eggs, milk, and meat and go off to deliver. It's no dream. We are helping our community with food.

They had a comedy of errors trying to get going this morning. The 10° cold kept their truck from starting; it has a poor battery. They had to start up our tractor to jump-start the truck, but starting the truck wasn't good enough. They drove it up to the house to say goodbye and stalled out again. Then the tractor wouldn't start. They finally figured it was out of gas and got it going. I told them where they could sell their hay, and they made the deal. They thought we'd want it, but we thought it a little too stemmy and dry when baled. For the same price Everett's hay is better.

January 14: The day started overcast and stayed cold for some time. Dee took the milk run. Sandy went along, and they then shopped for baking pans in town. It's been many years since the square, king-size pans were new.

Jon and I killed the mother pig. We skinned her on a scaffold at the pen. We quartered her and hung the meat in the root cellar to cool. I skinned the head to boil. Sandy came upon it unattended on the circle table and got upset. I got a little of the tasty meat off the hide to fry.

January 15: Halfway through January, nature finally breaks the spell, and we have a snowstorm; it's a fine-grained snow in a soft constant wind. No mountains or sky are visible—just very low clouds. We are immersed.

Jon and I brought up the pig. Jon quickly got most of the meat off the bones—Jason helping to clean more off. I cut up bones, ribs, and chops, and Sandy cut up many packages of pork cubes and strips for Mexican and Chinese-style dishes.

Our visitor Joel left. Then another guy Bill came up; a husky fellow and very crazy. We asked him to leave. Jon got up very close—in his face— suggesting he stay away. We don't want this fellow. He made us all nervous. Lots of talk of death and electrocution and very incomprehensible constant rap. We gave him a place for the night and two meals.

January 19, 1978: Here at New Buffalo we are in the midst of our best storm yet. The weather has been teasing us, but tonight we are getting a fine but persistent snowfall. Our prospects are looking much better.

Jon and I discussed barn plans today. We'll go for the simpler flat barn design. We then discussed our plans with Marie Kimmey, a draftsperson. We'd like to start work in April when concrete can be poured.

We packaged more hamburger for sale. Dee made sausage and put about sixty pounds in the freezer. The sausage machine is a handy invention. The mixed meat goes in the hopper—intestines over the spigot and crank. We first clean the intestines by rinsing and attaching them to the faucet and running the water through like a hose.

Tomorrow morning we'll have baby Emil wake us with his cheerful morning talk, and we'll have a white world to look out on. I'm immersed in the commune, and I like it.

JOURNAL 22

January 21, 1978: We have hired Marie Kimmey to make a barn blueprint, which will be essential for getting a grant or a loan. One way or the other, I'm determined to start building as soon as we can this spring. By this time next year, we should have a license. I've gotten more pressure in town to show a license. So no more cows until we get the barn. Jon's the same way. It's do or die. To do dairy we've got to have the facility. I spoke to Keith from Lama. He said they borrow money.

Sean and Patrick were over and worked on the new schoolroom by putting some mats on the floor and sort of smoothing it out.

We had another guest come and go; a young longhaired fellow on bicycle with pack and two instruments tied on. He had plenty of dreams of things to create—not practical ideas—doesn't like kitchen work. He was off this morning after two days. Wizard was the name, a wanderer seeking a good life.

January 23: Last night as the sky cleared and the sun was setting, the mountains reflected a purple glow on their frosty sheen—the purple mountains majesty of the national anthem. In the morning we were enveloped in another storm.

Last night a car pulled up. Sandy excitedly said, "Oh, maybe that's Larry!" And sure enough, it was! We're all glad to see our friend. He's staying in his old room. We discussed our doings this past month; we've been busy. We went over our latest plans for the barn, and we made some estimates of materials we'll need. Wow, Larry's back!

Sean Kimmey moved in today. He is fourteen years old, well built, and willing to be quite conscientious, becoming a part of our little farm family. I showed him the cows and the different groups they're kept in. Then we cut wood.

The "school" had a meeting here today. It's an idea I like. There could be many schools, especially at places where things are being done and young people can see firsthand how many things in society operate. There were six teachers present; groups of two will take charge of a day. I've got Wednesday afternoons for physical education and work detail.

The school is in a very formative stage—so far no money. But there is a staff and schoolroom, and it could grow to be regular and professional. As our consciousness is just forming, so are our ways of educating. We'll see what develops. It's going to start next Monday. Only a few kids, so far, are enrolled.

I think I made it quite clear that I'm a bit skeptical, and that we are concerned what will happen to our home. But if enough people want to make it happen, it could be a good thing all around. It's certainly more creative than an empty room.

January 24: Finally got a real snow, about seven inches. Sausage and eggs for breakfast with our enlarged family. I set up a little shelter for Crystal the Jersey cow, just big enough to keep her out of the blanketing whiteness. Sandy fed the chickens inside their house, and we put Beth the cow in the corral. Larry packed the truck as the snow fell thickly. We put on the chains, and Jon came along on the milk run. We got home early, just as the storm suddenly cleared. Jon chased some unwanted cows out, and I went up and fed and watered.

Sandy and Dee have got the seed order ready. They are developing a closeness. And Dee is quite close with lucky Jon. She must be some woman to take on such a strong young hunk like him. With these storms we can think about spring planting.

January 26, 1978: After the storm, we had absolutely clear sky. Temperature dropped to 8° below zero. I brought the meat to be ground out of the refrigerator truck. The Dodge won't start in the morning; it was too cold. Larry's going to take over the chickens again. Seems he's slipped right back into the groove. A sane decision, I think.

During the day usually we can set our pace. Slavery and wage slavery and so many kinds of constant labor used to deprive many of a healthy long life. Our life here gives us quite a bit of time to choose what to do. It also gives me the chance to be with my little son during some days. It's a help to mom, who cares for him so much, and I'm sure it is good for Emil, too, to be with a man part of the time.

The greenhouse sun porch is looking very fine. Alyssums with their many tiny flowers are spreading. California poppies are coming up, and Sandy puts out her flowering geraniums each day. I worked with Jon on his greenhouse collector; we're getting close to having it sealed.

One of the most immediate problems is to get electricity out to the barn site. Larry says we've probably got sixty amperes of electricity available at our power pole, and our present setup uses about all.

A new day: We talked to the electric co-op—Mr. Ernie Santistevan. He says go ahead and put in our electric line and set up our electricity, and if more power is needed, they'll change the transformer.

Sean Kimmey has unfortunately gone. I'm not sure why his dad, John, didn't carry through with the school. It's so easy to talk about ideas, but when it comes to the physical work the enthusiasm fades.

This is my proposal for the corporation reorganization Statement of Purpose: Goals: To further peace in the world, brotherhood, generosity, sharing, and freedom. To develop solutions to social problems such as unemployment, alienation, and hatred. To join with people of like minds to create a good home and life. Bylaws: We will have monthly meetings to review finances and review new members. Secretary's responsibility to see it takes place.

We are on the verge of success. Another year of great effort, and we should have a more complete scene. It's a challenge—a creative endeavor. As science, technology, and medicine have their points of challenging research, we are development in the social arena; we are at a creative place. With hard work and some reorganization we should yet be able to establish a good home and ongoing farm. I still believe, definitely, although that was a hell of a blow Reb and Lena gave us and the whole way of living.

February 2, 1978: Had the vet up to test Candy for TB. This we should have done right away but didn't because of money pressure with Rebel and Lena, especially after near $600 was spent on jewelry supplies. There was pressure for no more money out. Never mind—never again.

Larry has come up with a new barn plan. Looks good. I've been making more cost estimates as we get more information and figure out more aspects. Sandy is cooking her special Mexican dishes again. She cleans the kitchen so well before cooking.

February 6: Bob Moore and Bob Dowling, from Colorado, have been here for several days, adding to the fun and good feeling. They know how to pitch in and also have been playing Risk with Jason and Larry. They're from the Ortiviz Ranch now called the Huerfano Community Farm. Fledglings like us—working it out. After cutting us a super supply of kitchen wood, Jon introduced them to our milk bottles, and they got a bunch of them washed.

Sunday Jon branded one of the steers. He and I then gravitated to the greenhouse. As we worked, we listened to the new Taos music station. Some people are doing a very fine thing there. We heard a lot of classical guitar. Marvelous.

I missed three milkings and went with my mom to pick up my sister Anne in Albuquerque. She was in Europe for four years, much of the time in school. Then, like I did with school, she dropped out and changed her life. Now she looks for something new.

The two Bobs started on the concrete and stonework in the new greenhouse and it looks good. They mostly used rocks that Red Jim brought up. We'll have to go looking for more.

Our friends, Ramon from the old La Bolsa days and Vree, gave me $200 today for the farm! There is generosity alive. Thank you. Our friends are being a big help. Our income is just enough to keep getting materials we need. The workers get to create a home; no pay 'til we get a lot bigger. Larry cooked dinner for us! So we keep moving.

Larry Taub said he should have our corporation papers ready for approval this Saturday.

A new day: It was fairly wintry today with a furious inch of snow at evening milking. The mountains were in a storm all day. This is good.

Jon, Bob, and I went and got a pickup load of rocks from down in the Rio Grande gorge. We noticed an ancient man-made wall in the side of the cliff; Jon suggested it might have been a cellar. Nice stonework.

The two Bobs are doing a great job setting the stones. One more door could go into the middle room. The three openings Ron created are essential to these rooms getting heated. That was a good job.

22.
Cliffs. Photo by
Clarice Kopecky

The "dynamic duo" cut more wood today. They put the bottles to the side of the milk room and cleaned the floor. Jon did the milk run in Hondo, and Lama Foundation came by, as usual, for eggs and milk.

Sandy cooked her Italian specialty tonight. Bob made another squash pie. Today, just for snacks, we ate a couple of loaves of bread with preserves. Our two guests help create the feeling of togetherness: the easy happiness, the healthiness of hard work, relaxation, and good food.

Kim just sent us some information about alfalfa fertilization. Larry has another drawing inked in and a partial cost estimate of $3,200.

February 11: Heavy clouds all day and more snow at the higher elevations. My sister is here. For something to do, she washed a lot of milk bottles and then cooked dinner. She's a quiet woman and very nice. Sandy fixed up my room with cleaning and flowers to make her feel at home.

My mom's got a party planned for here tomorrow. With Anne and the Ortiviz Bobs and now Peter from Germany, the house is cheerier. Hard to dispel that hateful vibe Reb and Lena showed, however. Five are too few adults for Buffalo; we need a stronger group.

February 12, 1978: Jon decided we should brand. In the crisp morning we made a fire and then branded our three young calves, including the two heifers. Afterward my mom had her little party here. Then my sister went home with her.

Life is better. In a book I'm reading about Africa by George Schaller, he states that in 50 B.C. the average human life span was twenty-two years. In 1800, it was only thirty-six years. He describes an area in the Congo that in 1898 was devastated by the cannibalistic Baleka tribe. Throughout the world, it used to be part of life that wars would flare through the villages. I think we are getting away from that in our modern world, I hope.

February 14, 1978: As the mountains accumulate snow, it continues to dry out down here. The fields are still very wet. Soon it will be time to plow.

Jon laid some rocks in the greenhouse. Peter mixed the cement. Peter, our new German friend who wrote us several months ago, is nineteen years old and speaks quite well *zee English*, which he learned in Canada.

Dee cleaned out the refrigerator milk truck, finalizing that meat trip. We need to get it running.

Wednesday: We remain in hot pursuit of our goals. I made an appointment to see a government representative about a loan, and at the same time I have started on an application for an NCAT grant—National Center for Appropriate Technology. We should be the type of thing they're looking for, so we've got a chance, maybe a good chance.

Yes, it's time to think about seeds. The snow scene is looking good, so I'm thinking we'll go full ahead and plant every piece of water rights we have. We were ready last year, but we didn't have the water. This year we'll get the chance to finally get near our maximum hay production planted.

We also may have found a solution to our city problem; we'll get a license for eggs and pet food sales. That should satisfy the fellow who has tried to stop us from selling.

February 16: Another day of snow. Jon and I cut two big piñon logs with the sharpened two-man saw. Larry is coming very close to being finished with the barn plans. They look detailed and very professional. He's got a good mind. I've drafted a possible grant application.

February 17: Jon and I sold milk and eggs. After buying feed and gas, we had only two dollars left. I recently sent $40 away for a new special milking can, which we are doing at the request of the Health Department.

Big worry—nuclear wastes—France. Reprocessing at Cap de la Hague being expanded so they can handle foreign nuclear wastes! French signed contracts with ten Japanese utilities to handle 1,600 tons of spent nuclear fuel over a ten-year period. They will bury some ultimate wastes underground or at sea! The most radioactive will have to go back to countries of origin. So much potential to fuck up and hurt so many.

February 18: At Buffalo I was just getting set up to mix concrete when Chet and his brother Bill showed up with Deek in a green van! Pretty soon the four of us were working in the very warm greenhouse, and we finished the stone wall. Next the pathway.

These traveling workers, Chet, Deek, and Bill, are tough-looking men with gentle hearts. They have big hands and full beards and not many changes of clothes. They are cheery, and we had quite a good time placing rocks and finding pretty colored stones for the finishing.

The weather has cleared. The spring winds are starting. We had our annual meeting. Larry McInteer is president. Dee Shain, treasurer. Art Kopecky is vice president and secretary, and Jon Taintor and Sandy Lopresti are directors. Sounds good. We still don't have revised bylaws from Mr. Taub to discuss.

February 19: We offered breakfast of sausage and eggs to our guests. I felt a little tired, but Deek was all enthused to work, and Bill, plenty willing. Then we set up the logs in place as the walkway border. Chet sharpened scissors and knives and fixed a sleeping bag.

After some homemade cottage cheese with preserves, we got down to concrete. With the extra help the work was "rather painless"; it's almost done, and we've shared our lives with some good friends.

February 22: We agreed to slaughter our biggest steer, Christopher. Jon shot him and Bill helped. They did fairly fast work of it and were done by early afternoon.

Sandy made wooden planting flats. Jon and Dee brought up soil from the garden to the new greenhouse. Deek turned it in—a big job. Larry, Bill, and I traced the Chevy engine problem to a leak in the manifold. Jon made copies of the barn blue prints. Larry also has made an electrical wiring estimate for the barn. I cooked a big pot-roast dinner, one of my very few specialties. We got quite a bit done today.

February 25: Grass is growing—ground is thawing. We put a few more posts in for the new garden fence, some more manure went to the field. Greta the goat had four kids at night. Jon dried them, milked Greta, and fed the kids. Two died immediately. Jon was right on the case as is necessary with these goats. On their own, they'd hardly have any kids survive.

February 28, 1978: The two baby does spent the night in the circle. In the morning they came into the kitchen. During the day they stay around in the courtyard. While I was off doing errands and milk run, Josy and Veronica goats both had their kids—four more females. We put notices up for free does; there's really no market for goat kids.

We signed a paper giving the electric company "right of way" to put electricity through our property to Tierra de los Rios, a development on the land bordering ours on the mesa top. Ten-acre tracts have been marketed. In exchange they will put an electric service at our barn site worth several thousand dollars.

I reviewed with Bill Betz the grant application procedure. He recommends a far more complicated and detailed application. We had a meeting to discuss that and to discuss getting a license to sell "pet food" and about becoming a center of Taos Learning Center, an almost nonexistent entity. TLC we put off. The license we're going to get, and we'll have to keep working on the barn plans and grant application.

March 1, 1978: Very heavy skies—mountains getting snow—down here getting rain. Jon got up in the night and covered some of the hay. In our little garden in front of the doors of our private rooms, narcissus are in bloom—white blossoms with bright yellow centers and freshly fragrant. The irises are sending up flowers too. Alyssums, with their hundreds of tiny yellow blooms, are billowing larger. The poppies soon will add their brilliant orange flowers.

March 2: Young Peter from Germany, who has lived on several communes in Canada and France, has returned. He spent nearly his whole savings on a car—plans to go to California next month. While here though, he is very pleasant and helpful. He's soft-spoken, quite down to earth, and he likes our commune.

March 3, 1978: Rain turned to snow over night. Two inches here and no break in sight. As soon as it dries enough, we'll be plowing.

In the news, January 23, 1978, *Newsweek* climate and weather report: By burning fossil fuels, man is steadily increasing the amount of carbon dioxide. This cloak produces a greenhouse effect that may heat up the earth, causing considerable changes, perhaps disastrous for some. Decimation of forests contributes, too, since trees breathe in a certain amount of carbon dioxide.

When the Industrial Revolution accelerated in 1860, the atmosphere contained 285 parts per million of carbon dioxide. These experts project the figure will reach 400 by year 2000 and climb to double that amount by 2050.

Chlorofluorocarbons (from aerosol cans) have similar effect. These are also a by-product in jet propulsion, I believe. Nitrous oxide, a by-product of chemical fertilizer, also has this effect.

How do I relate to this and many other pressures of the industrial world? One thing is by believing in the power of the communes—people sharing— many people less dependent on the giant industrial machine.

The grant application needs more work. Larry has to make a good drawing of the solar collector and especially the water heating system. He'd rather just build it. Actually, he's just done a lot of plans and needs to take a break. But we also need a verbal description of the solar system, which Larry should best do. It is very modern—a black painted insulated attic with a collector for roof. He saw the design in *Mother Earth News*.

March 7: The storms are past. Pretty dry already here, but the high mountains look extremely snowy.

Yesterday Mick came over, and he, Larry, and I butchered most of the steer. He is very skilled with a blade, odd for a one-time seminary student. Always good for some philosophical discussion, Mick lived here a few years ago.

Jon and Peter towed the wreck out of our field that was abandoned there in the fall when Tahiti smashed two radiators. Jon had to change a tire, unarm the transmission, and lower it down the one hill instead of pulling it, because it had no brakes. Very good that he got it out of there. We can't have junk cars abandoned in our fields.

Larry and I took a compression test on the Rizzo delivery truck. Seems good. Then he took off the manifold and made an aluminum-foil gasket for the one intake manifold housing that was leaking. Now it works well. Larry also fixed the crank on the tractor and gave us a scare by running it without water for a bit. Lady Luck is with us, and we've still got our excellent little tractor.

It was a marvelous day. The grass is really taking off. More and more plants are visible where we've established them in previous years. It's exciting now to see.

A fellow Pat, with red hair, was here for two nights and days. He was from a country community in Missouri, which they couldn't buy, so they had to abandon it. He and Peter left together.

March 11: Last night, we had a meeting to discuss and adopt our new by-laws and articles of incorporation. They sound quite good. We are becoming more businesslike, getting an organization together that is more likely to last and that will accept members in an orderly fashion, and hopefully, attract serious, mellow people who will want to make the commune their home.

Sandy and I put up about twenty feet of aspen-pole fencing near the newest greenhouse. Though we'll use barbed wire for much of the new fence, in a few places the pole fence will be much more attractive and less dangerous. It does look good, and we can have sweet peas and other flowering vines climb them. Soon the lilac will start to swell.

Dee wrapped up all the hamburger and put it away—seventy-five pounds—a nice stash. Sandy has planted broccoli, cabbage, tomato, and pepper seeds. Dee has tomatoes and peppers started. She also has nasturtiums up. We're eating lots of homegrown lettuce now. Also got some nice carrots out of Jon's greenhouse (Mike Pots's old room) tonight.

The grant application is not complete yet. I've been investigating the floor pouring. We might include hiring a supervisor in the price.

March 14: Larry and I, in spite of the cold wind, put in twelve more fence posts. Now most of it is done and it looks great. This fence around our new garden—cutting off the animals from our trees and flower gardens—is attractive and will allow us to grow more things faster. The front terrace, with its big iris and phlox beds, is included inside.

Sandy started putting Varathane on a little cabinet I made for Emil.

March 15, 1978: I did the milk run and got a town license to sell pet-food milk. This should take care of our problem with a town official that has stopped me twice.

Larry and I talked to Larry Taub. We're getting our bylaws and incorporation papers amended. We now will have official membership and control of the organization by the members. We hope to get tax-exempt status.

We copied another set of plans and then discussed the concrete work with Cipriano Medina in Cañon de Taos. Cipriano seems a good man, and the floor can be done in one or two days. He is willing to give us advice on how to work up to the point where he would take over. This is the man we've been looking for. This is progress.

Larry and Sandy finished putting in the fence posts. Fantastic. I hung the one gate I made, and I sunk a post and made a gate for the entrance near Dee's new greenhouse.

Huge Beth looks good and healthy and maybe one week away from dropping her calf into the world. The Brown Swiss with light-brown color and dark highlights are very handsome. She is far and away our best cow.

March 18: Our big cow separated from the herd, found herself a cozy secluded spot, and in the afternoon dropped a beige heifer for us. This is fabulous. She's big and sturdy. I couldn't get her to suck on Beth, so I milked Beth on the spot and bottle-fed the calf.

Sandy put in a fabulous day of work putting up many pole railings for the fence out front.

March 23: Big Beth is giving close to seven gallons. We start bottling her milk for sale tonight. We have nearly twenty gallons of colostrum milk stored for the calf. The first few days a cow's milk is yellowish, very rich, and has antibodies for the calf. It is advised to get the richest colostrum into the calf within an hour of birth when absorption of antibodies is greatest. Jon and I cut off a little vestigial fifth teat from big Beth's calf yesterday. "Immediately" is the time for that, says the vet. This husky heifer can grow to be a magnificent dairy cow.

Jon and Dee are going to Albuquerque, Santa Fe, and Lamy tomorrow. They will be gone two days. Going to see if Lalo is interested in buying our entire goat herd for $300. Jon's not happy about all the noise they make. I'm not happy about all the #1 best hay they eat. "Goats in the courtyard!" Attacked our two cherry trees. They are so mischievous—so labor intensive.

They are a lot of work for $20 profit a week, at best. Lalo does have a yearling heifer that might make for part of a trade.

I worked all day doing adobe parapet building for $30 with Kemal. Dee picked up a big order of food. On her way home in the night, she ran out of gas. As soon as she walked in, Jon and I went out and got the truck back. There's a brief moment of helplessness when stranded alone on the highway on a cold night. One must rely on the generosity of strangers to help out. A few of us, hitchhiking home, have had narrow escapes.

Just about a full moon out. The world is luminescent. Spring is beckoning. Since the bad incident with Rebel and Lena, we have been blessed with considerable harmony at home and good luck in most aspects.

New day: Today Dale Berry from the Health Department was here to discuss our plans. He says he's anxious to see us finally go into business. Us, too.

We have much to do on that score. We need a typewriter so we can start typing the grant application. We need to fill out the IRS tax-exempt status application. Larry needs to draw up an accurate water-heating plan. I've got a letter to be rewritten to Mr. Sherwood, a solar expert who is advising us on the solar aspects, and who would recommend our system to NCAT if we did a few extra things, such as make a more complete system by adding storage and/or a backup heating system.

With the pickup in Albuquerque, we decided to use the Rizzo delivery truck to do the first full-size milk run. We went over the route and the list of proposed customers. We've got the funny license now, too. I would like to get pet food labels. But we've always played it close, and we've been edging upward with concentrated effort—cooperation—and a measure of God-granted good luck.

I'm sitting at the desk for a few minutes between chores. Emil likes to climb on my lap and have his own pen and paper. At night, when we read, he likes to get a book, lean back and study it, albeit upside-down.

March 25: Larry took that first big milk run in. And in the effort to sell all the milk, he ran out before he could get to a bunch of people who expect us, but several gallons of goat's milk came back. Now it seems quite certain we'll sell the goats—a smart move.

Easter Sunday tomorrow. It doesn't mean a holiday for us. Jon's got the pace and so do I. As soon as he was back from the two-day excursion, he was right back milking and plowing.

Jon and Dee had a great trip. Stayed at Brian's house and went to three dairies. Got more bottles, cases, and soap. They also sold $50 of candles. That goes to keep our treasury afloat.

Sunday: Sunny warm days without much wind. Except for the top garden, we are done plowing. Now we have to drag, plant, disk, and put in irrigation lines.

A flood of milk—never had so much on hand. Larry took fifty-five gallons to town. Jason went with him. Sandy made about nine gallons into hard cheese, cottage cheese, and two pounds of butter. She's been feeling good—Larry too—all of us. We eat well, sleep soundly, and work hard. Jon is quite cheery.

Larry, after looking at the plans sent us by the University of New Mexico, came up with a very good suggestion for a milking pit design. This is likely what we'll do. I've got a letter off to our solar consultant Larry Sherwood. Dee typed the introduction for the grant. We've got to get that together, preferably soon.

The fields are getting greener. Eight-year-old Jason baked us a cake for dinner. Baked potatoes are his specialty.

I'm up late, thinking about this marvelous journey I'm on. Such a precarious perch—so much luck needed—yet such a solid thing on the Mother Earth we're trying to create. Something we can rely on for our survival.

I ran the fields over and over in the starlight.

April 4, 1978: The one cow has so changed our production. Now on Tuesday we've got nearly sixty gallons to go! On each run we make a few new contacts.

Great news! Larry sold over fifty gallons! He also picked up some blank sticky labels and a date stamp—ordered a PET FOOD milk stamp. Now it will be more legal and clearer.

As the milk kept pouring in, I felt a little apprehension, since we weren't selling all the milk. Though logic said we'd work up the business, it is the proof that counts. Now in three runs we have done it. That's a good sign that our cow's milk is popular, and we're onto a good thing.

On the world front: Good news from China. Moment of triumph for Vice Premier Deng Hsiao-Ping—age seventy-four—whose pragmatic ideas have been endorsed by the National People's Congress. They move to more of a socialist democracy—recognize the need for material incentives—improved education and freer cultural climate.

In our own little revolutionary scene we are pragmatic too. We must make a good living. We constantly work to produce food. That is pragmatic.

We are very aware of the work-a-day things we must do to make our little economy function and make the grounds look fresh and picturesque.

In China there is a major concession to the peasants, allowing them to sell handicrafts and farm produce from their private plots. China's graduate institutes of history, law, religion, philosophy, and economics will reopen—closed since 1966. That's good—that's huge.

Thursday: Busy day. We unloaded manure on the garden; Larry disked it in. This is very good stuff: rich, dark, and crumbly. Then Jon, Larry, and I—along with a visiting young Frenchman, Xavier—seeded the big new alfalfa field with two hundred pounds of oats, thirty pounds of alfalfa, and seven pounds of brome and Timothy-grass seed. The alfalfa seeds are tiny. That thirty pounds will turn into a vast amount of hay for many years. Our guest is a very nice fellow with red curly hair and not too much English.

Emil is walking quite a bit now—a late start. We spend a fair amount of time together. He sometimes stays in the dairy when I do clean up. He stays in the truck cab when I load manure.

April 11: We now have three foreign guests; Xavier from France; Stelios, originally from Greece; and Peter from Germany, who was here a few weeks ago. Also a lady, Mary Anne, is staying with us a bit. I'm working on a grant application.

Saturday we cleaned the main ditch. Monday the ditch came on, and we started running water, cleaning ditches, and destroying prairie dog tunnels that got ahead of us last year.

April 12, 1978: For $170, the remaining herd of goats went to Lalo Cordova in Lamy. So quietly came to pass such a momentous moment. We are now firmly dependent on the cows for milk and dairy income. There will be less noise, fewer attacks on our shrubbery, and more hay for our basic enterprise, cows.

Thursday: Springtime! The days are longer. With the goats gone, the farm operation is simpler and much less time consuming for Jon. We watch the cows carefully. I visit them out in the fields, count them and look them over. This is the best graze, but it can kill a cow from bloat in short order.

One day Larry ran the tractor in the garden without water. Because the radiator is old, it leaks and is not really fixable. So we must remember to water it each time we use it and drain it each night. Recently we noticed water in the oil—a cracked block. We take the news as a matter of course.

Xavier made chicken and banana for dinner with soup, rice, and salad—quite tasty. His presence is very entertaining with his funny English, European charm, and magic spirit.

Our four friends are still here, and they play Monopoly with Jason and Larry at night. They have been very good about helping keep the kitchen clean. Mary Anne washed most of the bottles.

I chased the water twice but never got any. One rancher, who's a friend, nevertheless felt he needed all the water—lazy-man irrigation using a giant head of water to flood the field instead of working a smaller amount and sharing the water. He said he'd be done in a few hours.

Sunday: After milking, I turned water on to the new field. It's hard work; the water on bare soil with seeds must be constantly tended or there are washouts and silt-ups. All day long the water gets spread by hoe or shovel and gradually the big field gets wet all over. For me it is deeply satisfying to work with soil and plants. This is the meditation, being useful in service with the earth. Modern psychoses are analyzed endlessly. To me it is only too obvious many people simply need a wholesome country experience, and it is only a philosophy of generosity away. There are ten thousand volumes written to justify greed and avoid looking at the obvious. They don't fool me.

April 18: We've got one grant application near completion. Habib was over here several times typing it. Dee took our new, signed articles of incorporation and bylaws into Larry Taub's office to be sent to the right authority. We have the tax money, but we need hay. And people are thinking about another cow.

Stelios, Jon, Dee, and I finished planting the fields. Still the irrigation ditches must go in, and then we can apply the water. It is a very big step between planted and watered. We've given ourselves the biggest job of irrigation ever. When I wake up, I think of the water, and change it in the dim light before milking.

Peter and Stelios fixed up the once-burned-out tower room very nicely.

April 19: Jon, Larry, Stelios, and Mary Anne are off to another wood run. Jon pulled these both off. He actually has a great sense of responsibility. I'm glad to have another member with the incentive to take out those runs. I know he likes the lunches! He also knows that our ability to carry on is partly how much firewood we have stockpiled.

A new day: Jon put in lines in one of the western oat fields and started watering it. I showed Stelios how to irrigate. Maybe he'll catch on. At first, a lot of people don't do a good job.

The big news is the garden. Larry really laid out excellent rows and now is making some flood boxes. I like the idea of flood boxes, because they get wet quickly and speedy irrigation is very important. Sandy and then Dee jumped at the chance to plant; onion sets, peas, carrots, lettuce, garlic, and beets went in. This is a very cooperative effort and should produce some fine results. What we need now are storms to guarantee more water.

No, that first attempt didn't work too well. With a good head of water, our new man Stelios only watered a small amount. So we lost the use of one day of water. Stelios, though, does want to help. It was ignorance, not lack of desire.

April 28, 1978: Friday milk run brought home over $100, plus some rods for Larry to make a new portable chick coop with. Mary Anne cooked. She is very good here. Larry seems to have picked up on her company.

We brought the bottling machine to outside the dairy room. Larry fixed the levers that turn off the water when opening the doors. I took several parts to town to get them repaired. Larry picked up a motor we will trade for with milk.

The first grant application is off to Shalan Foundation. We've got such a unique arrangement and such a good chance of being a success. I'm sure, with enough grants sent off, we'll get some help. Now to get the NCAT grant together.

I spend a lot of time with Emil. He is having a very good life. Filling these kids with lots of love and happiness is a way to a better, more peaceful world. That is a definite thing about working at home. The father can spend more time with the children.

Stelios is twenty-one years old and a good worker. He is not preoccupied, as Peter is, in spending weeks and weeks unraveling his personal problems. He quit Greece because he did not want to be inducted into the army. Peter says that is why he left Germany too. Stelios has a philosophic mind. He is troubled by the world—lonely—troubled by people not getting along better. But he is not pessimistic; he has belief there is great love in humanity. We have had some little discussions. He likes the idea of the open house and has a little difficulty relating to our having to influence the flow once in a while. These discussions seem important.

This life is invigorating; we do a lot of physical exertion. At Circle we can be very thankful we each are in good health.

May 1, 1978: In the morning descended a complete storm. We are buried in clouds, and it's cold and snowing. In the afternoon when I started to work on the grant application, the ditch came on strong. I surmise that Des Montes community turned off their half of the water to clean their ditch. Yesterday the flow wasn't even reaching us; now it has turned into a torrent. So one day completely changed our water picture.

Peter and Stelios left. Peter, we were not too happy with. While he had money, he ran around, bought a car, and traveled thousands of miles. Then when broke he hit here and pitched in but not very much. No, he certainly wasn't aware of helping the commune.

Stelios was a help, but he felt that by not taking in every person who showed up, regardless of anything, we were not for him. So they left. Goodbye friends and good luck.

We've now got two new gentlemen: Gene, who washes the dishes and is helping irrigate, and George, on vacation from Michigan. Fellow Paul appeared too. Mary Anne, it seems, is going to stick! Yeah! She's tall, with long brown hair and glasses, rather quiet.

Tuesday: Larry took in the milk run on this snowy morning. The ditch continues in a torrent. For the night, it is bypassing the bare field and is going to the alfalfa and grass below.

On the water front we are lucky. On other fronts, we have problems. Candy still shows no heat and her milk is down, very likely because of her cut teat. Right now this prize cow is a problem.

And Larry hit a parked car today with the heavy Rizzo truck. This is a great fear; that we will have an accident. As soon as we get professional and are earning more money, I'd like to insure the truck. Until then, we must go on luck. Larry was a bit careless, and today it cost us $100 to sell milk, and a terrible embarrassment. Thank goodness it wasn't worse. It's a head-on collision on a narrow street I worry about.

May 3: We work to the sound of hard snow pelting the greenhouse. I put in some work on the grant application. Larry got his chick coop together, and we moved it over to the hogan.

I showed visiting fellow Paul some lines of fence that need stringers, and he set to work with baling wire to weave the fence more cow proof, happy to be able to be put to work.

Thursday: Larry got the electric motor mounted on the bottle washer after hours of work. Paul worked on the fences all day, making real progress. Gene washed bottles for us. Next he took cedar bark and wood chips out of the woodpile and made some extensive paths to keep us out of the mud. He doesn't have to be directed to see what needs to be done; he can see it. This is a consciousness that is fairly rare.

Jon, Dee, and Mary Anne made a quick trip to Santa Fe with all our candles. They sold out, bringing back cheese and noodles, and the treasury has $119 in it. Good.

Candy, our bit of a problem cow, is way down in production. I have taken over milking her; Jon was getting too uptight. So he agreed he might as well take a break, since it was turning milking from a pleasant task to a real bummer.

May 8: The sun is out—the storm passed. Fellow Paul left today, and Xavier returned. He has got a job possibility in Colorado. He asked if he could stay a few days. Of course. I mentioned to Gene that he would probably be well accepted here if he'd like to stay. Another batch of candles is ready for delivery. We're having trouble getting wax.

Sandy and Dee planted more lettuce, spinach, peas, and carrots. The first planting is showing up. Spinach is up in a nice neat row. Inside all tomatoes are surviving.

May 13: What's new at New Buffalo? Very quietly a transformation has taken place. Brother Gene has slipped into our lives. It's a wonderful thing that we are an open community so that new people can join us. The return should be some marvelous people.

Last night I couldn't face the night dairy cleanup. But the chores got done. In the kitchen the two senior ladies were squawking about the dishes. I have a suspicion Gene later cleaned up in there too. Gene's wiry, but he's got the energy. He is one of the very few people who have come here that has picked up on the irrigation. We truly needed the help of some gentle folk, and we've got it. Leo gave him a baby lamb yesterday.

Larry is going to Oregon with Mary Anne to get her daughter! They bought wax to earn money.

May 14, 1978: Fabulously beautiful days. A quiet gets pressed on the country. The sun intensely covers everything. Combined with the wet soil, the huge fields of green absorb the rays and almost grow before my eyes.

Sandy has transplanted most cabbage and broccoli into the garden soil. Onion sets, beets, and peas are up. I've made a little more progress on the NCAT application.

Sunday we finally gave red water, blackleg, malignant edema, and pasteurella shots to four milk cows and two big steers. It's pretty easy to get nicely kicked. They forgot to teach this on the subways in New York. With more practice, we'll get faster and surer. Kemal gave us the serum. Thanks.

We need another cow. Because we are too dependent on the four we have, May 23 we will dry up half our herd and have about nine to nine-and-a-half gallons a day. But when they come in July 23, we will have about sixteen gallons—$32 a day. So we have $26 worth of milk after feed. If one cow goes down, one-forth of our herd, that would make a big difference. Too much rests on a single cow and everything can happen to livestock, so if we are smart, we'll start saving in July for another cow, which is probably $700. When I was down in Albuquerque, dairymen said cows went up. If we don't invest in cows now, I don't think we'll make it. The money we do make just supports us.—Jon

Tuesday: Larry and Mary Anne took off in the Grey Ghost to Oregon. Good luck and safe driving. They expect to come back as quickly as possible. I did the Tuesday run. I gave Leah $60 toward her damaged car.

May 18: Time advances. The day dawned clear and remained absolutely brilliant. Still frost in the mornings. I don't expect that to end as a rule until around June 1. It's such a fine line; it is so close to losing our frost-free days entirely. The hot weather has just started. Today Sandy got me to turn on the garden ditch, and she and Dee did a thorough watering of the two plantings that are in. There is talk in the news media of another Ice Age. Eighty-nine thousand years ago, an Ice Age developed in a period of just a hundred years.

Gene noticed one of our delivery refrigerators was smelly from spilled milk. He washed the refrigerator and taped the holes. Jon got the loaded truck out to the place we'll manure, then he called a tractor junkyard in Alamosa, and seems they do have a dump rake. Great! Next week we'll go for it.

May 23: Ditch came on strong last night. I discovered this morning that we had a lot of water. On the one front, our land is having a great year. We have more crops on more acres than ever. The amount of perennial hay is much greater with the new field getting better established every day.

On the cow front, we've got three heifers growing up and two due to freshen soon. Still the herd looks frustratingly small, but it is bigger and more valuable than ever. Beth, our super cow, gave thirty pounds tonight. She's doing great.

On the barn effort front, there is some progress. I have a complete application made, thirty-eight pages plus some appendixes.

We've got some Community Action Program people aware of us. In two days they'll get someone out; we hope to get a letter of recommendation. Seems they'll be helpful. Already they made two copies of our proposal. The County Extension agent will be here next week to see our farm. He'll lend his support, too. Hopefully, we can get a really good application off in a week or two.

Larry came back alone—without Mary Anne! This is the second married lady who's had a fling with him then returned to her husband. One of these days though, he'll be in love with a gal who will really appreciate him.

The good with the bad: Our fields are great; this is very significant. But our main piece of equipment, the tractor, is ruined; there is still water in the oil. A new tractor, we just can't afford.

On the good, Candy cow finally came into heat! But when Tieder went to breed her, he found it impossible to enter the cervix; he had to deposit the sperm outside the cervix, giving us a poor chance of getting her pregnant. So it's a bull for her next month, and if we're lucky, she's already pregnant. The odds are against us. Here we are milking but two cows. For two months we'll be in quite a poor situation for money.

May 29: Jon looked at and measured Carlos' iron rake wheels. One is so sure to fit the mower in town that we saw, that Jon bought the mower and brought it home. Friend Chet and lady friend Tracy came by this morning. Chet helped Jon retrieve the rake.

In the garden, Sandy giving the peas a nitrogen boost because of some yellow leaves. She also cultivates and weeds as she mixes in the nourishment. The greenhouse porch looks very good. Tomato bushes are growing. The marigolds are getting big.

May 30: Jeff came up and put in the new water-line trench that Sandy and Dee wanted. The centralized water faucet in the courtyard will now make it easier to water the greenhouses. Sandy ordered a very long rubber hose of excellent quality from the Sears Catalog Center in Taos.

From NCAT (National Center for Appropriate Technology) we got a response to a letter I wrote. It says they ran out of money in March. They hope to get refunded in June, and they will send us a copy of the up-to-date application when they have the money. It is a good thing that I wrote to them before just sending off the application. I did pick up ten copies of our barn plans from Community Action Program in Taos. They've been helpful.

We found an Allis Chalmers engine at Durand's in Albuquerque for the cost of $500. I think we can get a complete tractor for that price. Ours is no smooth road to success. But great things achieved usually are not done without numerous obstacles.

May 31, 1978: Today, Sandy, Tracy, Chet, and I planted green beans and brought water to the garden and the new alfalfa field. A bunch of us finished installing the new courtyard faucet. We had some very hard ground to pick through. Finally Jon attached the two pipes, and the faucet is working. Our company really helped out. A new guest, young man with very red face—fell drunk asleep in the sun.

We are quite mellow. Our very busy Mr. Larry did mess up some this past month. The tractor cracked, and lots of expense to try and fix it. And then the accident, hitting a parked car. But Larry is essential here, so we have hardly mentioned it at all. We need to keep each other feeling good.

June 6, 1978: Lots of thunder and threatening clouds in the afternoons. No rain—irrigation continues. Dee is off to get her two sons in San Diego. Jon, Deek, and Chet are mudding the floor in the room that will be for them to live in. Yes, Deek, good friend of Chet and of ours is here.

Two ladies spent the night. One of them, Robin, helped in the garden for an hour and did a very good job weeding the little carrots. Her friend Page helped George, while Larry and I dipped candles.

George is not the usual fellow we meet. I like greeting a variety of folks. George has short hair. It's normal for him to be employed often. He's got some clothes, car, bike, and a little bank account. He's friendly—quiet— likes Jason a lot. He bought some fireworks for Jason's birthday. Now Jason is away with Bob Moore on a visit to the Ortiviz Ranch. He went up with a truckload of people, your genuine hippie caravan. A few of them looked awfully dirty. That does not appeal to me.

June 11: My sister came out with her beau, T. Ben, and spent the night. His mother, Ruth, is Clarice's good friend. And here's Jim Preston, very excited to be back at New Buffalo. Good that he likes us so much! He's milking Candy now, and I'm off of milking for a bit.

Sandy and I took a short trip to Ortiviz—the Huerfano Community Farm—our sister commune. I saw a number of the people there that I know: Daddy Dave, Steve Reins, Pat Reins (New Buffalo originals), Jeff, Susie, Raz, Elaine, Peter, Red Rocker Peter, David Henry, Sage, Tomas, Debra, Paul, Mei Hua, Arnie, and other friends.

Like us, they need a tractor. Until then, a team of horses will get them by. They have put more energy into separate dwellings, and their central place remains rather neglected. The garden is excellent, and they boast a new chicken coop that has separate facilities for different birds and different age groups. Susie does great stained glass, but it's not like our candle shop, where several people know the craft and it provides a constant income.

The Bobs showed me some terrific double thermal pane windows for their future houses. My own consciousness would be to get that central building together with hot water and washing facilities, not think of more houses.

America. It is an unusual situation; a lot of people do have little share of wealth. Steve Reins, who was at this commune and Libre, is now with a gal named Lynne, who was also into communes not so long ago. She's got some money and bought a good little alfalfa farm, and they live there. Tomas and Debra, who lived at Ortiviz for years, now have their own little farm with help from her Dad. I think Tomas will do very well. He's thinking of raising heifers for sale and doing custom farm work. Beara has got some land too.

I'm so conscious of how close a thing it is we've got. Our tractor is screwed, and we have about $100 savings. Only two weeks until hay cutting; we play it very close. Deek and Chet have been rebuilding Chet's engine. They've got it almost done. Tracy has been a great help in the garden and is a very cheerful and attractive twenty-one–year-old gal. Bubbly and vivacious, she is a compliment to the scene. She and Sandy have fun working together.

The tractor, now that the head has been taken off, does not run well, says Jon. I'm going to talk to our neighbor Al to see if he will be on standby to help us in a pinch.

June 14, 1978: Candy cow seems to have come into heat. We suspect she got bred by a neighborhood bull that broke in overnight. We herded him down the road and out the gate to find his way home.

Nature gives us lots of water. But she has also sent a terrible infestation of some insect, the worms of which live on the upper part of the alfalfa. The damage is extensive, so we've decided to cut. This should kill the worms, and hopefully the next growth will not be so infected.

Progress: The electric company advance man, Bob Gowing, was up today. We have to choose where we want our new pole at the barn site to be located. This means it is going to happen.

Just as it should be, there's a crew fixing the building. Gene, Jim, George, and visitor John are continuing the mudding of the south wing in the bright sunshine.

Jon and I got the mower and tractor ready; she started right up. And she does fine; that's a relief. I half expected her to quit. But no, except for the water in the oil, she's normal, which is terrific. The mower, too, worked fine.

Deek left with Tracy and Chet, who say they'll be back but also may find something else. Sandy wants them to return. Chet left his truck here because it still was leaking a lot of oil. It may have other problems too.

In the kitchen Mr. Gene keeps the counters clean and does a very thorough job washing dishes. We only have one lady, Sandy, here now. But she needn't feel burdened, because some men have taken responsibility to see that the kitchen is clean, dinner is planned, and shopping keeps happening.

Friday: With today and yesterday's sales, we somehow made a little money. We won't have a decent sort of income until our Guernsey and Jersey freshen. The pasture is plenty adequate in grass. The meadow is a fantastic resource.

We picked up the hay today that was cut yesterday. I like making the first cut in the good June weather. It should always be done. College Jim and I did more mowing. We cut the fields with the worst damage. The tractor is working fine. We need more pitchforks.

The haystack is neat. Only one person is on the stack as it is built, so it doesn't get too compressed. Then the sides and top are open to this baking sun in a blue sky, so the hay continues to dry, making it very high quality. Haying is beautiful.

The ditch is on just enough to slowly water the garden, a very little bit, but it keeps coming. The rest of the place is drying out under a pretty intense sun. The land is in good shape; new fields are established enough so they can take this continuous sun. Soon all the water will be shifted to the western fields.

Sandy works in the garden every day. Gene washes kitchen dishes every day. I get something started for dinner any night there isn't a cook. Now nine years old, Jason made a big pot of bulgur and a golden bowl cake, playing his role to help us out.

June 23: All our new plants are being saved with some irrigation from this hot sun, which is baking us for weeks on end with little sign of clouds. I am enthralled being out under the blue sky in the dry air. How can people love concrete and asphalt and sit in traffic?

Jim nailed up the first chicken wire for the south-wing retainer wall. Gene oiled and tarred the five canales. It feels good that we're making progress with fixing up our pueblo; that wing looked like it was falling apart.

George baked some cookies. He's been taking Jason out quite a bit: to a movie, to bike ride at the airport, and to the rodeo tomorrow.

June 24: Wood run to Garcia Park for aspen poles for the proposed new corrals. Jon, Larry, Gene, and Jim went out and got a full load. Great.

June 30, 1978: Big storm the last few days. Dee has returned. When Jon picked her up, he took candles to Albuquerque, sold out, and got some potentially big orders from a number of shops, expanding this nice little business. Jon's anxious to "buy cows." Both of us are anxious to be really producing dairymen, doing the business we have talked about for some time.

Larry and Jim jacked up the big circle-room roof after Larry repaired the hydraulic jack. They cut a hole in the support, put a brace through it, and lowered the log onto two supports. The ceiling was raised nine inches—no small trick. Good job. I put a little more chicken wire up for the concrete cap on the south wing. Also started making a desk for Jason.

July 1, 1978: We had our monthly meeting. It costs about $600 a month to keep us going. These meetings are a good idea.

Coming up is the finishing of the south-wing retainer wall. College Jim says he'll help buy cement and sand. Also coming up is the constant candle production. We got more orders from Taos. Jon hopes, in thirty days, to have $1,000 worth of candles. A cow and Lascolite plastic to cover the greenhouse, he proposes to spend it on. Thank goodness we have two cows coming fresh soon. That will be a big help.

At the house is fellow Jack. He's very tan. The good fellow's been camping out alone by the river for months. He comes up here once in a while. Last few days, he's been staying here. He has a bunch of colored wooden beads. He made himself a necklace and is stringing another.

July 2: Gene put a motorcycle wheel on a stand, made wooden parts, then used clutch plate springs, electrical conduit, and some oak boards to create, with some help from Larry, a very fine candle-dipping machine! Today a crew made 240 pairs of candles. And they dyed them! Almost every day, candles are made or colored.

My sophisticated friend Charles Haseloff from City College days spent a few marvelous days here on vacation from New York. We did some hoeing in the sweet corn together. My first memory of Charles was his ordering vermouth on a plane when we were both headed for Europe. Charles has an obvious German accent. Being the avante garde artiste, one wall of his apartment was decorated with children's dolls he had found on the streets of New York; a little macabre for me, but he's a lovely fellow.

July 6: Retainer wall is all ready for concrete, but there is no cement available in all of northern New Mexico! That is very odd.

Life is pretty relaxed as the summer advances. Our barn project is stalled, but many good tasks that we've set for ourselves are being worked on. We're not too rushed. We have the time to leisurely do some of the fine-tuning that makes the place improve. Larry is at the chicken coop, redesigning and putting up new oiled roosts. There is good cross-ventilation now and more room.

I read a lot about space travel and adventure. When off with a group to meet many challenges, it is important to have cleaver, resourceful people. For us it is true too. When you do get together with a competent group, it feels great. Such should be the eventual reward of making oneself useful and skillful.

July 9: A hot summer continues. We picked up hay bales with neighbor Carlos Trujillo—storms threatened—no rain though. Carlos is trading us a cattle rack for helping pick up his first cut. We really enjoy working with Carlos and having a good lunch with him and his family.

Carlos has worked very hard to make his little ranch prosper. He's sixty-two years old and has about thirty-two cows and several horses. He shoes horses for income and has a little welding shop. Carlos has a very neat, low-ceiling house, neat corrals, and small barn. He's an expert with horses and ranching.

In the news a story I like, Howard Jarvis in California leads successful tax revolt. Voters reduced property tax by 57 percent and mandated that it would not rise more than two percent a year. A big block of voters is seeing if they can control the government. Good.

Jarvis has a fantastic story. A retired successful businessman, he has campaigned long and hard against the inhuman raising of taxes by bureaucrats in their fancy county seats. In one year, his cause escalated to terrific success after a long period of sticking with it.

What I would like to see: Instead of government taking money for massive social welfare and services, have the people be more generous, more thoughtful in how they use their money; more imaginative in seeing what good they can help accomplish in the world.

July 10: Storms threaten. Recovered the hay and even got a sprinkle. George, Gene, and I got the front end entirely back together on the truck except for adjusting the brakes.

George baked two terrific loaves of bread. It is quite nice having him here. He's quiet, courteous, mature—over forty—likes the kids, and has a childish youthfulness about him. But Sandy had some words with him. She is concerned he spends too much time alone with Jason. Enough!

I spent some time with a frail nervous fellow who was here overnight. He seems rather inexperienced but is making an effort to learn to live more outside; do more camping and live cheaply under the sky and whatever little shelter he can find. He talks to himself a great deal, but can talk directly and perfectly coherently to a person, too. Good luck. I hope he can feel good in this beautiful land.

Last summer for the dairy we got some basic equipment. This summer for the dairy we are adding greatly to our hay and pasture. The barn, though, is stalled for lack of funds. The kids are having a fine summer, and we are enjoying our little extended family. We're doing well together.

July 13, 1978: First adobe bricks of the season were made yesterday. Two German visitors came and a fellow named Skip—a country lad—and since we don't have much else to do, we cranked up the mud. Jim and I fixed two hoses with parts that Mike Pots had bought. Then Larry did a little plowing, and he,

Jim, and the two visitors made bricks. In the afternoon a big storm rolled up and this one hit us. Some of the new bricks were ruined. We did get the hay and the dry bricks covered.

Tonight, miles away, a terrific storm is letting loose. Tons of lightning—a strong wind blowing—all hell breaking loose someplace but not here.

July 17: Crystal cow gave us a heifer calf Saturday afternoon! She is very cute, dark brown, and seems fine. This is a little more like it; now we've got four heifers—our future.

Gene and I cut and raked oat hay, and we brought in both western fields and stacked them. Each day storms threaten and a little spray hits us but no rain, and we are able to bring the hay in. Each day dawns clear. Then around three p.m. the storms are swirling around us.

Neighbor Manuel Martinez had a ewe with a prolapsed anus. His wife didn't want it, so he very nicely gave it to us. Jon and I slaughtered. Next day I butchered and froze it. Sandy froze peas and broccoli for winter.

Jon and Dee loaded $600 worth of candles into the pickup. They've got all our money. Jon wants a cow, and he's putting his effort on the line. Good luck. At worst, they'll come back with a bunch of money. Finding a good-quality cow is not easy.

Visiting German student Gilbert, Larry, College Jim, and I stacked the 840 bricks that were made in the past days. Now the fields are clear for another batch to be made. This is some progress toward our barn. Jim has great enthusiasm and energy. Of all the teenagers in the USA, at least one has found us and contributes a lot.

The new little heifer is doing great. She's lively and has learned to drink from the bottle. Her sister Rikki is looking terrific, more and more like a milk cow. It won't be too long, and we'll be breeding her.

July 21: About midnight the pickup rolled up. They did it; sold out and brought home a cow! It took four full days. The cow is a good-looking, six-year-old Holstein. She seems quite gentle. From our old friend Leo Rizzo, we got her. She's pregnant—due in December. Bought for $650. I haven't heard all the story on the cow market, but Jon got the best he could, I think. So, we'll be milking five cows very soon for a record amount of milk for our farm. That's great.

The sky was very cloudy, and we got a little rain again in the afternoon. The hay needs some sun to get it dry. Our alfalfa fields are a sea of green;

23. *The new kitchen garden. Photo by Sandra Kopecky.*

they're just about ready for cutting again. We'll have to look for a break in the weather. Sandy froze up broccoli this morning. The garden got relief from all this sun by getting rained on.

Personal sketches: Gene, he's strong enough though very thin. He has a little beard and fairly long, light-brown hair. He's very quiet, but we are getting to know him. When he first came, he told me he was in the Navy and spoke about the process he had to go through to psych out. Very difficult.

Recently Gene lived in Hawaii; had a child and woman. Then later traveling alone with his backpack, he decided that living alone was not where it was at for him. He went to the Farm in Summertown, Tennessee and said, "I want to grow with the farm." They said it wasn't good enough, and after a week he left. Now he has found us, a little family that deep down is craving some good consciousness; some people from out there who can appreciate the life New Buffalo offers. After the trauma with Rebel, it seems necessary to our survival, as a group on this land, to be more discerning about who moves in.

Rebel and Lena are back in town and plenty belligerent evidently. They are camped just opposite us on the other side of the Hondo gorge; the only people who have viciously turned against the commune, and they own an acre almost adjoining us.

Pepe, my good friend and idol, fed Rebel's gangster instincts with his careless talk of "Let's take over the commune." Reb got so out of it, that he then announced to the Mabel Dodge commune that they could move out to New Buffalo now that he'd cleared it of some of us scum. Rebel's mental balance is delicate, and he makes me extremely nervous. Jon and I reviewed the operation of our few firearms. Rebel can be expected to come up here—armed—if he is in a bad mood and wants something.

Thank God we've got a good household. I'm very glad Gene has found us, and young Jim is just great, and I don't want him to leave us and go back to school. The commune needs to be nurtured; needs to have the energy of good-hearted, optimistic people. So many have left us. Let's make it a productive and happy place.

Larry, Jim, and Gene went off to Carlos's and worked most of the day picking up bales. Larry and Jim had their first taste of the Trujillos' country hospitality—a real treat.

Can we do as well? It is up to the people—the people who see New Buffalo and want it to live. This is definitely a challenge. Our love and perseverance in our work should weigh heavily in our favor. Kachina and Carol are here. She's been having a difficult married life with dear John, whom she loves.

Maggie (roommate of Brian's in Albuquerque), who is spending a few days, and Dee picked peas. Maggie, Dee, Sandy, and my mom, Clarice, shelled them. My mom spent the night. I'm very glad she does come out and enjoys our home. Jon mentioned to me what a nice group we have this summer. Yes, I agree.

The financial challenge: We owe Rizzo $50, Jeff $10, the vet $35 and Leah $20. We need a generator for the delivery truck, a tire for the pickup, a tire for Larry 's car, and $30 for ditch fee so we can get water. Soon we should have sixteen or more gallons per day of milk.

A multitude of ferocious storms swirled around us this evening. Our oat hay, just about ready for picking up, got a little wet. Yet, with luck, we will finally get it in tomorrow.

July 23: We did a little mowing for neighbor Manuel and had to clean the spark plugs to get the tractor to run. For a moment, we thought it had breathed its last. We got most of our hay in today before another short, light rain stopped the work. We were picking up the fourth and last load when we had to quit.

Rebel, reminding me of his return as he sits across the valley with his rifle and takes shots in my direction. I keep doing my work in the fields, sure he won't actually kill me, but it is unnerving.

July 24: We got the rest of our oat hay into the big stack just as another storm approached from the east. The wind blew hard, the clouds got dark, but the storm dissipated; we never got a drop.

More peas got frozen—beans and squash are flowering. The storms are cooling the weather; it's the old race with the frost now. Lots of tomatoes on the vines, peppers, and some eggplants protected inside the greenhouses.

Our barbed wire fencing has done it again! Our new cow—big, quite attractive, and with a big udder—was charging away from a giant horse fly and swung her bag alongside the barbed wire and got one fairly bad cut.

She is gentle and pretty easy to manage, but she's never been hobbled. This is the first cow we have been unable to restrain. Jon milked her last night and got kicked several times, one kick glancing his face. This morning she was not milkable; Jon got a little, but we let her go. Some day we'll get rid of all that barbed wire.

Around noon we brought this cow up and had a calm session with her. We put a lasso around one kicking, giant hind leg, and this restrained her enough so that after a dozen passes or so, I was able to milk her out. Jon ordered a Can't Kick restraining strap and hopefully it will work. Until then, we'll just have to milk her as a group effort the best we can.

But, we have noticed a bad feature—leaky teats! This makes the cow very susceptible to mastitis, I imagine, and she may not even be able to keep a full bag without losing it all day. It's very tricky buying a cow out of someone's milking herd; Jon may have been just a little over anxious. He did see some nice heifers, but he wanted a milking cow. It's experience.

Gene has improvised halters on the two new heifers, which are doing very well; they're getting lively. I'm training Abby, the Holstein, to lead and eat in the headstall. Gene's got a halter on Jessica now. This training is very important.

Carol, Kachina, Jack, Maggie, Sandy, Jason, Jon, Dee, Larry, Gene, the two kids, and I are here at New Buffalo. We're waiting anxiously for Kim and Peggi to pay a visit. We pooled our money and paid that ditch fee and got the water. We were still working on the sweet corn when we set up for the night. This was an important watering for the garden.

July 29, 1978: Bricks were made, hay was cut, and then the wooden pitman arm on the mower broke, and we spent several hours custom-making a new one. We're ready to cut again tomorrow.

Dee and Sandy bought some good little peaches in town and canned them up all day. In the winter it's fine working around the huge, hot, wood-burning stove. In the summer it is sweltering work.

Fellow Lee staying here in his trailer. A big fellow—quiet, serious, and quite nice. He's been cleaning out the barn and bucking up our fallen-down cottonwood tree with his chainsaw, taking in hay, mounting Dee's tires, helping with firewood and granola preparation.

Out in the field I was moving the water with a shovel when two shots rang out and the dirt a few feet away spit up some dust—Rebel taking some long shots at me from across the valley. I intentionally kept working for a while, but this is not what I got into the movement for.

August 3, 1978: Two pretty ladies were down from Lama Foundation. They shop for hundreds of pounds of food on Thursdays and get ten gallons of milk and up to twenty dozen eggs from us. I'm really anxious to get Grade A before getting bigger.

Got the Miracle Cow Can't Kick device. The new cow's milk tests negative on the California Mastitis test; a very good sign because of her leaky teats. Today there was no leaking until just about milking time. It seems she is rehabilitating quickly, after only several weeks on the farm. Her appetite is fine. Her milk production has gone up.

We are now getting up to twenty gallons of milk a day. We drink several gallons ourselves. Dee made yogurt cheesecake, and Sandy is making butter again. It will take a month or so to clear away debts we've accumulated, and get things like new tires that we've been putting off.

Had our monthly meeting. Gene is now "officially" accepted as an equal member. And we have a new man on the scene. Lee's a big man, with a well-trimmed but full beard. An unlikely fellow (we are all unlikely characters) who was thinking of hunting coyotes if things didn't turn out positive at the commune, he lives in a camper with several quality possessions. He carries tools for the tree cutter's trade. And he feels he's been spiritually directed this way. Pepe and I were going to disappear into the desert ourselves when our fate brought us to New Buffalo's gate.

The weather plays further games with us. We finished bringing in the hay, over half of which is of very good quality. It takes years to learn to do it right. We will judge as we cut through the big stacks.

August 8: We now have the water; a very strong stream is in the ditch. We are moving forward in the grand attempt to do a complete watering of all our irrigated fields. Fellow Tony is helping me. We have to move a lot of dirt and plants to keep the long ditches big, so they can carry the water to all the spots. Cutting through the alfalfa plants is especially difficult. I keep an eye to the other side of the valley for Rebel. I don't say anything to Tony, like "Oh by the way, someone may take some shots at us; don't pay him any mind!"

In the clean kitchen, though very rustic, are a bowl of carrots and peas fresh from the garden and rows of colorful, newly canned vegetables. The flies are not so bad with our many screens. A porch (as what Reb had in mind) would make the kitchen more fly-proof. Before the screens, a couple of people would create a walking barrier of flapping towels, propelling the flies northward out of the open windows and door, an excellent technique for removal of flies in mass quantities.

Bricks are getting made, and our grant application will go out this week. Bob Dowling should be down to help pick up the pace and make bricks. Jim Preston is determined to get that job done before he returns to the college campus and his many friends.

We now have new man Tony here with us. Tall and handsome, he walked with the Indian-Cross-Country Walk, protested the Trident Nuclear Sub and worked with the L.A. Catholic workers. He also worked for a rendering plant in Michigan. He's in the tower, which George just moved out of. George found a place in Arroyo Seco.

August 11, 1978: Three days of irrigation with two good streams of water pretty much irrigated the entire western section, about fifteen acres. At least five times I cleaned long lengths of clogged ditch to get full pressure to a certain area. Tony picked up on it a bit. He's away to Hopi land for a few days. Jon is not impressed with Tony.

Dee's boys, Steven and Matthew, are living here now. Steve, the oldest, is very considerate and interested in the farm. Matthew is a great friend with

24. *The tower. Circa 1990. From the personal collection of Chamisa WeinMeister*

Jason. He's got lots of energy. Dee and Jon fixed them up a very nice room—simple used furniture—clean and spacious. It's good to have them here; they seem to like it.

The NCAT—National Center for Appropriate Technology—grant application went out. So good luck to us. Hopefully someone will pick up on the potential we have and give us that extra lift.

Daddy Dave was here; we spent some time together. Razberry was here too, my old friend from the early Bolinas, California, days. They are some of my basic family.

JOURNAL 23

We are part of the evolving, living consciousness of what peace means.

August 20, 1978: We got a short hit of water today. Sandy made me go send it to the garden. We just had time to irrigate most of it before the water stopped. Good thing she insisted!

Jim, Tony, Larry, and Lee made over 400 bricks. We're getting close to 5,000 for the new barn. Chet's brother Bill arrived and gravitated toward some mechanical work.

Lee cut a pile of cedar wood for the kitchen with his big saw before he left to return to his lumbering job. They cut all trees over six inches in diameter. They get ninety cents per tree regardless of size. Too bad he left. Another good man gone.

August 24: Good life on the farm. In this plentiful season we put away the fruits and vegetables. Beans and tomatoes have been canned in the last few days. Today we have a big effort with Art, Jim, Bill, Sandy, Gene, and Maggie picking and then freezing a dozen or more big quarts of cut-off-the-cob sweet corn. The work is easy as a group endeavor.

Jim and Larry made the last adobe bricks. Then they called it quits and brought back the tools. We had eggnog and brandy, and all got happily tipsy to celebrate the occasion. We wished Jim a good year at school; he is leaving us soon.

September 6, 1978: On August 25 I took off hitchhiking and dove into the world—off to Fort Worth, Texas, for what turned out to be fourteen days. It took me four days to get to Mel's, 800 miles away. I ended up hitching 460 miles, walking great distances—watching the traffic—working two days for some kind people and taking a $48 bus ride to get where I intended. I was a bit homesick the while and just a bit uneasy, since we've had some unsettling things happen still not so removed. But I thought I should go, and such was popular opinion too.

I spent some time with a good friend and met a number of his friends, and I helped him work on his house. I'm glad to be back, and there's a lot to do. Happy to see Sandy—haven't seen Mr. Emil yet; he's asleep.

Things are good here. Our life is not dull. The circle started to fall in again. There was some altercation over Tony, but he has stuck through it. A few frosts have occurred. No water has been gotten. It's very important now that we do get water; it's overdue. Also it's time to cut, but we do not have a spare pitman arm or spare knife; that is not very prepared. Neighbor Al, though, will probably be able to back us up.

New Lascolite is on Dee's greenhouse. The concrete work has started on the retainer wall. There are new tires on the pickup truck. We're getting over a hundred eggs a day. Still a good flow of milk.

September 7: The fall colors are coming in; the green weeds are burning to a dull yellow. The chamisa bushes are flowering, tinting the countryside gold-yellow. The land is terribly dry in many places. Around the house I watered some of the green grass that was dying off. The garden and the new fields desperately need water; they needed it two weeks ago! Right around the house some extensive weeding—tidying up the grounds—has happened. A Puerto Rican fellow was here for three days and did a nice job.

As soon as Jon and I started to cut, another piece broke off the mower! I gave Jon and Bill $90 so they could go to Alamosa to look for a variety of parts for the mower so we can just mow without interruptions.

Crystal cow was down and had some cheesy stuff in her milk—a worry. Emily, the little heifer, has a loose and light-colored stool—another concern. Jenny cow's milk is down from two weeks ago. The garden shows great sign of heavy frosts, but the greenhouses are excellent.

September 8: We seem to have found the problem with Crystal. Gene changed a technique without mentioning it! He squirts a stream of milk out of the teats before drying the udder and teats. He did this to clean the entrance, but it is the opposite of clean. Germs move much more freely in the wet environment. Ideally, no milk should come out until the teat is clean and dry.

We discovered a mistake and corrected it. But we have a sick cow; one quarter is congested and needs treatment. It will cost us money, and we will lose at least three days milk. This dairying is not easy.

I gathered the water and got permission to use it after speaking with Melacio, who had it. I have become friends with both sides in some of the local water disputes. Melacio has a good-sized ranch that he manages tightly, so the water is extremely important to him. And he has occasional differences (we'll call it), with the Ortiz families who are upstream of him. A good mayordomo, who knows how to manage water, is essential at these junctures. Anyhow, when I first was crossing Melacio's lands, he objected to me, as a public official, carrying a hunting knife. I saw his point and didn't wear it after that. Since then, Melacio has hosted me for lunch at his farm home several times.

Thank goodness the crops are hearty out here. Our little orchard grasses and crested wheat, our new alfalfa plants, and the burned-up pasture below the barn are all still alive, though parched, and if need be, they'll take more of the same if they have to. I walk and run around and get down on the ground.

If I hadn't gone away, I would have gotten the water. A fleeting opportunity was missed. Now the ditch is low, and we are virtually cut off—not a big-enough head of water to reach us.

September 11: The season has changed to fall. The many big chamisa bushes are in full bloom, adding bright yellow to the thirsty landscape. Today the wind blows under a clear blue sky.

The pumpkins are turning color in the garden; the Hubbard squash are a vivid orange. There are hundreds of big marigold blooms—what a picture! Our new, twelve-foot-high Chinese elm trees make a green backdrop for them. One corner of the pueblo has seven-foot-tall hollyhocks in bloom, with poppies and phlox displaying a riot of color among them. Some areas though still look crappy, barren, and weedy. The two long greenhouses, attached to the rooms, could hardly be more glorious, mostly vegetables with a variety of flowers. The cross-ventilation worked extremely well, keeping them cool this summer.

Several visitors are here: Louis and a young lady; a tall fellow, Michael; Bob Dowling from Ortiviz; and young Hans from Germany.

September 13: The sky remains totally clear—the air delicious. Today we take in the last of our hay, and tomorrow the cows get the fields for grazing; they need it. Jon is off to the mountains.

A Hereford bull got into our herd. Jenny was in heat and may very well have gotten bred. Too bad. Gene, who was here and knew a cow was in heat, wasn't aware enough to prevent the bull getting to her. The fence was fixed today.

Event! Larry bought electrical supplies, and he started right in to drill holes and cut wire channels in the mud walls—a modern convenience to be brought to each room. One of our guests cooked a big vegetable soup with more gleanings from our garden.

September 14, 1978: Yesterday we did an oak and pine-wood run to the nearby San Cristobal stash. It was easy going and a pleasant time in the dry, aromatic forest.

The concrete work on the south-wing retainer wall is just about complete. A visitor, who might like to stay, named Michael Gibson, asked me for something to do. I got him to load manure. Michael is tall, fairly thin, quiet, and seems like quite a sensible person. He's been working in town as a carpenter. Hans also wanted to keep busy. I showed him how to clear weeds and revive some of the grass we've got planted in some of our desolate places.

Dee's canning pickles, tomatoes, and applesauce; Sandy's bringing in more onions, squash, and the last beans. Four big trays of diced onions are in the solar dryer. The heavy odor wafts across the land.

Bob brings word that Peter and Elaine, a very sweet, quiet couple, are leaving Ortiviz! So many sincere people have put a lot of energy into these places, received much from them, and then left. The income is so low, the facilities primitive, and personal relations kind of rough. I hope our communes survive and get better. Bob cooked us a very good dinner. He's got a lot of good energy, happy to be among us, and we're very glad to have him now making a regular thing of coming down from Colorado to work with us.

Finally, rain! About ten p.m. last night, Bob and I went and covered the hay as best we could. Sure enough, thunder, lightning, and rain followed, and the sky is now completely overcast as we start Sunday morning chores.

Tony has gone to Oregon. A nice guy but somehow Jon has taken a strong dislike to him.

September 18: Sandy and I mixed up a big boat of mud, at her request, and we mudded the archway and the western doorway. I made an improvement on the end piece of roof; it's sturdier and now looks better. Sandy helped by throwing dirt up on the roof.

Michael finished putting up a new guardrail—hitching post—outside the kitchen to protect plants from vehicles. Big Bill found a wood stash by accompanying some locals on a wood run over Pot Mountain way.

After several years, we're going to make a resolution of the little land dispute we have. Someone is building on a piece of land that is on our deed. I had been told that Justin, Max, Dave, and George from New Buffalo had offered to resolve it in their favor. But they were leery of dealing with hippies, and no formal settlement was ever reached.

Larry continued working on installing electricity. Thanks to Bob, who left this morning, the wire was already buried in the trench when Larry got to the west wing. Carol baked bread. Several of us helped with dinner.

September 21: Sandy got me to move some very dusty rugs out of my room, and then she did a thorough cleaning and rearrangement so my sister would have a nice place to stay when she visits. The simple little room looks quite nice.

A gal Edie, from Kansas City, is staying for a few days in her travels to several communities. She worked with a group in Kansas City that bought several properties, including apartments, and ran a restaurant, a school, and other things. Much is still going on. Some of the people were marvelous. But losing money, too many plans without enough workers, and some con-man type hassles made Edie decide to look further. She seems a powerful, intelligent woman who has really gotten involved in alternative community-type action—just our type. She's been helping do mud work—soon to drive off to California. Too bad.

September 23: The fall season. The sky, mountains, and emerald fields of our valley make a tranquil scene. Our house looks well kept. But underneath not all is peaceful—people—difficult for them to live together with concern and peace.

Jon has been very uptight about Tony. He wants to have his way about this, though the rest of us were being quite friendly with Tony and enjoying his company. Part of the problem was we didn't see how strongly Jon feels. When it comes down to it, we won't make a division over it. Therefore Tony, good man he may be, is rejected. Jon, I guess, still felt his presence, because Tony may be coming back.

So Jon got to shooting his rifle off around the pueblo a bit. "If you don't care about my feelings about Tony, then why should I care about your feelings about guns?" Then it all came out with some shouting—Sandy scared and upset—Jon a bit enraged. Larry, Dee, and I were there, and little Emil, stumbling about the sun porch. It ended with a big hug between Jon and Sandy. Our visitor Edie thought it was good—out in the open.

So this did resolve an issue; Tony will not be invited to stay if he returns; shooting will move, once more, off the property. Perhaps we'll have a weekly talk session. Good idea. We can improve our ability to communicate—to articulate; this is a type of self-improvement. We do have to do some novel things to get us closer—higher—more conscious of each other. Jon went off with Michael to start a job. Feelings are well resolved here, for which I am very thankful.

I hate to even mention it, but Rebel is still making his presence felt. He hit David Pratt, one of the peyote church leaders, at Dennis Long's house just to vent some feelings.

We want things to resolve peacefully in our community and our world. There are so many really peaceful people—most people are. Consciousness is heightening and awakening, but there is violence. As we read about it in books and the magazines, so we also live with its presence. And we persevere and wonder and hope. Some pray.

Will our prayers for humankind be answered? I believe so. Will, in time, an Aquarian Age resolve into a more peaceful world? I believe so. We are part of the evolving, living consciousness of what peace means. A commune tries to apply it in the everyday life. It requires more caring, nonviolence, consideration, quiet, and sharing. Often it does not work. The general consciousness is not good enough.

Living in this scene can be difficult. Our life is sacrifice in some ways; an uncertain gamble that one's life will be secure and rewarding. I still can believe and say all the faithful things, but I am less naïve, a little less positive. My world has been shaken a bit.

I look for good things to happen, too. And I see perseverance as one of those virtues that help create the solid type of happening I want to be part of. What does it matter? It always matters how you conduct yourself.

The electricity is in. It's good to have constructive things to do. There is lots of winterizing going on. The place really has never looked better. The greenhouses are a tremendous improvement; the retainer walls were absolutely necessary to keep the houses from falling apart.

Michael Gibson bought two sacks of concrete on the black market for $5.50 each. My sister and her beau T. Ben and Mom were out last night. Good to see them.

September 25: We got quite a good rain lasting over two nights and two days. This takes pressure off of getting the irrigation water. I love to walk the fields, especially the new ones, and see the wonderful plants that make valuable pastures out of formerly barren ground, with only an occasional tuft of poor grass.

Another day: The vet says Mabelene is not pregnant—duh. Also her teat ends are like deep wormholes. It is obvious that they are abnormal. But he says, "Yes, Candy is pregnant!" That is very good news.

Larry's got a daughter in Oklahoma City! Marilyn says she knows that Larry's her dad. I'm sure the right woman will join Larry some time. Such a loyal husband he would be. Meanwhile, his romances have given him a rough time, except he doesn't show it too much. He's quiet, self-contained, and has the power of a deep religious conviction. Good man. But having a daughter that he can't be with, that's got to hurt.

Carol baked bread. The homey aroma of bread and cedar wood is suspended in the warm air. Maggy churned butter; this is country living.

News: Revolution in Nicaragua; in Iran many angry people, too. Once again, it's a revolt against a very wealthy man.

My own optimism about people is getting that little beating. Feel uneasy about a few in the neighborhood who are against Sandy and me—controversy and especially violence and aggression. I'm more determined to be peaceful myself: cooperative, gentle, never short or angry. And Rebel, again, has been showing his true colors with rifle fire directed my way while I was out in the west fields.

At the commune, we have our new friend Michael Gibson. I'm glad he's here and getting along well. He's got a good mind for mechanics and carpentry and has a good consciousness.

September 28: As of this evening, I have put some antifreeze in each vehicle of our six-vehicle fleet. The red truck and the tractor have the worst radiators and must be watched closely.

We recently got some land survey help for free. The neighbors do have a legal claim to the disputed three acres, so it is no simple thing to settle. We are learning more about our boundaries.

The kids are very glad to have electric light in their rooms. Welcome to the modern era!

September 29, 1978: I asked Gene how he likes New Buffalo. "The greatest!" he said.

We came out a little ahead on the milk run; the dairy had $90 and the treasury has over $200. We shipped Mabelene off to market with Sonny Wetzel; she may bring near $500, or we may have to take her back and brand her.

Sandy and I would like to get a car or truck of our own. After seven full years, I want to save some money for me and the little family. I've used mostly hand-me-down clothes, taken my vacations with $20 or so in hand, and constantly applied my earnings to what I thought were the most needed things here. Now I feel the need for more independence. If things really turn against us, I want a means of moving. Never have I considered this sort of idea until Rebel turned violently against some of us.

Still I believe in the commune and have obligations to people and the farm and the Grade A project. And I like my home. "I have a dream." Martin Luther King, Jr. made that remark famous. I have a sense of that too. As a matter of fact, that's a reason I write—to work it out—just what it is that is a better world—a fairer, happier world at peace.

Another commune-type scene dissolves. Ramon used to live at La Bolsa, a small ranch with a hip scene; that is, young people—changing people—lots of projects. And they helped us out by letting us pick fruit several years that Ramon was there. The property had four hundred fruit trees, good bottom-land, graze for a few cows, a riverfront property, and lots of tools. Now near deserted, only one renter is there. Trees are being cut out. No irrigation happening and no harvest. The place was never made into a corporation. The owners live in Santa Fe, the nearby city.

Family news: Pepe's recent wife, Jennifer, is due in town soon—alone! Pepe's in Texas.

Pepe was the person I was closest to for some time. I consciously thought of myself as serving him. I saw the greatness in him, the possibility for peace in the world, in how he had matured in our fast-changing free world. What role will he play? Will he help our consciousness toward peace and friendship? Will we still be good friends? I certainly hope so. We should be able to have a meeting of minds. We lived together and shared this dream for four or five years. We helped each other—led a fabulous life.

The dream of life. I am prepared to speak very highly of Pepe. I wonder if he will feel positive about me, or if he holds a grudge because I stood with Kim once, and Pepe felt betrayed.

Jon tried to take out a kingpin on the Dodge. But the bolt that holds it in is old, and we couldn't figure out how to get it loose. Larry joined in next day. With pounding and guided blows, they got some grease in without ever taking off those kingpins. Good work.

October 7, 1978: Each morning is now cold. The harvest moon is growing each night. For us in high country, harvest is really over, except we've got apples yet to pick.

Michael Gibson has been adding mud and chicken wire around the alcove and candle-room upper walls. I've been getting ready to do more stonework pathways. The kitchen floor, the circle floor, and roof all are in discussion for remodeling. And we discuss further solarization.

Yesterday Dee and Maggy did the milk run, and Gene, Matthew, Michael, and I took off to the woods to scavenge dry, hard, pine firewood. The forest was very beautiful, and we fortunately found some good wood. My back hurt a bit, but as we got rolling, I felt fine. We managed to break two axes and lose one. But we had a good day and brought in a good load of wood and a big bonus of large flat rocks. The woods were so nice, I'm going to take Sandy and the kids up there tomorrow.

Jon and Larry figured out a good place to hoist the carcass after we kill a steer. Then Jon and Larry plugged in the refrigerated truck, and we are ready to proceed. The meat can go in the new freezer we bought.

I'm reading about Muhammad Ali—world heavyweight boxing champion—in his very well-written autobiography. What a man! He had to face a lot of hate, as do so many black and brown people in the USA.

October 10: Jon has got a job for a few days. Gene and Maggy are constructing a solar collector on the front of their room, adding a door that goes into the alcove instead of directly outside. Good idea. Already the area in front of his room looks more attractive. Before it was just totally ignored.

I've started on a stone-and-concrete entrance walkway that leads to both the kiva and the greenhouse sun porch. This will be the start of some long walkways.

October 12: Michael, our newfound friend, is now helping with the dairy cleanup regularly. The milk run made enough today to pay some of the vet bill. We voluntarily ordered $40 worth of testing; it is well worth it.

Everett, my friend—owner of the Feed Bin—celebrated his birthday today. He told me that, as a boy, he worked after school for a neighbor milking two cows, cutting firewood, and doing other chores for twenty-five cents a week! He saved and saved to buy an eight-dollar bicycle.

I felt good today—did some exercises several times. My plan for personal betterment now is to start making some chairs. First I will finish Jason's desk. Also I will do more stone work. Each additional area enhances the looks of our communal home. If people put some creative effort toward it, in this world there could be a lot less tension and anger and a lot more generosity and happiness. Still the optimist.

I'm in quite a good frame of mind. I dipped another set of candles and cooked dinner. Sandy has not been feeling too fine though, even with me being quite attentive. She's a little burned out on the commune scene, which does have its tensions. It is a pioneering sort of venture—not terribly easy. America does offer now a pretty relaxed comfortable life for those with a little home, a little family, and a little means of income. To trade that for a scene with its potential explosions and rattling of the nerves is difficult.

Then there is the vision of the greater world scene and our changing society. I have had a strong drive to play a role in this. Not to retreat to a comfortable niche, but to take the opportunity and try and do something good that can extend to other people. When we can reach out with our love and wealth to the other peoples, then we can have world peace.

So today I take Sandy and the boys out again. My immediate family needs to feel my love. I believe in the idea of little communities, but it does not negate the need for a close nuclear family, which is one of the greatest things we have.

October 16, 1978: Michael, Sandy, and I butchered—nice neat job. Larry worked on installing an overhead light in the circle—a great move to help us use the space. We were just discussing it, and Larry took action. He also wired in another outlet for the new freezer.

We filled out our 1977 corporation income tax with the help of our lawyer friend Larry Taub. Only a few years ago, this process was an unorganized sort of farce with few records and very little income. Now we're more organized and earning more. This is progress for the commune.

Many others and I have worked not for money but for an ideal—for the commune—for the idea of helping a good thing grow. A Buddhist monk does not figure his praying in terms of an hourly wage, nor the Christian monk or nun. There is a long, if small, tradition of working in service. We, too, work for something that is not figured on an hourly wage basis.

For an ongoing scene, we must be able to provide some money for the members. The candles and dairy will help do this and any other crafts we develop. Also there is the option people have of working jobs as Carol (nursery) and Jon do. I've been getting in a few days of work, too.

Mel came up and also some other friends. We spent some time looking at our greenhouses, which Mel helped build. He joined me in some more stone walkway work and helped with a chef's salad dinner I'd planned. Very quiet around here.

Larry installed a light in the big circle room. Sure enough, it drew people in to have dinner. It's a good move.

October 20: Gene and Maggy got the glazing on their new solar collector today—looks good. The new system should definitely be much warmer.

Jon took Dee to see a doctor in Española, about sixty miles away. She's had some terrible pain these last days. Sandy too, continues to suffer from some pain in her teeth or left side of her face. She has some bad nights.

October 22: Yesterday the clouds descended, and it rained for several hours—a very needed heavy rain. The mountains remain immersed in storm. The earth's plants rejoice. The cows stay out during the day grazing. We continue to pick tomatoes, cucumbers, and peppers for salads. The fruit and other trees and shrubs—displaying fall shades of color—slowly change to dormancy.

Cows broke a post and marched into our hay corral with the four big piles of hay. We got them out. Gene made a temporary fix.

October 23: High dark clouds continue to dominate. Larry is putting the solar panels back on his collector. Another warm season is just about passed. Outside the greenhouses, the wind blows cold.

Michael and I dipped 120 pairs of candles after Dee dyed a batch. Maggy painted a colorful symbol on the new door Gene put on. He did all his construction from what we had available here.

Larry packed up the red truck with the bucked-up cottonwood tree, and we unloaded a full load of it into the woodpile—needs a year or more to dry.

Cottonwood is the traditional wood that is burned inside the teepee during a peyote meeting.

The cows look good. They're rugged.

October 25: Heavy skies continue with their dramatic, brooding colors and ever-changing patterns. Chet and Tracy returned after nearly five months away, hitchhiking in the Northwest! Tracy is fixing up the tower for them. Good.

Sandra has got a very severe head pain. She has been pressing flowers, making colorful quilted baby balls to sell, sleeping fairly well, but the pain sometimes is terrible. She has seen the dentist and doctor several times. She's holding up quite well, but says sometimes she's scared. Tomorrow she sees a neurologist in Santa Fe.

October 28, 1978: The other day Dee took Sandy to Santa Fe; the doctor seemed to think she could be cured easily. She has been feeling a bit better. Dee packed up candles and took them along. They made $143. And we may need the money; Jon took the red truck to his job, and it stopped working; the engine may be shot. Chet and Michael went and dragged the truck back the twenty miles.

At the Oest's Valdez orchard we went and picked juicy, sweet hard apples, six hundred pounds for $33, and we got more for squeezing on a deal to give them juice. The apples look so beautiful.

In the courtyard, the kids, Gene, and Chet started right in to press apples when we got home. I did some grounds upkeep, moving several things out of the courtyard, including Xavier's snake cage that was three months lying around—junky wood and broken glass. Larry starting on a solar water heater out of scrap.

Story from Brazil about homeless children: Over two million have been abandoned by destitute parents; another 14 million children live in terrible poverty—one third of Brazil's youth! It's things like this that have urged me to find a way of life that tries to reach out and share.

Saturday: Storm cleared at dawn, magically creating a warm morning. Ditch came on strong, and I moved the water again to a new location.

I put off starting the building of my second chair and instead started to take out the red truck engine. With help from Chet, Larry, and a good idea from Gene, we got it out before sundown.

Gene, Michael, and the boys got a free, no-muffler, old motorcycle running. The boys are thrilled; some of us could do without the noise.

November 6, 1978: Sandy is craving a more normal life with a nice little place. I can hardly blame her. I want her to be happy, yet I'd like her to stick with me. I wonder if this grant will come through; I want it to. Along with Michael we looked at a van over in Arroyo Seco. We were ready to buy and tow it, but the papers weren't quite right. We have to wait a bit.

We got the red truck engine out, and the next day, completely taken apart. Tomorrow Larry will take in some parts and get info on the rest. Perhaps we can have all the parts by Friday.

November 10: Cold in the morning but fine in the day. Sandy made Emil some little moccasins, and Jason, a fine red shirt. She's pressing flowers and bought frames to make flower pictures. I've got a second chair about done. It looks much better than the first, which I am fixing up too. We made a set of candles and colored them.

Nice international traveling couple here for a bit. Sabina has taken the burden out of our dishwashing, and Felix has gotten us ahead on the kitchen wood stash. Tracy cooked a fine stew and an apple cake for dinner. The boys are playing poker in the circle where we had our first fire in the heat stove. It's really raining.

> From an interview in *New Age Magazine*, May, 1977,
> with Margaret Mead:
> *New Age:* I've seen so many intentional communities start
>   and then fall apart. . . .
> *Mead:* They fall apart because they have no sense of responsibility
>   to the larger whole. The ones that do not fall apart are
>   the ones that have a function in the larger society.
> *New Age:* This sounds true to me.
> *Mead:* We need communities that care about the problems
>   of the world.

November 14, 1978: In the greenhouse sun porch, summer flowers persist—purple irises blooming; nasturtiums, bright and scrambling; calendulas and others sprinkled among the still-ripening tomatoes. On the other side of the plastic, snow has coated our world.

Just the beginning of winter and the larder is quite full. Also there is plenty of wood. We have some pleasant company and a pretty full house.

November 17: Ten degrees above zero. The mud is frozen for several hours after sunup. I left to do the milk run before the thaw; Sandy and Emil came along. We can hardly reach half of our customers now, because we only have about nine gallons a day.

But on the dairy front there is news! The National Center for Appropriate Technology (NCAT) has recommended us for a grant! Yeah! They're smart because we have a lot of talent here that could blossom into a great little creation. And it is support for me and some good ideas I espouse. Plus Taos County will get a dairy! It is not completely final yet, but pretty sure.

Also speaking of success, Pepe has returned to Taos and has brought several woodwork art pieces that are some of the most terrific you will see anywhere. One is a long box for carrying a heavy silver concho belt. His wood engraving is detailed: dragons, trees, clouds; earth, sun, and moon symbols; and all sorts of legends and figures are carved in.

Jon and Chet have been successful working, and I'm going on the job tomorrow, too, if the boss will take me. Oh, we do need good things in life to happen to us.

Dee had her first day at work at the local cooperative food store. Good. She wants a little money; she probably needs an operation, and the co-op is a good thing to be involved in. Part of her acceptance was a result of her rap about cooperation and experience in the commune. She also worked in a health store in San Francisco.

Felix and Sabina have been accepted to stay until Christmas. Both are conscientious and happy. Felix has been traveling and working around the world for twenty-one years. He is an industrial mechanic by trade and has done sailing in Malaysia and has been in much of Africa. He has been seeing this old colonial world change extremely rapidly these past twenty years.

So the grant! This could be a tremendous boost for all involved. It makes sense. I never thought I was into a false effort; now we may bring to fruition the dairy project and help the commune and become a more stable, contributing part of our society.

I see *Communities* magazine is still coming out. They even mention directly "commune movement." They are conscious of a good thing happening.

November 20: Blessing to the Lord. We are moving along. A lot is happening;

Neil Svenningson is staying with us, which is nice. He's happy we're still functioning. Holly, whom he lived with and married here, is back on the East coast.

Sandy and I drove to Santa Fe, eighty miles away, and sold candles. Our little business is good for a little cash. We bought wax and went to some new shops. We went back to the neurologist, combining it with the candle trip. By good luck, Sandy's tooth cracked and a piece came off, confirming abscess. That was good, so Sandy needn't seek a cure for something else. Thanks to Medicaid, a government-paying program that covered the two hundred dollars spent seeking expert advice.

Coming home, we picked up a good friend of ours, Billy Whelan, who was hitchhiking, and we took him to his very nice home.

Billy has gone through changes and much to the better. He's been in the thick of the scene and was very rebellious and bitter with modern America. Now he has a more understanding, accepting view of money, electricity, and marriage. He found a wonderful wife, and they want to work with kids and are willing to work with retarded, abused foster kids. They are willing to devote themselves. And Billy has several good crafts; he can teach jewelry, woodwork, and goat husbandry, and Susan is very organized. I'm sure they will find a vocation in this, won't have to hustle the buck so much, and will be able to devote their time to the kids.

Billy was very lucky to catch our ride, because we picked him up just before the onset of a very cold and dark night. And then the good Lord or good luck saw us home. The generator failed seventy miles ago, but the car didn't stall out dead until we got inside our gate!

The other day Sandy bought the van we were looking at, and it is here. We must work on it soon. Chet gave me some advice on how to start. The previous owner—attractive young gal—we were just informed, committed suicide!

My little wood works are coming along. I've got some more ideas. I need lumber and time.

Thanksgiving, 1978: We have a biggish gathering here; neighbors coming— Dick and Kathy, the Kaplans, Bruce. Dee's parents and sister are here too. I like the big family. It's a good feeling to get together for a holiday.

Next day: With the irrigation water, I flooded a little prairie dog village yesterday. Though few people get involved with it, there is always work to be done with the land. This fall we did more ditch cleaning than ever. The land and irrigation system were never in better shape.

I hear guests discuss the commune when here; they compare it to their own comfortable life and say, "No, I won't trade." It never comes up, it seems, to consider doing something besides getting happy. There is more purpose to the commune than just getting the most comfort for oneself. There are broader considerations. Nevertheless, our struggle is in part to make our community have an outstandingly good life—so it does appeal—so people don't lose the good life by doing a sharing thing.

Sandy and I dipped and colored a set of fabulous rainbow candles. Had a big pile of Swiss steaks for dinner cooked by Tracy. She's been working in the kitchen a lot. Sandy is very happy Tracy calls this home.

November 28, 1978: Vehicles: Our world-traveling guests had a bit of a laugh. Jon and Chet came back from Albuquerque. Jon got a good pickup truck—1968 Dodge—same year and engine as the New Buffalo's Dodge. But in the morning when Jon and Dee tried to take off for the milk run, the Dodge would not work; the battery mysteriously blew apart, and the starter motor is not working correctly. So we start the big Rizzo delivery truck with a jump from Dee's car. But that truck is mysteriously out of oil. Good thing Chet checked it. Then Larry's car we had to jump-start too. Finally got going.

Mabelene cow, taken to market, has sold for $580! Money first has to go through the bank.

A big crazy group of Americans in Guyana, South America, called Jonestown, have gone completely off the deep end into murder and mass suicide! Very disturbing. Real gangster people, they killed a congressman and three reporters. Very upsetting. We must try to do well and be gentle in our lives. This violence is alarming. Mayor of San Francisco was murdered just the other day also.

I'm reading about Alpha Farm in Oregon, similar to our farm. They began with thirteen people from the Friends Service Committee. "We began to see that the renewal of the social order must begin with ourselves." They're doing well. Sounds good.

At night, alone in the kitchen, I speak softly with Larry. We have our troubles with Rebel and tension with Pepe. Now this mass suicide in a community seems to ring a death knell. How can we overcome this? I see the difference between them and us. We are open, involved in the community—

not paranoid and shut off from society. But this Jim Jones and his Temple of Doom have done so much damage. We had enough to overcome already.

A new day: Fieldwork has stopped; the ground is freezing. The ditch water is off. This is winter now.

Event! Our monthly meeting started something new; and a great sign of progress it is. After eleven years, the group paid the workers a little return! It is a great monument to the good spirit in people that New Buffalo was built and has functioned for fourteen years without paying anyone.

At this meeting of eleven adults, we had nearly $700 out on the table, this mostly from candles. And people were paid according to the candle-making schedule that had been lately filled out. Our temporary members Felix and Sabina were able to earn money too. Felix said they would spend it here. The group makes good decisions that I feel are better than any one person would come up with.

Michael, Gene, and I had a long talk at night around the fire in Michael's room; there is no dispelling the black cloud of Jonestown.

At least in the morning a big snowstorm started just as we got up to milk. It snowed heavily for about half an hour as we milked in our open-air shed. A good sign to us from our Heavenly Father.

December 4, 1978: The storm cleared. Last night the tomatoes froze in the greenhouse. Sandy promptly took them out and turned over the soil. The ground is frozen quite hard at the barn.

December 6: Jon and Chet are off to work in the ski valley at $5 an hour. Dee is off to work at the co-op.

As I milk, the snow blows around in every direction, and the mountains appear and disappear. I'm quite comfortable in my hand-me-down ski mobile boots, hand-me-down navy shirt, and Kim's old military arctic coat. In the mornings our smiley boy climbs into bed with us. We have a very nice little family. Jason is very caring of his little brother.

We got a letter from George. He found a Taoist-oriented community in Colorado on 180 acres that has a Chinese leader. Sounds very good.

December 8: This morning was clear, the mountains shimmering cold with puffs of mists. Twenty degrees below zero here; the snow sounds crunch as we walk to the barn. This is some real cold. We have a good stash of hay though not enough. We have a good stash of food, also not enough to get through to May.

December 24: Pepe was over to visit us. Good. But bad, he got in a fight and got thrown out of a fancy bar in town. It's part of his fun, but it's ugly, and it keeps him apart from the closeness that sometimes he wants. In part, he is a visionary of the new man. Part of him is still in the backcountry fighting for respect.

December 26, 1978: On Christmas day we took two families into our home for the holiday. My mom, sister, and T. Ben came over and Pepe, Carol, and Jenny, too. One of the two couples is leaving today. We didn't know them before, but still they spent a nice holiday with us. The other couple is moved in. This is real Christmas, to be able to share on this level.

January 21, 1979—Sunday: We've got a real winter—lots of snow. It is just about guaranteed to be a spring with plenty of water. Once we can start farming, it will help us feel better. Still no word on the barn grant—sure is taking time.

Sandy, kids, and I have returned safely from a California trip. We saw old friend Wind, a gentle, strong lady who once lived here. She has a daughter, Christiana, whose father is Bob George from the Huerfano Valley. We stayed two days at the Fairway House—a commune—in Soquel near Santa Cruz. They have good clean, peaceful togetherness there, about fifteen adults and a few kids.

Back at Buffalo, they had just gone through a tumultuous event with some visiting guests. At the place where Wind lives, it takes a unanimous decision to admit a new person. Lama Foundation has a similar policy. We need a regular way of dealing with it too. And by explaining ourselves to new people, we will better understand and shape our methods of creating the group scene. Good luck to us. There certainly are some nervous, psychological tensions that have been part of our changing home.

While we were away, for the first time since the Pride family arrived at New Buffalo eight years ago, the kitchen scene fell apart for a bit. It can revert to an "every person fend for yourself" sort of thing when not enough people make it their concern to see that dinner is cooked. Chet cooked the night we got back. Sandy cooked next, and I'm fixing dinner tonight.

25. *Wind and daughter Christiana at the Capitola, California coast.*

Larry has been feeling low. Life has too many challenges. At times it seems an overwhelming effort. But we can do it if we discipline ourselves, make our health as good as possible. I hope for this barn project to give Larry a great achievement.

January 30, 1979: Since Sandy and I are back, the kitchen scene is running smoothly again. Together, today, we colored some candles that Michael dipped. Good to have at least one well-established craft to do on cold, snowy winter days.

Gene is sort of back but is drifting away. His big goal is government money: social security insurance and food stamps. He considers himself mentally incompetent to work—a poor attitude. He broke several bottles of urine in his little greenhouse—kind of extra weird. Now he's cleaning his room back up. He's confused, I guess, as are many. In the next few months, he'll figure out what he's doing. It appears Maggy has fled this situation.

Sandy is concerned we're getting older and getting nowhere. Often she thinks it's a dead end, this New Buffalo community—no security for later. It has that possibility. After many years here, we were just about forced out by some violent, hateful people. The structure, though, has changed since then, to give more stability to those who make the place their home. I still believe I'm pretty young—nearly thirty-five years old—and that there is a great future in this scene. Not just New Buffalo, but the searching of many people for greater community. This year will be decisive. I cannot stay so poor for much longer nor go without a breakthrough on the major project, the dairy.

Life is a struggle; there's really no getting away from that. For me what we are trying to achieve here is a very good thing to struggle for. And it's going to look just great in the coming spring. For now, in our poorly insulated dirt buildings, we sleep under lots of blankets and sleeping bags.

Chet and Tracy are accepted as members. We had our annual meeting, and it was quite good. We've got nine members. Gene, though, is pretty much dropping out of the work come spring; he's going to live off alone in a tent. Tracy, too, is planning to be away for two months this summer.

I can't believe it! Jon has mentioned he may leave! He finds too much anger—too much not seeing things done as he'd like. It is a difficult task to compromise and persevere, wait and be tolerant. That is one of our prime chores though, to get along well together. Larry is planning on being here. Dee has been feeling good.

February 10, 1979: Another day of sun. Now we're finally getting some heat. I can hear the drip, drip of water coming off the roof. I also heard some drips coming down my stovepipe. Matthew and Jason are giving Emil sleigh rides down the driveway. Good friend Eric, who has been here with us, is recovering from an illness. Usually he's very fit. He has the Nordic Viking look with the blond beard and robust build.

Dee, though she has seemed happy on the surface to me, talked to me yesterday about her nagging desire to leave! I hope she doesn't go. Certainly a reason for being here is not that it offers the most comfort or privacy one can find in our society.

Jon spoke up for the community of New Buffalo. He thinks it's quite good. At twenty-one years old he's not quite sure what's best for him. The social consciousness angle is kind of new to him. He likes the farm. He doesn't like the personal conflicts, which make him very angry.

The thing with Tony upset him. Now we have more structure to deal with that problem. Then the other day, his good friend Chet got angry at him because Jon wanted to postpone butchering and therefore wouldn't buy some wrapping paper. Chet got unreasonably mad, I heard, and said something like "Well, you can just go down the road if you. . . . " That is a particularly poor choice of words in our situation, and Jon was made very irate just over some $3 worth of paper! This is exactly the sort of thing that Jon does not want, on a perfectly nice day to have an angry confrontation over a very little matter, and with someone who hasn't given one hundredth of the effort that Jon has.

But we all will say something stupid once in a while. So far Jon has controlled his reaction to these confrontations. Good, good. With Larry, Chet, or some others, and I guess even me, he is once in a while tempted to do physical harm. This is a very difficult thing to live with. He knows he put us through a scary scene when he was shooting off his high-powered rifle around the pueblo over the issue of Tony.

Back into the cold to milk and feed some more of our precious hay to that hungry group of cows.

February 14: Larry and I spoke to an insurance agent and an NCAT representative in Montana about our contract. We got most of our questions answered satisfactorily. I wrote down the questions and answers in the secretary's notebook. Tomorrow I have some more questions to ask at the Employment Security Commission, and then I'll send the contract in.

February 17, 1979: To dampen the good news of the barn grant, Chet went out and downed a bunch of beers. He was in and out of the property several times driving the corporation's pickup truck. At 5:30 a.m. he walked in all bloody. He had picked up two hitchhikers while cruising around in his boozed-up state, and they robbed him! There was a scuffle while he was driving, and Chet crashed. We found our truck hanging off a bit of a cliff.

Chet evidently got a tax return or some kind of check. He hasn't been drinking for weeks, but when he saw that money his poor mind flashed booze, and he went on a bender. It cost us $65 to get a wrecker to bring the broken truck back.

I sent the contract in—signed.

February 21: The nights are now around 20° above. Larry hasn't had a fire in weeks; his collector is doing a fine job. He has been reviewing our barn plans and cost estimates. The future looks so bright and exciting. Thank goodness this grant is coming through.

We had our mid-monthly meeting. We tried to create a rule of no driving corporation vehicles when drinking alcohol, but our reaction has been very nonhostile toward Chet, who did do a very stupid thing.

I'm letting a visiting lady stay in my room for the moment; Rebecca is her name. Gene appears only infrequently. He does little annoying things, like putting things away in new and hard to find places or smoking at the barn. He's a sweet guy, though, and we've agreed to wait and see if he does get something better arranged. I finally did a little cleaning in his greenhouse where he had a lot of trash.

In comparison Sandy keeps our greenhouse sun porch neat and well cared for; the lettuce is all newly cultivated. Dee's greenhouse looks good, too, though without much of a crop at present.

February 23: Last night I checked Big Beth cow at 2:30 a.m.—no sign. This morning there was a thin new covering of snow, and Jon found a new, wet heifer! Jon milked out some colostrum, and he and I fed the calf; she drank right away. In our cold living room, the circled kiva, she's staying for now—so precious—excellent dairy stock.

March 1, 1979: I went to work on a job for the second day and didn't come home until late. Sandy fixed dinner again because no one else was doing it. This is a problem we have not solved very well. Larry is almost completely out of doing any kitchen work. Jon is the same. They cannot be depended on to pitch in if no dinner is coming together, or if the dishes get piled up. Michael has done some meals. Seems he's quit washing dishes, too. Chet simply doesn't "do" dishes and rarely cooks. Gene hasn't cooked ever. He can't be counted on for even the simplest things because he's just not here.

We've got a new approach that we are an educational scene. I'd say we have learned that we all have to pitch in. Our scene shows that it takes a lot of work. Somehow, still, we're always on the brink of disruption because we don't have a regular way of handling these responsibilities. Tomorrow we'll have a meeting, and I hope we can make progress on this. The volunteer method I like, but lately most people simply don't volunteer. Sandy's not happy about not being able to depend on some of the other people for this

26. *Greenhouse sun porch*

very basic stuff. At the community we visited in California, the kitchen work was assigned. Eric, who is leaving, has been doing his share of cleaning the kitchen. It was he who finally cleaned the pantries the other day—a terrific friend.

Some people want spaces for teepees. This adds more social issues, which we must discuss. And Sky wants to purchase Buffalo land on the mesa top. And what about Gene, who has a room but doesn't work?

Friday: Gene is playing on some minds here with some craziness. He came with me on the milk run. We talked; I can enjoy his company. I think this settled-down, serious farming or homemaking is not what he wants. He is applying for social security as mentally incompetent to work, and he's got a problem there all right. Anyhow, I stopped to help an old guy whose car was stuck, seventy-one-year-old Gordon Stevenson. Turned out he needed more than a little help; he didn't know where the battery was! He wanted to go 30 mph in town so he could jump-start his car. He wasn't clear on the name, or where he was going, or where his money was. Poor guy. So Gene stayed with him, and I continued our business in town.

A new day: Gene and Gordon are out here. Their "how-dee-do" was waving a bottle of vodka in a cheery way to Dee and Sandy. Gene is so blind that he doesn't see that that is a sure way to make at least some of us nervous and very much wondering what is going on in our home.

Take your pick: They are going to Hawaii for $1,000 or going to Colorado. Or the old man is going to buy a pickup, having abandoned his VW, which has a blown engine—maybe—he's not sure. He's not even sure if the car has a clutch or not. He is flashing a little money. He put Gene in some of his clothes and took him out to dinner. So Gene is going to grow pot here, live in a tent, but he must get to Hawaii. He's already given up his room (not really). Gee wiz, a lot of people in our dear world are pretty mixed up.

From Gene's room came an assortment of junk. He kept a collection of useless stuff: empty wine bottles, broken milk bottles, empty cans, old dirty socks, abandoned sandals, shoes, two big cans of ashes, last year's marijuana stems, broken radios, and my poor unrepaired 12-string guitar in many pieces. I really should be pissed at that. Good luck, Mr. Gene. He had a great opportunity to resolve his worries through work, but he couldn't get behind it—too boring. So maybe he will help old Gordon. The fellow is emaciated. It's just possible he hasn't been fed decently for a long time. Gene is more likely to pick up on more vodka and cigarettes than fruits and good food. But people make choices; we all have several opportunities.

Tuesday: Sandy and Tracy colored the last batch of candles I made. Sandy also sawed and chopped kitchen wood, as she often does. Chet and Jon went off looking for jobs. I worked on the gate that will seal off our gardens from the front of the pueblo.

We saw the rock musical *Godspell* fabulously performed in Taos by a group of local people, many of whom we know. Terrific to see people doing something so fine. And the theme of the Gospel according to Matthew is a good message: love thy neighbor; share with the poor; the riches of heaven are to be valued more highly than earthly acquisition; be good to each other; turn the other cheek.

March 24, 1979: The UNEXPECTED: Big Jon was moving out; he felt too much aggression toward me—rebellion against authority, personality clash, lack of a basic respect, something. He was leaving with a bad feeling—Dee unhappy to have to go. Jon's buddy Reb, always needling him about what a pain I am. A real enemy this Rebel has made himself.

The unusual early banging of the courtyard bell brought all the people together. Rebel pacing and yelling—challenging—they announced it in the courtyard: Rebel, Jon, and Chet are taking over—Goat John, standing behind, his presence quietly backing them up. Sandy and I are "Out!" along with any one else who doesn't like it! They're going to help build the barn, but not with us here! Reb says he'll make our lives miserable if we don't leave—Chet reinforcing him.

Sandy and I have had enough. Within two hours we have some stuff packed and go into Taos. But Jon gets a shock of conscience, comes to my mom's house, apologizes, and urges us to return. I urge Jon to stay; I never wanted him to leave.

A new day: We are moved out and into two small, derelict rooms in the center of town. With our little bits of furniture, plants, and pictures, we made an instant home in a day. Sandy's got a gardening job, and I've been working—working our way up. Larry brings us eggs and milk.

Days later: At Buffalo they had an open meeting in the circle, which we were encouraged to attend. But it gave another opportunity for a particularly threatening and ugly show of the "get rid of Art" spirit. Rebel shows up—pistol in boot—puts on his most rabid, hateful performance, promising unending interference and threats. He got into Clarice's face, blaming her for "spawning" me. Great guy. Chet being the tough guy, too, continually sharpening a stick with a hunting knife. More resentment than support seemed to come out generally. There was no definite rallying behind Sandy and me. Rick Klein was there but maintained complete neutrality. Mick Kitts was there but used the moment to air some mindless remarks.

We had become too dominant—too closely associated with the image of New Buffalo. When we came, there was no formality, so it was like I have just dominated—made my ideas project over others. . . . Jason is now staying in Hondo with friends so he can continue with school.

So, after all these years, we are finished. Jon and Dee are staying. Good. Larry is very anxious to do the barn. There are plenty of workers, and Goat John will be coming down to help. Jon is new project manager and dairy manager. I have written a very nice letter to get NCAT to continue their grant.

I wanted to see fields and a prosperous Grade A dairy. This is still coming to pass—maybe. I expected to have met more similar-minded people by now. Instead I seem to have caused hurt and aggressive feelings. Some have treated us in a shitty manner. So we are going to make a new start. New Buffalo has lawns, gardens, bushes, fields, dairy, and a "Grade A" grant.

Perhaps it's the basic democratic impulse of the place that won't see one individual have too great an influence. Lack of organization—the original group abandoning the place with no set method of choosing the new people who have responsibility. It's also a power play, and some people can be a whole lot meaner and uptight than I. Jon said the day we were ordered out of New Buffalo, "I just can't help it, but I think Buffalo is better off without you." So the vigilantes come in to test the theory.

The Fate: Most people who have lived at New Buffalo have left. The first four years saw hundreds of people coming and leaving, including all the originals. Not propitious really. I came along with a lot of idealism, developing a theory of the good of the communes and the way they can work. I had youth and energy. Larry is one though with whom I have found a common cause.

Now I would never enter a group as I did in 1971. It was very inviting, of course. But at Buffalo, I was sort of joining the originals in absentia. They were already gone. They didn't keep a structure nor pass on duties or offices. There was no way to be admitted because the board of directors was gone. In the last few years, we have improved the organization. But recently, again, the rules weren't respected; a few members and a few nonmembers came in—threatening—proclaiming the new order.

June 29, 1979: My big concern since I was in my teens was peace—better sharing of the world's wealth—extending love and material help to the less fortunate. These desires led me to the effort at New Buffalo, which I finally left because it was such a crazy scene. Instead of idealistic, humanistic workers, we got more unstable misfits: some vicious, some drunkards. I had meetings in college with close friends, but we never got anything solid together. Then at New Buffalo, I was not able to inspire people. We got plenty of people going through, but they did not pick up on the idea and left to pursue other goals.

So now Sandy and I make a new start. I've got to get something together for my immediate family. Then later I may be able to find another approach to inspiring people.

August 1979: Bauer Dairy, Gladstone, Nebraska: Living proof. . . . Living by example not effective where I was—no longer at New Buffalo. Those dreams and efforts rather smashed. We now live privately in a trailer and with a steady job in the American heartland of Nebraska, on a two-hundred-cow dairy. The milkers just quit—no notice—disappearing in the night. The owner and I are really working now: up at 4:30 a.m.; home after 8 p.m. Big tomatoes coming in from our garden—chile peppers, cantaloupes, broccoli, and eggplants these days.

Surprise, surprise! A visit from our good friend, college student Jim Preston—out here on the plains to see our little family. He was at New Buffalo, and it was kind of him to say that the commune just isn't the same with us gone.

October 1979: News from our old home New Buffalo! Barn work continues. Big Jon has most responsibilities: milking, building, and selling milk. Larry sadly has left—not happily. He, too, must start fresh. Oh, good luck, Larry—just the right sort for communes: peaceful, clever, earnest. But he, too, attracted dislike and bad feelings from a number of people. We simply didn't have enough folks of like mind to make a happy home.

Unstable people. Goat John supposedly had a nervous breakdown—fights terribly with his new woman. My dear, good sister Carol was so very ill. She passed away after we left New Mexico. Brain tumor claimed her life. The HUGEST of losses.

Chet, who was there when we were threatened, is already long gone. He went to drink, worse and worse for a while, until he finally left. Rebel and Lena reportedly are getting divorced. Jon and Dee are committed to see the barn done.

This year, New Buffalo decided to continue with its famous Solstice birthday party against our advice. A tragedy occurred when a little boy, playing on the roof, fell through a skylight. There were some paramedics at the party, but they were unable to save the child.

At the Bauer Farm I have gotten a raise. I'm more confident and able. I know the 118 or so cows that come through the milking parlor twice a day. I'm helping train a new young man. I feel good physically. I like the greater responsibility of knowing the job better. My mother Clarice is here visiting from Taos.

November 1979: My first half-year is past—working toward our new goal—some pleasant acres on the west coast, where we can build greenhouses, plant gardens and fruit trees, and have a workshop and home. Boy, have we got the energy to do that now. The job here is good, but in the wrong place. Sandy is lonely and doesn't like having to sleep with the boots on during the tornadoes. Jason doesn't like the hundred-mile round trip on the school bus.

Here I am, the conscientious worker, engrossed in my job for the moment. I spent so much time at idealism, voluntary labor, and the communal effort—in order to communicate my concern—that now I must make a real effort to at least care for my immediate family. Starting again at thirty-five, I feel confident.

July 22, 1980: Bloom Dairy, Meacham Rd., Petaluma, California: I have found a good job—the herdsman on a large dairy in the rolling golden hills of northern California. We're to have the original old farmhouse with the backyard right at the dairy. It's a beautiful location only twenty miles from Bolinas, where ten years ago I set out. I was looking for a job near Petaluma, and incredibly I've got one. A connection I made one year ago with rancher Don deBernardi helped.

At New Buffalo, life continues too, though rough. We hear Rebel was put out, Lee put out, Pepe has moved out, and Jon and Dee talk of leaving because of an opportunity to build their own home. There is a new, old tractor and big water troubles. I could have been a permanent mayordomo. As a private owner in the valley, I would have been, but personal shit drove me out of the group scene—unappreciated—very small-minded, ugly feelings got the upper hand.

Fellow from NCAT told Dee that they never would have given a grant to a place like New Buffalo, except the application was so well done and thorough. The "thanks" is a kick in the ass! Some thanks for success in the endeavor to start a real business. They still drive the Rizzo truck—great buy—but it caused hate for me; Goat John was so jealous. Teaming up with Rebel gave him the entire scene. Yet through it all, the place continues. Best is if it

27. *Arty, the*
   professional
   herdsman

continues and eventually prospers and puts that valuable, still uncompleted barn to long and good use.

Tomorrow I start work. I'm anxious to be a few months into the job—accepted—getting ahead—knowing the job. Just got to work at it.

Year of 1985: Ielmorini Ranch, Chileno Valley Road, Petaluma, California: A summary of events: Telephone rings in our home nestled in the coastal, rolling, green and wooded hills of the rural countryside; a surprising call from Taos, requesting our presence at a New Buffalo meeting of the Board of Directors, to be held in the parking lot at the Taos County Courthouse!

It appears that Rebel and John have placed the property up for sale, asking $1,000,000! They say that they are not cashing out, but are moving New Buffalo commune to Oregon where it is easier to farm and make a living, because it can't be done here!

In the six years since we were expelled, these people's true colors were revealed. The farm is defunct—cows and equipment gone. In their chaos they abandoned doing the annual reports of the New Buffalo Corporation, thus they were never the legal board of directors. Those of us who were on the board in 1979, legally, are still the board of directors!

Sandy is off to Taos, flying courtesy of those in Taos community who oppose what is occurring at New Buffalo. She is staying the night in Albuquerque with Mick and family, our old commune brother. Larry is picking her up in the morning, and they will cruise up to Taos together for the meeting.

Next day: *For security, the corporation meeting is held in the parking lot of Taos Courthouse, attracting curious bystanders and police officers on the periphery. Familiar faces—a few that once helped banish us from our home—some looking nervous, and some now looking eager for a common goal: to rid New Buffalo of the negative element that now resides there; the place derelict—prosperity extinguished—rumor of heroin use. Only a few people living there, with the gate closed to visitors.*

It's decided. Remaining residents are expelled from New Buffalo— sheriff to post eviction notice—Sandy.

Rick Klein eventually reinherits his donation to our alternative society. As it should be. Let it rest. A great gift he gave to us; the people failed to make it prosper. The end of an era.

June 2003: Sebastopol, Sonoma County, Northern California: Here in the land of the diminishing apple and the growth of the vigorous vine, the telephone rings and the answering machine records a message from a man who says he has just returned from a small town in New Mexico that we are familiar with, Arroyo Hondo. And as of July 15, 2003, Rick and Terry Klein will be leaving, and he, Bob Fies, will be the new owner of New Buffalo, now reduced to the pueblo and ten acres. The passing of the torch. He just happens to live in the same area as we do, and he is looking forward to meeting us and seeing the book!

August 23, 2003: A computer message from some friends in Taos: *"On Saturday, David and I were at New Buffalo for the first time in many years. The*

28. *Lama and Tibetan monks with Bob Fies. Courtesy of Bob Fies*

courtyard is covered with a bright green lawn now, but everything else is much the same as it was thirty years ago. We went in the circle, which was adorned with beautiful silk hangings. Tibetan monks were creating a sand mandala in the center of the room. I cannot describe how exquisite, beautiful, and intricate the work was. It was like creation itself. In your old room, behind curtains, the lama, an old man, stayed. People went in and he performed a ceremony of healing and protection. The most amazing thing was on Sunday. The mandala was completed at about 3 p.m.; then the lama gave a healing for all the people who had gathered; then the incredible work of art was swept away, nothing but colored sand in an urn and carried with banners and chanting down the New Buffalo driveway to the Rio Hondo, where it was given as an offering. I thought you would like to know that something so wonderful just happened at New Buffalo.

There are strong forces and good magic around.

Love and Peace, Kathleen Woodall (Catalina)

CONCLUSION

The experiments with the open-land idea were not sustainable. A more organized approach to intentional communities, however, is very much alive and growing internationally. The wonderful *Communities* magazine functions as an information and education center. Groups like the Occidental Arts and Ecology Center in my neighborhood, or Housing Works in New York City are far ahead of the old funky communities.

The Farm in Tennessee has been able to adapt and carries on its mission. In addition, there are now many works being published about this pioneering of a new culture. A bit of a ground swell shows, sparks of Aquarian light are more frequent. And I get to add my voice. This sharing of property can be done; it needs to be done.

We came close. If the liquor and drugs had been kept to a minimum and if the people had put their resources into the central effort, so much more could have been accomplished. These are not impossible wishes. A more disciplined group could go so much further. Which brings us back to idealism and faith. The major religions have called for devotion, nation states have called for sacrifice, and so the Aquarian Spirit calls for the strength of idealism. Not in a battle with weapons of destruction, but with devotion and dedication nevertheless.

Present society has one thousand weak points. The debt balloon is vastly huge and stretched thin. Yet borrowing is now called upon to solve all problems. There is too much greed. Every day we are bombarded by incessant advertising, endlessly enticing us to spend and spend, and with money we don't even have. Oil is running out. The glaciers are melting. A vast gulf separates the wealthiest from the rest. No social services can keep up with an ever-expanding population, yet no one addresses that issue. The roads and freeways are all clogged. Again the ever-expanding population negates all improvements. And again no one seems to speak of this. They've always got a plan, and it always gets worse. Just when science should have given us a good life, the list of worries has gotten very long. I need something in this landscape to give me hope and inspiration.

To conclude this volume we present a few essays that illuminate this notion of turning a very strong tide in human affairs.

ESSAYS

The Rise of a New Paradigm

Now thirty years after the fading of the counterculture, we see that it coincided with a weakening of the progressive forces in American politics.

In the later part of the journals, I am trying to reach out—to inspire—to find allies. But there is the foreboding sense of being in a sinking ship—the people were not ready—the ideas too odd. The times were not ready—the problems not critical enough for a new paradigm to arise. The challenge was so huge—the shift required, so immense—that more time needed to pass. Now some time has passed.

What is this shift to a new paradigm? Here are a number of the elements.

The Left consciousness that arose around Marxism disparaged religion as the opiate of the masses. The new paradigm accepts all religions and holds spirituality as very important. The New Age is distinguished by its belief in the one-world family. There is no longer a need to out-populate the competing groups, for we must see ourselves as the same group on the only planet we've got.

From the earliest times the different religions incorporated admonitions to procreate—have more babies so they would have more warriors and followers. Thus was born the notion that God "collects" souls. In the modern world, religions passed on from the ancient past are thus against birth control and homosexuality. In the new age we recognize all religions are true; none is the one true religion, but we still hold onto spirituality and honoring people's beliefs.

We do need to recognize in the new paradigm that no one speaks for God. No one knows what God wants. Does he (she) want planes run into buildings? Does he (she) want more souls in order to be happier? In all cultures, the tomes of religious writings were written—guess by whom?—by people. Of course it is difficult to convince true believers of any faith that their beliefs don't come from God. Ah, humans. As soon as someone purports to know what God wants, you know he (she) is going to be very difficult to talk to. In the new paradigm we've only got our God-given brains to figure things out, as was meant, and we have to judge beliefs on their merits. We still need to be thankful; we still need to be reverent. This is not an easy thing, but it can be achieved. It is a major challenge of the new age.

The Left consciousness sponsored and instituted thousands of government interventions. These innovations, started in the Roosevelt era, improved American life immensely—so much so that the Republican Party finally accepted and usurped and expanded the programs.

The new paradigm starts a new trend of self-reliance—to quote a recent article, "it is time to pay for the revolution ourselves." These times are not those of the *Grapes of Wrath*. Millions of people have benefited from America and have considerable wealth. The government meanwhile has become ridiculously in debt. No founding father could even begin to understand these numbers. Where are the citizens who say, "I've had the good life; don't give me more"?

The Left consciousness saw free enterprise as an enemy. The new paradigm accepts the value and necessity of free enterprise. It recognizes that many millions of people have become prosperous with the development of democracy and human rights, and it is happy about it. The new idea urges people to use their wealth and enterprise themselves, not depend on government to deal with all the big issues.

The old Leftist ideas called for violent revolutions, the raising of anger and overthrow of the state. The new paradigm promotes change through service and example; encourages the higher consciousness of peaceful action and the power of compassion, generosity, and enlightened self-interest, even love. There is so much hate and anger, we just cannot add to it and get a good result.

The new paradigm would see some of the people devote themselves to larger nonrelated families. It is understandable that the more stable members of the counterculture took the opportunity offered by America to create a little nuclear family. But the larger cause was left neglected. Correspondingly, the communes, which I see as the spiritual centers of the progressives, faded, and the power of the progressives faded too. They lost this approach to wealth sharing and proving the goodness in human nature.

Here's another element that is so hard to shift to: Right and Left both have been wedded to the idea of constant economic growth. The new paradigm promotes the concept of sustainability; it offers sharing as a counterpoint to the trickle-down theory to raise people out of poverty and accepts the impossibility of exponential growth. This belief can even see the slowing of city building in favor of preserving eco-village farms. Some group has to face up to the impossibility of solving all economic problems with growth. It's not doable. Full employment—a good job for everyone regardless of how many people there are—that is not happening either. Simplify the medical and legal systems and reduce government employment, all things that will have to happen at some time, and you've got millions more not employed. You need some really new ideas to reinvigorate the progressive side and face our new realities.

Now there's a bundle to think about.

Do We Make Progress? 2–27–05

To see generosity and service as major motivations in human affairs takes quite a leap. It sustains my faith to view the progress humankind has made. Here are some examples.

Through most of history, up until the modern era, slavery was as common as sand. In addition, serfdom, a form of slavery, held millions of peasants for millennia. In India and Japan a caste system kept a large population in a subservient status. The Bible accepted slavery as part of the natural order.

The idea that all humans come from common ancestors, that none are naturally inferior, is an extremely modern notion. In a few generations it has become thoroughly accepted that slavery is wrong. This change is most encouraging.

Likewise, through all of written history, women were almost always considered inferior in intelligence and legally had inferior rights. This is perhaps the central issue of difference with the Islamic fundamentalists, so the battle for women's equal rights continues. But in the non-Muslim world already the modern belief of equality of women is broadly accepted. This is another example of a vast change in the popular consciousness, which in my mind is to the good.

In my lifetime a number of unpredicted wholesome changes have occurred. In the 1950s and '60s the Soviet Union and the United States competed in an awesome arms race. Khrushchev spoke of burying the capitalist system, and we came within inches of nuclear war at least once. Yet under Mikhail Gorbachev, the Soviet Armies were withdrawn from Eastern Europe, the Berlin Wall came down, and then the Communist Party lost power. With these changes the most likely scenario for World War III evaporated.

A transition as significant as any in history took place in a basically peaceful manner. The process is not over, but Soviet communism passed more quickly and quietly than anyone imagined possible. Thanks are owed to the millions of people in those countries who somehow collectively reformed the Soviet Union and Eastern Europe. Often I have heard it suggested, and I believe it, that rock 'n' roll and the uniform world-youth culture played a significant role in the change.

Who thought Nelson Mandela would walk out of prison in South Africa and become prime minister? Who predicted apartheid also would be ended without a violent revolution? This is another very significant change.

They say as many as forty million people died in World War II. Fascism came within a breath of ruling the world, but it lost! Many millions suffered in a truly global epic battle. Yet the power of democracy is such that very quickly Japan and Germany were accepted back in the family of nations. Both have become democratic, prosperous, and free. The significance of this transformation cannot be overstated, I believe.

At the same time, the European empires, with their theory that the white race carried the burden of ruling all nations, evaporated in a generation. These nations are still finding their way, but there is no going back. History indeed has moved quickly in the modern world.

When I was in college, China was predominantly a country of poverty. During the chaotic Chinese Cultural Revolution, they descended into a totalitarian nightmare. Yet a few decades later the Chinese spirit of pragmatism and enterprise has come to dominate. Though we are in a new arms race with them, we are also tied together in ten thousand ways. I predicted that, but no one was listening at the time. It took Richard Nixon to break the ice and fly to Beijing to start the new era. Another scenario for WW III was averted.

We are also still in the throes of a titanic change from the 40,000-year rule of superstition to the age of science. It is only in the last two hundred years that all the sciences, medicine, astronomy, physics, agriculture, and so on have become guided by reason and have taken leaps of knowledge of gargantuan proportions. With the advent of electrical power, mass transportation, and advanced machinery, the backbreaking drudgery that was the lot of most people can be lifted. We can view the galaxies or the structure of the atom—worlds that were not even imagined a few decades ago.

Against this backdrop, my flights of fancy are not out of step. If you see with me the changes that are necessary in our culture for survival, there are plenty of precedents to demonstrate that sea changes can and will occur.

29. *The sand mandala. Courtesy of Bob Fies*

ABOUT THE AUTHOR

Born in New York City in 1944, Art has lived on both coasts and in the Midwest. He has traveled extensively in Europe, studied Chinese language, and has looked at clouds from both sides now. Art worked in service to build an alternative culture and then made a success, with Sandra, of the more common American dream of building a pleasant home in the country while working constantly. Well preserved by hard work, Arty AnSwei Kopecky had not read these journals himself for twenty-five years. "They have had a rejuvenating effect on me."

Amidst the little farmsteads of Sebastopol, California, Arty and family have made a new home for the past twenty years after adventures in New Mexico and Nebraska. With skills as a finish carpenter and with a contractor's license, he works freelance. Arty also continues to work with soil and plants in fabulous Sonoma County, where he and Sandy have a small bonsai nursery and a virtual botanical garden.

Now the mandala turns further, and what was nearly lost may yet be found. What was begun can yet be improved upon.